Information technology and workplace democracy

Information technology and workplace democracy

edited by
Martin Beirne and Harvie Ramsay

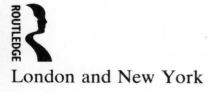

London and New York

First published 1992
by Routledge
11 New Fetter Lane, London EC4P 4EE

Simultaneously published in the USA and Canada
by Routledge
a division of Routledge, Chapman and Hall, Inc.
29 West 35th Street, New York, NY 10001

© 1992

Typeset in Times by J&L Composition Ltd, Filey,
North Yorkshire.
Printed and bound in Great Britain by
Biddles Ltd, Guildford and King's Lynn

*A catalogue reference for this title is available from
the British Library*

ISBN 0-415-00417-9

Library of Congress Cataloging in Publication Data
Information technology and workplace democracy / edited by
    Martin Beirne and Harvie Ramsay.
        p.   cm.
    Includes bibliographical references.
    ISBN 0-415-00417-9
1. Information technology—Management—Employee
    participation.   2. Management—Employee
    participation.   I. Beirne, Martin, 1960–   II. Ramsay,
    Harvie, 1949–   .
HD30.5.I529   1992
658.3'12—dc20
                                    92–1005
                                        CIP

Contents

Figures

Tables

Contributors

Peter Bain is a research fellow in the Department of Human Resource Management at the University of Strathclyde. He served an apprenticeship in the Clydeside engineering industry and worked both on the shop-floor and in the office. He is currently researching trade union recruitment strategies and the recent history of the print union SOGAT.

Chris Baldry is Senior Lecturer in Industrial Relations in the Department of Human Resource Management, University of Strathclyde. His teaching and research interests include technological change in the workplace and comparative employment systems.

Martin Beirne lectures in Organizational Behaviour at Glasgow University. His research interests range broadly around the theory and practice of worker-participation schemes. His doctoral thesis offered a critical view of participative approaches to computing systems design.

Anne Connolly recently worked as a full-time researcher at the University of Strathclyde on a project examining the impact of new technology systems in local government. She is now employed as a corporate planner in the Town Clerk's Department, City of Glasgow.

Peter Cressey is Co-director of Inspire, a research group at the University of Bath mainly concerned with the relationship between participation, industrial relations, and employment. He lectures in Industrial Sociology and Industrial Relations and has an extensive research background in the areas of worker-participation, new technology, and industrial relations. He has recently co-authored two books: *Agreement and Innovation* with V. D. Martino, and *Industrial Sociology and Crisis* with J. Eldridge, and J. MacInnes.

Professor Stephen Deery is the Director of the Centre for Industrial Relations and Labour Studies at the University of Melbourne in Australia. He holds a degree in Economics from Monash University and a Ph.D. in Industrial Relations from Latrobe University. His recent research and publications have been in the areas of trade union membership, absenteeism and employee turnover and industrial relations in Asia. He is currently working on a project on unilateral and dual commitment in the Australian motor vehicle industry.

Patricia Findlay is a lecturer in Organizational Behaviour at the University of Edinburgh. She has previously researched and written on the subject of employee responses to closure and on the role of gender in industrial action. She is currently writing a book on employment policy in the Scottish electronics industry. Her main research interests in addition to this are, at present, in the areas of computer systems design and employee responses to performance appraisal.

Cliff Lockyer is Senior Lecturer in Industrial Relations at the University of Strathclyde. He initially worked in the car industry before entering academic life. His current research interests focus on employment and labour market activity in Scotland.

Harvie Ramsay was on research secondment to the Industrial Relations Research Unit, University of Warwick, until October 1991, after which he returned to lecturing in Industrial Relations at the University of Strathclyde. He is the author of numerous contributions, most notably on the subjects of worker participation and employee involvement, and on labour in multinational companies as well as work on new technology, some of the latter being reported in this volume.

Lynn Valentine is a television researcher currently working for the BBC's parliamentary unit. She previously carried out film research for the BBC breakfast programme.

1 Manna or monstrous regiment?

Technology, control, and democracy in the workplace

Martin Beirne and Harvie Ramsay

The question of technological change, as with most questions in the analysis of work and workplace relations, takes on a different cast depending on whether it is asked from the standpoint of capital and management, or from the view of labour and the employee. For management the primary issue is whether the productive benefits of technology outweigh its costs, and therefore how to realize and maximize those benefits. For labour, the chief concerns relate to the consequences of technological change for work experience and control – and even for the very existence of many jobs.

This book is predominantly concerned with the latter vantage point, with the consequences for labour of a particular set of technological changes created by information technology. However, the persistent and vexatious need for management to gain co-operation from the work-force, and related issues resurrected under the currently popular label of 'human resource management', leads to common areas of concern around questions of work content, experience and decision-making. Despite this overlap, though, the terms of this shared contemplation are rarely compatible, as evidenced by the contrasting claims for 'involvement' from management and 'democracy' or 'participation' from labour.

In the text, we use the term 'information technology', or IT for short, because the alternative, 'new technology', is inexact and potentially embraces all technical changes, not just those arising from the development and integration of microprocessor and communications devices. That said, the range of applications of silicon chip technology is now so great that a very wide range of contexts and effects must be considered, a fact reflected in the variety of contributions to this collection. While the information-handling capacities of the technology make it particularly direct in its impact on work which performs this function – namely office work – the ability to instruct mechanical actions has important implications expressed in the more popular, dramatic image of 'automation' and the 'robot', while the ability to read and process codes is transforming checkouts and stock control in the retail industry, for instance.

We should be clear that this book is not yet another attempt to map these general changes. Rather, it focuses on the question of workplace democracy (WD), and examines the relationship between IT and the various dimensions of WD identified below. In this, it brings together two related themes high on the current agenda of concern, since the political and socio-economic conditions of the late 1980s and early 1990s have seen a revival of attention to the condition and interests of the employee.

Another point to make at the outset is that the book is avowedly empirical in its approach, the emphasis being on the explanation of observed reality rather than the theorization of abstract possibilities. In this introduction, however, the wider concerns will be considered, and the contributions set in the context of that overview. To set the scene, we begin with an analysis of existing perspectives on the technology–democracy relationship.

DETERMINISM OR CHOICE?

Early studies of technological change tended to treat technology as something fixed, exerting a neutral 'impact' on work organization and experience – the machine as a *deus ex machina*. In its crudest and most expansive forms, this vision presents whole eras of social change as inevitable reflexes of technological development. This genre is represented on the left by restrictive readings of Marx and Engels, with communism as the ultimate and unstoppable end-game: 'The hand mill will give you a society with a feudal lord, the steam mill a society with the industrial capitalist' (Marx 1847). From a different angle, the liberal right have recast the future to be read off from technology as pluralistic post-industrialism (cf. Bell 1973), while pessimists present more of a '1984' image, especially given the potential use of IT for surveillance and monitoring.

Of course, these images of IT or other technologies as exogenous but potent moulds for social relations have been partly modified by analyses of the social production of technology itself. Thus when Carchedi (1984) argues that computers are unsuited for socialism, his argument is based on an analysis of computer technology as created under capitalist social relations, and so being designed as a tool of class domination. In a less sweeping fashion, Noble's classic 1979

analysis of the management decisions behind the design of numerically controlled machine tools in the US after the Second World War
combines the sense of structural constraint (through management
control and the purposes management are required to serve) with the
sense of process and agency, and the way these squeeze out what are
in abstracto technical *options*.

Braverman, whose discussion of the 'labour process' inspired the
work of Noble and has provoked the most active debates on work
organization in the last decade and a half, presented his arguments
concerning the deskilling effects of technical innovation as a critique
of the evolutionary determinism of Blauner, Woodward and others
(see pp. 9–11). 'In reality,' he insists, 'machinery embraces a host
of possibilities, many of which are systematically thwarted, rather
than developed, by capital' (Braverman 1974: 230). In order to
distinguish between outright technological determinism and accounts
like Braverman's of systemic constraints on the application and
design of technology, we will refer to the latter approach as *social
determinism*.

Once the possibility of variation in the development and use of a
given technical object is allowed, however, further exploration of this
uncovers ever more complex sources of that variation in practice, and
so casts in ever higher relief the apparent indeterminacy or, put in
more active terms, the potential for social choice in technical design
and its consequences. This has led Wilkinson (1983), like many
others, to reject what he terms the 'impact of innovation' approach
to analysing technological change, styling it as a depoliticization of
the real processes involved. Differences of interest and deliberate
choices by management in their own interests are obscured by the
impersonalized view of IT, argues Wilkinson, especially when the
new technology is presented as inevitable, as an 'advance', as
something which it is in everybody's interests to accept for the sake
of keeping up with or getting ahead of the competition.

In this context it is interesting to consider the siting of socio-
technical analysis, as developed by the Tavistock Institute of
Human Relations, among these approaches. This is worthwhile
partly for illustrative purposes, but chiefly because socio-technical
analysis has exerted a great deal of influence in the field, including
recent approaches to computerized information systems (Beirne and
Ramsay 1988).

On the one hand, socio-technical analysis advocates the 'joint
optimization' of any work system, implying that machine and human
variability are both adjustable to each other. In practice, however,

it may be suggested that Tavistock consultants have always treated the technology as fixed, and sought to adapt recalcitrant human employees to it by varying working arrangements around the equipment (Hyman 1972; Kelly 1978, 1982).

This reflects two problematical aspects: the pollution of theorized possibilities by the consultancy role (which renders the replacement of equipment impractical as a suggestion to those who paid for it, and for the consultancy); and the conception of the social and technical systems as externally rather than internally related to one another. The eventual solution is also remarkably consistent, whatever the context. As Kelly (1978, 1982) has recognized, it comes down to the practice of mounting a critique of the set views of Taylorism only to substitute a different 'one best way' of group working. The socio-technical tradition is after all one of adapting to the 'impact' of technology: 'a change is required in the work culture from a man-centred [*sic*] to a machine-centred attitude – a *machine culture*' (Trist *et al.* 1963: 259). Of course social choice accounts themselves recognize more than one source of variation in the development of given technologies. First, there are those beyond the control of actors within the organization – namely, the environmental conditions under which IT is adopted which dictate the degree of room for manoeuvre, such as the intensity of cost and/or quality competition, for instance.

Second, there are the strategic choices open to management (Sorge and Streeck 1988, Child 1985, Friedman 1977), who may emphasize a variety of deskilling or enskilling potentials of IT in their recruitment and labour utilization policies. While certain options may be more likely under particular conditions (such as the pressures created by the different product cycle phases of manufactured goods, for instance), these authors none the less emphasize that alternative potentially viable choices are always open to some degree.

Third, there are variations introduced by labour resistance to management policy, and the subsequent negotiation or battle for control of how IT is operated. This contestation of outcomes is often elided from managerial writings, and sometimes from labour process accounts.

Unfortunately, social choice on these combined dimensions is often taken to extremes, becoming so dominant in causality that technology appears almost infinitely elastic in its nature, barely sustaining an existence in itself. For instance, in one widely used textbook on organizations it is suggested that 'we should not be studying technology at all . . . we should instead be analysing managers' beliefs, assumptions and decision-making processes' (Buchanan and Huczynski 1985: 221). This reductionism is also threatened by recent attempts, stimulating and insightful though they often are, to analyse technology as a 'social construction' (for example, Bijker *et al.* 1989).

In a useful corrective to this, it is riposted that the 'technology baby should not be ejected with the determinist bathwater' (to slightly rephrase Clark *et al.* 1988 and McLoughlin and Clark 1988). They observe that many of those who have set out to modify the simple causal model running from technology to social relations have none the less noted elements of 'constraint' or 'rigidity' in a given technology. Moreover, studies of technology show that just as it is not produced in a social vacuum before entering society, so it also develops from past technological and scientific understanding, preventing there being scope for infinite variation and recasting at any given moment in time. Technologies can also prove faulty, especially in the early years, and this imposes significant unintentional and unpredictable effects on work practices beyond the control of anyone in the innovating organization.

In any case, much new technology (whether microprocessor based or not) is itself produced by a few firms and sold as a package to others, seriously limiting the scope for local management or employee manoeuvre – a phenomenon particularly evident over many years in the computing field with the dominance of IBM, for instance. In a number of ways, then, technology does arrive from outside and has an 'impact' from the point of view of management or employees in a given organization. Ironically, an emphasis on the social production of technology may highlight, in important respects, the limitations for choice at the local levels by those applying it or experiencing the consequences thereof.

While social choice approaches remain more flexible and persuasive than determinist ones in our assessment then, the limits and constraints of choice remain in need of being charted. Many writers present cautious assessments of 'potentials' created by microprocessor technologies, for networked and more open access to data in an information system (Mumford 1979, 1983), or for diagnosis and reprogramming by operators of robots or CNC tools, for example (Jones 1982). But the slippage from this to insistence on the inevitability of such change is often swift and near-total. The sense of social structure as contradiction and constraint for such policies is abandoned too readily, as (to anticipate) our review of real-world outcomes demonstrates.

OPTIMISM OR PESSIMISM?

So far our discussion has provided glimpses of positive and negative implications for workplace democracy, but the determinist and social choice perspectives both contain contrasting assessments on this score. To get to grips with the issues of particular concern to us, then, we must introduce a cross-cutting distinction between optimistic and pessimistic predictions for IT users. If we persist for a moment in treating this (and the determinism/choice dimension likewise) as a straightforward continuum, it becomes possible to produce a simple diagram (see Figure 1.1) onto which it is quite instructive to map different commentators. The result shows how alliances may emerge on one dimension between writers of markedly different persuasion (a picture which should be enhanced if we could superimpose the third dimension of political standpoint).

Optimism or pessimism may be seen as shaped by either technological determinism, or (in a manner perhaps a little less narrowly determinist) by what we have called social determinism. Thus the mapping of approaches on Figure 1.1 reflects predictions of the enhancement or debilitation of workplace democracy derived from

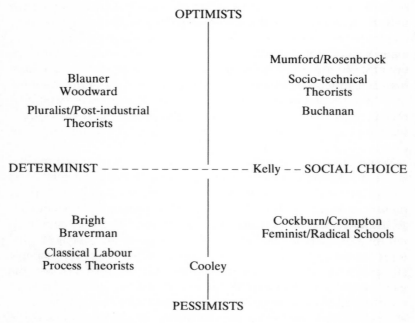

Figure 1.1   Images of IT

both arguments about the inherent properties of IT itself, and of the degree of structural constraint in the settings within which it is produced and introduced.

This distinguishes a writer like Cooley (1980) from someone like Rosenbrock (1982), for instance. In many respects these authors offer a similar debunking of the 'expert' ideologies of systems design that justify non-participation and minimal job discretion for the user. However, the former locates this campaign for alternatives within an awareness of the wider structures of capital imperatives and management objectives which he sees as promoting the low-skill options, whereas the latter offers no such analysis, leaving the impression that the failure to use people's capabilities fully is a consequence of no more than a misguided myopia.

The difference between these two approaches is one between liberal voluntarism and Marxist structural determinism. In this, it echoes divisions in the wider participation debate of the 1960s and 1970s, between the radical liberal participatory theorists such as Blumberg (1968) or Pateman (1970), and Marxist writers on the subject. The criticisms of existing management practice as 'pseudo' participation were very similar on many points, but the source of the limits to genuine democracy at work were never located by the radical liberal approach, whereas Marxists (sometimes rather blithely) could attribute them to the nature of capitalism. This debate is explored in Ramsay (1982). Meanwhile, to examine these various expectations further in the context of IT, we need first to specify what is meant by workplace democracy. The next section addresses itself to a simple classification.

IT AND WORKPLACE DEMOCRACY: DIMENSIONS OF ANALYSIS

In order to unwrap the optimistic/pessimistic predictions further, it is necessary to clarify what aspects of work organization and relations we are concerned with here. Broadly, it is necessary to distinguish between the direct implications of IT for work organization and experience at the *individual and work group level,* and the degree of influence which is exerted by employees at the *representative or collective level.* This analytical distinction is heuristic; it carries no implication that these are two discrete 'spheres' of action. Indeed, it will be argued throughout that the maintenance of such a distinction as real tends to occlude many of the important issues of power and democracy, a point explored further in the section on control (see below).

At the workface, so to speak, discussions examine the skill content of jobs with IT, and the degree of employee control over or discretion in carrying out the immediate labour process. 'Skill' itself is a sticky topic, and has generated an involved debate (c.f. Manwaring and Wood 1985, Rolfe 1986, Martin 1988a, Phillips and Taylor 1980), particularly around the extent to which it can be defined in terms of task content or is socially constructed. The former view invokes aspects of work content such as dexterity and co-ordination, task complexity, task range and variety, knowledge and training requirements, and may add elements of discretion as discussed below (see pp. 14–20).

The social construction critique, most ably articulated by feminists, suggests that rather than skill defining power, the reverse may occur; employees with a power base are able to have their work defined as skilled. Thus men and women performing tasks fairly equivalent on task criteria may find themselves graded very differently, due to gender inequalities in the power to define the job advantageously.

This important and undoubtedly valid argument demonstrates the link between different aspects of influence or control, and we shall return to it later. It does not entirely invalidate the need to identify objective task elements, however (indeed the demand for equal pay for equivalent work assumes that something of skill content can be excavated from the mystification). Thus we retain the notion of task content (or technical skill) as one aspect of our analysis. The problem of reading off from typical data on skills is more considerable, since these data are often already suffused with social definitions.

If we turn to the control aspect of work organization, this too presents various elements, Rolfe (1986) identifies the extent to which employees exercise judgement and decision-making, their scope for control over how the task is organized, and the degree of restriction by supervision. The amount of self-determination or autonomy in the work task must consider these aspects, then, though too narrow a focus may obscure constraints which the employee operates within (which may be so evident as to be taken for granted rather than articulated, or may be internalized as duties and values and so no longer seen as constraints).

Once we extend our remit to the *representative or collective dimension*, this question of control becomes still more complex and muddy. Broadly, there are two approaches to representation: first, through the union or other collective basis for *negotiation*; and second, through company channels for *consultation or involvement*. While these two approaches are not hermetically distinct from one another – since consultation may take on a tacit bargaining style, or negotiating may take a highly accommodative, 'integrative' form – nevertheless they do broadly represent competing participative paradigms. The first can be characterized as labour-oriented, emphasizing differing interests between employees and management. This conflict may be pursued at the level of work group or workplace, or it may be examined in terms of trade union influence and activity.

By contrast, involvement exercises reflect prevailing managerial views of participation, seeking to communicate and justify programmes of technical change in order to gain the acquiescence or, better still, the motivation and active support of employees. Hence, while certain areas of employee input to decisions may be entertained, these are marginal to management objectives and are means intended to facilitate rather than restrict management control. Consultation usually involves a formal procedure for communication, which also implies some discussion (though consultation may also extend to the union and so overlap the two categories). Several authors have recently described processes whereby managements have sought to avoid union influence by consulting directly with work groups, presenting this as a means of giving more 'involvement' to employees (Lane 1988, Daniel 1987, Martin 1988a).

The empirical studies in this volume each examine various aspects of this range of approaches. The emphasis throughout is on the extent to which genuine democratization occurs, but the focus varies. Several studies map the influence of trade unions, specifically Deery, Findlay and Cressey (both). Others, including our own (Beirne and Ramsay, Ramsay *et al.*) examine involvement or consultative programmes. A third group – the chapters by Bain and Baldry and by Valentine – focuses on the individual and task control aspects of the subject. The purpose of this chapter is to integrate these and other findings into a fuller assessment.

WORK ORGANIZATION: A NEW ERA?

The managerialist optimism that pervades much of the literature sustains many accounts of the inherently enskilling nature of IT. These assessments are in an established tradition, supported by the arguments of writers such as Woodward (1965) and Blauner (1964). Both of these authors regarded the onset of automation as a basis for better working conditions and workplace relations. In each case, it was suggested that machine pace became decoupled from work pressure as operators became overseers of the equipment rather than having to match its speed, and that worker–supervisor relations could improve in the new circumstances. Both saw the chemical process industry as the vanguard of this change. In contrast, Bright (1958) concluded from observing the engineering industry that fragmentation and closer supervision was the consequence of more automated techniques, indicating the need for a less sweeping and precipitate judgement.

A contemporary example of vulnerable optimism will illustrate this. Numerous writers have harboured the expectation that the powerful and increasingly influential computer operating system Unix – designed to allow multi-user access by a community of users exchanging ideas – would democratize information and increase the scope and individual choice of work task. Unfortunately the reality is rather different. Unix becomes a very restricted tool in modern networked systems which contain certain bars to information for users but allow centralized monitoring and direction by a 'super-user': integration turns from shared to concentrated control (Woolley 1986).

Unfortunately, the prevalence of one or another version of a social choice perspective over any narrowly determinist account entails that the soundest answer on task enskilling or deskilling is equivocal: 'it depends . . .'. The question is thrown back – reasonably enough – to an assessment of what the outcome depends on.

Here the difference between optimists and pessimists becomes important. For the optimist who leans towards a *social* determinist view, the good news tends to flow from an image of progressive and enlightened management. In the 1970s, a left version of this would have emphasized employee power to drive back the 'frontiers of control', but there were few such optimists in the 1980s.

For other contributors, however, management enlightenment is a practical, not normative, matter. Dankbaar summarizes this argument:

> Improving the quality of work, however, is not a major goal of management – it is, if it happens, rather a side-effect of management's efforts to reach higher productivity and profitability . . . the literature on new technologies and new production concepts is arguing that it is management itself that should be interested in diminishing the division of labour, in reintegrating tasks and therefore in improving the quality of work.
>
> (Dankbaar 1988: 26)

The advocates to whom Dankbaar is referring here represent probably the most vocal set of viewpoints in social science literature at present. It is a set of viewpoints rather than a single viewpoint, as is illustrated by the debate over the appropriateness of terms like 'post-Fordism' or 'flexible specialization' (see Wood 1989), but the shared element is the presumption that the efficiency advantages of Taylorist and Fordist methods, with their associated degradation of jobs, have now evaporated. This has been occasioned by the combination of a new environment (highly competitive and rapidly changing markets), new concepts of work organization (particularly from Japan, for example Just In Time and Total Quality Control), and the enabling capacities of IT.

The pessimist is much more likely to be in the Bravermanian mould, emphasizing the ultimate dominance and aims of management, and their undemocratic consequences. One revision of this offers a restrained optimism, arguing that, none the less, management will find it advantageous to hand over control and enhance the skill profile of employees to promote 'flexible specialization', thanks to the adaptability and co-operation employers need to respond to rapidly shifting product markets and technical content. The extent to which this post-Fordist model applies in practice, and across what sectors, thus becomes an important matter to assess.

However, it may also be argued from this less sanguine perspective that the supposedly 'new' management techniques associated with IT and work reorganization are actually far from novel. As Hyman comments: 'there are uncomfortable parallels between some of the current rhetoric on "flexible specialisation" and the traditional literature on "participation" and "job enrichment"' (Hyman 1988: 54). Indeed, we would argue that the parallels are not only legion, but that this is traceable through the resuscitation in the IT literature of human relations and socio-technical approaches which are refugees of the debunking research of the 1970s in particular (Beirne and Ramsay 1988, Beirne 1991). The revisions to adapt the arguments to the fresh context are often minimal (the ground rules having been laid by Blauner and others for this).

If there is any truth in this 'old wine in new bottles' view, other questions follow. Are the reconstituted approaches producing the same patterns observed by critics of their forebears (see, for example, Kelly 1982) – seeking in practice to intensify work effort, increase flexibility, and reduce worker resistance in a way which offers no threat to management control of the production process overall? The term 'controlled autonomy' has indeed been used by some writers to describe the more recent changes and their ambivalence for employee control (Dohse *et al.* 1985, Dankbaar 1988). In other words, have we moved far from the Chemco worker who commented, in a widely quoted interview, 'I never feel "enriched" – I just feel knackered'?

If this remains the case, we could simply label the outcome 'manipulation', or (after the earliest efforts to describe a technically driven revision of established work organization) 'neo-Fordism'. However, the further analysis of such methods also revealed constraints and contradictions, arising from the very lack of substance in the changes they purported to bring. If there is not, after all, a fundamental shift in organizational principles, then the problem of obedience and co-operation may not be so readily resolved and continuing difficulties will arise. The oscillation implied by Hyman will persist:

> the discretionary exercise of some form of expertise can be found in virtually every labour process. But conversely there are few (if any) workers whose voluntary commitment requires no external reinforcement. . . . Shifting fashions in labour management stem from this inherent contradiction: solutions to the problem of discipline aggravate the problem of consent, and *vice versa*.
>
> (Hyman 1988: 52)

These competing visions can only partially be addressed through existing evidence, due to the limited scope of research to date, but once the questions are posed in this way the interpretation of findings may be more discerning. Most of the studies reported below are British, this selection allowing some filter of the enormous volume of research emerging on the subject. The typicality of British experience will be considered later (see pp. 44–8).

SKILL AND JOB CONTENT

The question of whether IT leads inherently to the deskilling of work has been answered almost unanimously in the negative by research to date. A number of extensive reviews of the evidence have appeared in recent times: McLoughlin and Clark 1988, Lane 1988, Martin 1988a, Jones 1988, Elger 1989. Notwithstanding the differences of emphasis between them (of which more in a moment), there is broad agreement with the assessment that 'there is no uniform trend towards either degradation and deskilling or multi-skilling and upgrading of responsibilities (Jones, 1988: 480). The questions, then, concern the balance of, and any patterns over time in, such changes.

Given the different applications of IT, and the contrast in many respects in the pre-existing application of technology, it is helpful to consider changes in the non-manual and manual work environments separately before making other, more general, observations.

Manual work and IT

Within the manual environment, the most extensive application of IT in a way that substantially changes the production process to date has been in manufacturing. As a result, most studies focus here, although it should be recognized that such 'shop-floor work' is no longer the dominant form of manual work it once was.

There are quite distinct applications of IT even in manual manufacturing (material processing) jobs. In broad systems terms, it is possible to identify numerical control (CNC where computer-controlled), robotics, flexible manufacturing systems (FMS), and computer-integrated manufacturing (CIM) (Jones 1988). Since these are generally thought of as marking increasingly automated extensions of computer control, an heroic leap might seem in order to treat these as indicators of long-term developments once all sectors move to CIM. This latter-day Blaunerism would be injudicious, however. All the technologies concerned are still being changed as techniques advance, all are still 'bedding in', and in any case there are very few examples of FMS (let alone CIM) to examine as yet. Moreover, assumptions that all production must gravitate towards more 'advanced' forms is perilous futurology, as past predictions have shown.

As it happens, the options identified and outcomes observed show similar broad patterns for each of these technologies. A potential for 'polyvalence' (multiskilling which includes assuming supervisory or decision-making functions) is identified, on an individual or work team basis, but is found to be rare or undetected in practice. In a number of cases, at least some jobs are reduced to feeding and monitoring, although robotics in the car industry in particular has reportedly reduced the number of unpleasant and dangerous jobs (in the paint shop or performing repeat welding tasks, for instance).

For maintenance work, one view is that skill (and status) increases with the importance of understanding the requirements of new equipment – as in the paper industry studies reported by Penn and Scattergood (1985). At the other extreme, maintenance tasks may be allocated to operators, or maintenance workers may be required to work on normal production jobs when not in demand, amounting to dilution and a reduction of status (Martin 1988a). From research to date, the latter outcome appears more likely, entailing as it does an intensification of use of working time, an issue we shall return to shortly (see pp. 18–20).

The variability of outcomes in manufacturing is echoed in the retail sector. Research on Electronic Point Of Sale (EPOS) systems suggests that the resulting enhanced stock control data can be centralized to intensify existing divisions of labour, or access can be given to store staff to enable them to make their own ordering decisions (Smith 1988). The tendency was for high volume/low price outlets to centralize decisions, while up-market shops which relied on staff service quality for sales were more likely to decentralize. In this way the impact of IT flowed from, and reinforced, the pre-existing 'craft' skills. Other examples of such reinforcement are to be found, the most telling of which relate to gender access, which will be addressed in the next section.

The pattern described above is confirmed, with perhaps some-what greater optimism, by two widely quoted surveys.[1] Daniel (1987) reports the second Workplace Industrial Relations Survey (administered in 1984) findings on technical change, relying on managers' and shop stewards' judgements of the impact of such change on jobs. The relevant dimensions here are 'skill', 'range of activity' and 'job interest'. He summarizes the results as indicating positive enskilling on all three, but the figures actually show increases for only two-fifths (or just over) of employees on each dimension, around the same with no change, and a small proportion (11–15 per cent) with a reported decline.

Shop stewards reported less positive results for interest than managers, but greater skill and task range changes, a pattern probably consistent with pay bargaining stances more than anything else. Sectorally, interest was reported most positively affected (by managers) in private manufacturing, where task range also rose most on these accounts; but skill level was seen as least likely to have risen there and in the public services (the latter, probably reflecting the consequences of restructuring and privatization threats, coming out bottom on all three dimensions), and most likely in private services, with the nationalized industries between the two.

Intriguingly, Daniel reports (1987: 153) that these 'advanced' technical changes were rather less popular than 'conventional' changes, though more favourable than other forms of work reorganization. This runs contrary to his own expectations, and casts doubt once more over the particularly positive potentials claimed to be inherent in IT by many optimists.

A survey of 1,000 shop stewards by Batstone and Gourlay (1986) reports broadly similar findings to Daniel. Examining four characteristics of work, of which 'skill' and 'effort' will engage us for the moment, they tabulate increases on average in reported skill for most production and maintenance groups, matched broadly by reported increases in effort. Skill reductions are reported by a small minority only in chemicals, electrical and non-electrical engineering, and food and drink, though they are noted by a third of stewards representing production workers in printing. Effort is reported to be higher by between two-fifths and three-fifths in every sector examined.

These findings are seen by the authors as indicating a trade-off, whereby employers forgo the deskilling option in return for greater effort. However, these results and those reported below on control are also consistent – arguably more so – with an *enlargement-and-intensification* thesis which we will examine at the end of the section on control. Suspicion of Batstone and Gourlay's own conclusions is sharpened by their admission that they were unable to specify the notion of 'skill' for their questionnaire, leaving its definition to their respondents: hence it need not imply 'enrichment' of tasks in the eyes of those respondents, or in the reality they are reporting.

Non-manual work

White-collar work is no more of a single piece than manual work for the purpose of IT applications. Indeed, since it deals with information, which is also the function of the technology, the range of innovations is arguably far greater, especially as office work has previously been subject far less than manual work to technological change. Survey evidence confirms a far higher incidence of innovation in non-manual work (Daniel 1987, Lane 1988).

As a guideline to the likely patterns of enskilling or deskilling in non-manual work, Lane (1988) argues that management strategy will vary according to the significance of white-collar labour in total costs (which will affect the importance of office labour cost savings), and the importance of the quality of service provided by labour. This latter point is consistent with the EPOS retail example cited earlier, and seems to fit the insurance sector data as well.

Jones (1988) suggests another key variable. The more jobs already specialized and fragmented before the arrival of IT, he suggests, the lower will be the leverage of labour (in terms of existing skills and control) to help persuade management to pursue an enskilling route. Where jobs were more integrated and less segregated previously, the reverse will apply. This analysis introduces occupational and work group power to the equation, and can help to make sense of variations in computer-aided design/draughting (CAD) systems or those between typists and secretaries discussed later, as well as of the more sweeping gender inequalities considered in the next section. A further elaboration would note the way that those who exert tight control over their work, and the means of producing it, are likely to experience any new equipment as support facilities, and to welcome rather than fear them (as with new testing equipment for electrical engineers, map-drawing micros for cartographers, or word processors and computer terminals for academics).

Lane's analysis helpfully distinguishes between areas, particularly in the finance sector, where computerization has been extensive for many years, and in those where its arrival on a large scale is relatively recent. Dealing with the former first, the current changes are often characterized as a shift from 'batch' systems (where employees prepare large data inputs for large mainframes) to 'stand-alone' or 'network' systems where the data are fed in more continuously, and where the technical potential for 'real time' data access and analysis by the operator is much greater.

Optimists (for example, Mumford) argue that these later systems can open up (even 'democratize') previously routinized, machine-driven and centralized arrangements. Lane does agree that work in the finance sector, especially computer-related work in banking, is often already highly 'Taylorized' and routine in nature, and while she is relatively optimistic about the effects of second-generation computerization, it is largely in the sense that matters may have improved somewhat rather than deteriorated further. The optimism applies more readily to insurance than to banking, she indicates.

In insurance, some integration of functions is reported (Barras and Swann 1983, Storey 1986), while where a degree of distributed information processing takes place, skill levels may rise (Gourlay 1987, Rajan 1984). This is seen as a reflection of the need for employee service skills in selling insurance, in line with Lane's analysis. This would, however, need to be demonstrated with reference to the quite different sectors of the insurance market (general insurance, life insurance and superannuation, health insurance, reinsurance, brokerage services, for instance), where the possibilities of automating decisions and the extent of reliance on personal customer contact vary quite considerably. Interviews by one of the present authors in the course of other research in the insurance sector have indicated contrasting demands and attitudes to skill needs and employee information access within computerized systems in different subsectors.

In contrast to the findings concentrated on by Lane, Crompton and Jones (1984) found high levels of routinization in computerized work in their insurance case study. This reflects their findings in a bank and a local authority (the last also having long established computerization of many functions, with due respect to Lane). They do not consider the impact of later generation information processing systems separately, though.

A project in the United States which examined job content under more recent computerization programmes (Appelbaum and Albin 1989) suggests findings compatible with this contradictory picture, identifying two options to organizational design and policy processing in the industry: algorithmic and non-standardized. The former centralizes most policy handling, reducing many tasks to data input, with the computer resolving most quotations according to a standard set of rules, and passing those which are exceptional to an exceptions underwriter. The result is a deskilling of most tasks. The alternative eliminates routine and uses on-line processing to support each quotation, thus reducing routine data handling and increasing skills (of those who retain jobs, at least). However, the authors observe that it is the algorithmic option which is seen as state of the art and is expanding in most large firms, while smaller, more specialist firms are more likely to consider alternatives, a pattern which also confirms the need for a more detailed analysis of differences within the industry.

Having said that, Crompton and Jones's findings in banking are more consonant with other work in the finance sector. Here routinization is already high (Rajan 1984, Loveridge *et al.* 1985, Smith and Wield 1987), though often unacknowledged, tacit skills are considerable (MacInnes 1988). The emergence of various automated credit transfer systems and dispensers (see Cressey, Chapter 6 this volume) has had mixed effects, but while the common conclusion is that matters have not worsened further, any added movement across tasks is more a matter of enlargement than enrichment.

Moving on to consider areas facing the arrival of IT more recently, the contrast between secretaries and typists mentioned above seems to illustrate Jones's predictions well. The main innovation for both groups has been the word processor. Early fears foresaw the deskilling of typing work itself, and a general increase in the electronic input rather than social content of most office jobs, reducing the differences between the two categories (Downing 1980, Tongue 1986).

However, this does not seem to have been borne out. Although the influence of both groups on change is already circumscribed partly by power factors relating not least to the gender-segregated, 'feminized' nature of the work, within this framework the distinction between the two is if anything found to be sharpened, and their experience of IT is very different (Webster 1986, Butler 1989). Secretaries, situated in a relatively high-status task where typing is only a fraction of their work, tend to use the word processor as a more efficient and convenient typewriter, if anything enhancing their status in the process. Typists, however, often already facing high levels of routinization and Taylorization of work (especially in large offices) may even find this worsened by the advent of the word processor. Standardization of work is unlikely to fall much if at all from existing high levels, and though task variety does sometimes increase, work intensity almost invariably does as well (Butler 1989, Webster 1986, Wainwright and Francis 1984, Buchanan and Boddy 1982).

The debate over one other area of non-manual work clearly illustrates the divergences arising from different analytical app-roaches and fieldwork findings on IT. This is the research on CAD. As Cooley has argued (1981), CAD has the potential to be used in enskilling ways, cutting down on routine work and allowing greater attention to creative design by the draughtsperson. Alternatively, it can centralize information and standardize drawings by storing for recall certain fixed and repeated shapes or component representa-tions, reducing the task towards one of diagrammatic assembly. Some observers have argued that CAD tends in practice to be used in a deskilling manner (Arnold and Senker 1982, Baldry and Connolly 1986), partly for organizational reasons to do with the prevalence of cost-accounted justifications of expenditure. Others have placed greater emphasis on the potential for enskilling (Wainwright and Francis 1984).

McLoughlin reports that the outcome is actually quite variable, the variation depending on whether systems are operated by dedicated or non-dedicated staff, and on whether work stations are centralized or decentralized (McLoughlin and Clark 1988). Dedication is not a matter of professional commitment, but refers to the extent to which use of the CAD work-station becomes the entire task of the draughts-person, who effectively becomes a CAD operator. The non-dedi-cated CAD user employs the system more as a tool for part of a wider-ranging set of tasks. The analogy to the typist/secretary experience of word processors will be readily apparent. Centralized work-stations also tend to reinforce the separation of electronic drawing from other work.

In a later contribution, McLoughlin (1989) suggests that there are two broad types of system architectures which may be applied to CAD – draughting systems (basically 'shape processors') and modelling systems (which allow more flexible use and input from the designer). The former type of system is more likely to create the dedicated and routinized option for the draughting job, with a process of 'distancing' whereby many traditional draughting skills are incorporated in the machine, rather than a 'complementary' enhancement of designing skills.

McLoughlin suggests that the potential for modelling systems and other 'complementary' work systems to emerge is high, leaning to the optimistic, Mumford-type view of the new technology. In practice, though, these potentials may be little exploited by management, an outcome which this type of approach is again poorly placed to explain. This conclusion is actually not so different to Cooley's (or Baldry and Connolly's), but it shows little appreciation of social constraints and priorities which Cooley suggests sculpture management policy. As such, McLoughlin's discussions clarify the nature of CAD work, but fail to resolve the issues he addresses.

Turning lastly to the two surveys whose findings we have already cited on manual work, Daniel (1987) confirms that the greater diffusion in IT in the office reported earlier is reflected in greater reported changes in task content there. Both his and Batstone and Gourlay's (1986) findings also suggest on balance an enskilling for non-manual employees. Daniel claims that the outcomes seem more positive for non-manual than for manual work, with enhanced skill and job interest (matched, too, by range of activity) reported by three-fifths of managers responding to the Workplace Industrial Relations Survey (1984), a reported decline on these dimensions being rare. As with manual work, shop stewards were more likely than managers to report skill increases, but noticeably less likely to report enhanced job interest.

Batstone and Gourlay (1986) also report that more than half their non-manual shop steward respondents in finance, the civil service, and Post Office Engineering Union (POEU) sections of Telecom claim an increase in skill has occurred for their members. Civil and Public Services Association (CPSA) Telecom employees fall below the halfway line (43 per cent) of reports on skill enhancement, but are also most likely (71 per cent of steward reports) to indicate an increase in required effort, where only a quarter to two-fifths of the other groups do so. A decline in disclosed skill levels is a little more likely than for Daniel's sample, varying from 10 per cent (civil service unions) to 26 per cent (POEU Telecom employees). However, in contrast to Daniel a comparison with the manual steward responses shows that increased skill is apparently *less* likely for non-manual employees; so, too, is increased effort.

Patterns and explanations

The overall pattern is remarkably hard to summarize, and certainly confirms at least the unanimous reference to variability, rather than some simple and determinate nature of outcomes on task content. An overview suggests a tendency, but rather thin and highly qualified, to greater rather than less skill, associated also with greater effort.

A number of factors may be suggested as possible variables influencing management policy on enskilling or deskilling. Martin (1988a) enumerates management values and objectives, product markets, labour markets, political regulation, organizational size and structure, and employee attitudes and behaviour. In addition, we have noted the explanatory strength of the importance of labour costs and the nature of labour's input (that is, the importance of quality); and also the significance of pre-existing task structures and occupational controls. These variables provide a useful starting point for analysis, but data is still thin for exploring the nature and extent of influence exerted by these factors.

It has been observed that labour costs (and labour management issues generally) are in practice very much in the background when management plan technological or product change (McLoughlin and Clark 1988, Martin 1988a). Willman (1987) suggests that the importance of work organization is likely to be greater for mature products, where cost competitiveness is predominant. Usually, however, labour utilization is apparently a residual issue for top management at least, left to line management to handle. The other side of this, however, is the predominance of financial objectives, and so cost control, in management's justification of capital expenditure. This may be expected to increase the pressure towards less innovative labour policies, especially in industrial cultures like the British which foster this accounting domination. Further consideration will be given to these issues, and to management objectives and decisions more generally, once the issue of control has been discussed.

CONTROL AND AUTONOMY

In many respects the issues of control overlap with those of task content, and the variable and inconclusive overall trends we shall report echo those we have identified on skilling. It is important to address control issues separately, however, since they invoke wider questions of power and democracy at work than we have hitherto addressed.

The concept of control

Put simply, control in the workplace can be understood in two quite different ways. It can be understood as the expression of power, as a concept which deals with the distribution of the ability to obtain the compliance of others in the pursuit of aims or interests. As such, it is a *relational* concept which is expressed solely in terms of dependency relationships between people singly or in groups/classes. Alternatively, control can be dealt with as a system property, in which those in a unit or organization are regarded as a unified entity seeking to manage their environment and achieve shared tasks. This usage is found in *functionalist* social systems analysis.

A shift to a functionalist use of the concept of control has a number of preconditions and consequences. Most importantly here, its very assumption of unity replicates itself, since control over, say, the market or the production process is seen as a common interest and allows advances in these respects to be represented as showing the 'positive-sum' nature of control (that is, an increase in the total amount of control, from which all may gain).

It has already been argued by one of us (Ramsay 1985, 1986) that this conceptualization of control is actually a dissolution of the concept, since in reality control draws its existence from dependency relationships. In fact, it would be better to insist that because of shared interests, relations are not ones of control at all. If the relational concept is sustained, however, then the distributive basis is restored: control is zero-sum by conceptual definition.

This requirement may be obscured by a further analytical device: that of distinguishing different spheres or levels of control, and attributing to them at least independence and perhaps even separate and distinct laws of motion. Just such a separation is threatened by the vulgarization of the distinction between 'formal' and 'real' (capitalist) subordination of labour in Marx, as frequently attributed to Braverman (1974). 'Formal' subordination sees the employer with little control over how the work task is performed, but controlling through the coercion of the employment relationship in a market system. 'Real' subordination supposedly emerges when employer control is extended to the direction of work itself, as attempted by Taylor. This is rightly criticized for creating a crude polarization between job control battles against 'real' subordination, and arguments that no significant change in control relations within capitalism is possible since 'formal' subordination remains all-pervasive (Cressey and MacInnes 1980).

None the less, just such a slippage between different levels and so meanings of control is apparent in recent reformist 'Marxist' views of job enrichment (Wood and Kelly 1982, Kelly 1985), and may be readily extended to the analysis of the potential and consequences of IT. It is also voiced with particular clarity and plausibility in the 'materialist non-Marxist' analysis of control presented by Edwards (1986). The terms for Edwards are 'detailed control', concerning the work task, and 'general control', concerning 'the accommodation of workers to the overall aims of the enterprise' (Edwards 1986: 6). Edwards goes well beyond Braverman, treating the two dimensions of control as quite independent of each other, and argues that 'general' control 'is not a zero-sum concept' (Edwards 1986: 79). He proceeds to argue that increases in employees' detailed control may enhance management's general control, as with increases in productivity achieved through such means as job enrichment, 'industrial democracy experiments' or quality circles. Much the same claim is apparently made by Jones and Scott in discussing flexible, automated systems, when in a parody (presumably deliberate) of a famous quote by Allan Flanders they suggest that 'management may need to surrender some power over their human factors of production in order to regain power over production operations as a whole' (Jones and Scott 1987: 36).

It is our contention that this is not merely a paradox, but if read in Edwards' (or Flanders') terms is a *reductio ad absurdum*. Such an analysis as that laid out by Edwards leads precisely to the functionalist slippage, and consequent reproduction of the unitarist assumption implicit in the concepts from the start. This is evident in his definition of general control quoted above. 'The overall aims of the enterprise' emerge as unproblematically (and managerially) defined, a classic functionalist reification. 'The accommodation of workers' to this sounds very like a process of (relational) social control, whether by legitimation or other means, once the unified aims are questioned.

It is the articulation of concepts like 'industrial democracy' in this context which not only strike the strongest resonance here, but also echo most hollowly. Democracy, after all, is precisely about the *distribution* of decision-making; in this sense it should be the antithesis of being controlled. But under the functionalist reformulation of general control it becomes a means for management to increase productivity, not in its most radical form a means for resetting the agenda of organizational objectives altogether.

The dangers of analysing control in the context of IT, as of any other variable in the workplace can be exemplified in terms of distinct arenas of task and organizational control by considering issues raised in other connections above and below concerning flexible working arrangements partly (but, importantly, not integrally) linked to IT developments. Consider, for instance, the characterization of new work organization arrangements as a 'flexible' cage' by Dawson and Webb:

> whilst staff may have greater autonomy over the pace of their work, they do not have any control over corporate policies or the oscillations in business activity and hence have to adapt continuously to environmental contingencies . . . [this] poses uncomfortable questions about the use of labour. The changes reported are consistent with the view that new production arrangements serve capital in the search for more efficient exploitation of labour.
>
> (Dawson and Webb 1989: 236)

The effect of greater autonomy at the 'detailed' task level here is to load onto employees the responsibility for coping with sudden demands, creating a precarious and stressful environment. The flexibility here may or may not be linked to the 'cage', to the transfer of pressures from management; the point is that the two are *not* on different dimensions but must be considered together.

Exactly the same points apply to the 'controlled autonomy' concept developed in the German literature (Dankbaar 1988). This is linked to attempts to analyse the Japanese system of work organization, on which one influential contribution observes:

> In our opinion, only a comprehensive perspective that includes both the organization of the labor process and the organization of labor relations can adequately explain the functioning of the Japanese model . . .
>
> . . . the labor process and industrial relations are so strongly interrelated in all important dimensions that an isolated consideration

of the labor process, as is done [sic] by management theorists, is impermissable [sic] and leads to erroneous conclusions.

(Dohse *et al.* 1985: 134, 140)

The 'harmonious' system of industrial relations is argued to be a result of management victory over militant unionism, with important (but not decisive) input from the state and from cultural dominance of certain ideas suitable to management, allowing in turn the installation of a series of controls over individual rewards and progress which makes flexibility and autonomy manageable (see also Batstone 1984: 334–41). Again, and even more extensively, the job level controls accruing to employees can only be properly understood in a wider context of power and conflict.

To conclude on the need for an analysis of control – and so workplace democracy – which integrates the different arenas of power, we come back to the British case. The introduction of IT here has also had a particular context in the 1980s, and to analyse task level arrangements and their outcome without reference to this is clearly to exclude a major element shaping them (Elger 1987, 1989). The acceptance of work intensification along with greater seeming task autonomy and flexibility by many employees who have experienced work reorganization along with IT innovations (see pp. 25–8) has undoubtedly been influenced by this visible pressure. Employees are thus accommodated to 'enterprise' objectives, and management control is increased via the particular ways in which effort is increased, whether this involves more or less 'task control'. Significantly, the apparent blindness to the 'broader power structure of employment relations' is also identified by Elger (1987) in his review of recent literature as a repeated feature, though taking various forms, in the analysis of IT.

This is not to argue that control in the job itself is unimportant – indeed employee attitudes and responses indicate that it is – but that it cannot be treated in isolation, particularly if we are concerned with questions of democracy. That said, we will none the less now review the evidence on IT and work control.

Control in manual work

It is interesting this time to begin with the surveys reported by Daniel (1987) and Batstone and Gourlay (1986). The relevant questions from the WIRS study here concern the changes in responsibility (not specified further in the questionnaire), control of work pace, the ability to decide how to do jobs, and supervision. The optimistic theories of IT would probably predict still more positive changes on these dimensions than for the skill elements considered earlier.

Certainly on managers' accounts supervision has at least not increased – it remains constant for two-thirds of responses, with increases or decreases roughly evenly dividing the remainder. A similar pattern emerges on responsibility, with over half of managers reporting no change for manual jobs, and a third reporting increases. In other respects 'control' variables show even less impressive evidence of improvement for employees, with almost half the management reports indicating no change in control of pace and decisions on work method, and almost a third in each case reporting a decrease. Only just over a fifth report an increase in control. Shop steward accounts roughly agree on pace and method, but are more likely to report increased supervision, and claim increased responsibility in 58 per cent of cases. Evidently the fact that responsibility is unspecified becomes important here, since being responsible for something (especially without greater room for manoeuvre in other respects) can be a pressure or burden rather than an 'enrichment', and might be a means to compel intensified effort as much as anything else. Unfortunately there is no way to decipher the appropriate reading.

Batstone and Gourlay's shop steward survey asks about 'worker's control' over their work, but again this is poorly specified and so potentially ambiguous. For all manual groups control was more likely to have risen than fallen, though five of the eight groups identified 'no change' as the largest category. Maintenance workers in particular fitted this model – over half of the maintenance steward reports in three of the four sectors indicating no alteration in control. For production workers around a quarter of reports indicated a reduction in control. For maintenance workers the figure was half this. Contrary to the authors' own report of a lack of pattern, then, the figures suggest that maintenance workers (typically with higher prior levels of control, it can safely be assumed) were also better able to at least sustain these. Union strength is found to be associated with steady or increased control, but this is mitigated by negative effects of tough management styles and large job losses. Whether union strength is the causal factor, or is co-variant with some other variable such as stronger shop-floor organization and ability to 'claw back' control for instance, is not considered by the authors.

Overall, these rather mixed survey findings must be regarded as lending poor support for the optimistic thesis, and fodder for the work intensification reading of the larger 'skill' and effort changes. The role of employee power to retain or regain control in the face of change also works contrary to the notion that greater autonomy is a product of management flexible-specialization strategies, reflecting their rational recognition of the mutual gains to be had through this approach.

The case study evidence on control proves even more inconclusive than that on skills. Buchanan and Boddy (1982) provide examples within a single firm, United Biscuits, in which control was lost to automation by operators at the mixing stage but enhanced through the ability to adjust settings at the baking stage. Wilkinson (1983) provides examples where management in a spectacles manufacturer sought to enhance employee involvement in an automated system through job rotation (though it is not clear that this amounted to control rather than intensification), yet in a plating company distrust of employees and tighter supervision via the use of new electronic equipment was observed.

An erosion of supervisory control has often been reported (McLoughlin and Clark 1988, Buchanan and Boddy 1982, Rothwell 1985), with control frequently being transferred to the pace and procedures set by the automated equipment itself. A more general inclination among the designers of equipment to view human inputs as an interference, and of line and financial management to seek to minimize any independence they see as threatening production and cost control, has been observed to play a role contrary to the optimistic scenario (Jones 1988, Elger 1989).

The other side of this coin is the ability of work groups to 'claw back' control over areas, especially (as is common) where the equipment fails entirely to perform to specification, or requires far more active human support than designers intended (Jones 1982, Wilkinson 1983, Buchanan 1985). Perhaps the most accurate assessment is that of Elger (1989) who concludes from his review of the evidence that polyvalent (multiskilled) teamworking in practice is more likely to be assimilated into existing industrial relations and occupational practice. It should be added that where this defensive control is ineffective, management themselves may well seek to be far less adventurous on control and autonomy even than they are on skill, and on balance the consequences for manual control (in a period of retrenchment) may well be negative.

Non-manual job control

The pattern reported by Daniel from the WIRS survey for office workers is similar to that for manual workers. Control increases are markedly less common than those for skill, though higher than for manual workers (39 per cent of managers reporting greater responsibility, 34 per cent more control over work pace, and 32 per cent control over work method). The modal response is no change for each aspect of work, and 70 per cent of reports give this response on supervision (with just 17 per cent reporting a reduction). As before, stewards are likely to report more responsibility but less control over work pace and method than management. Once the ambiguity of increased responsibility is taken into account, it is again hard to see much evidence of democratization or team autonomy here for those working with IT.

Batstone and Gourlay differ in reporting less favourable results for their non-manual and public sector samples of stewards than for their manual groups. The main direction of 'worker control' is found to be downwards, especially for telecommunications and finance sector clerical workers. Again, as for manual groups, heavy job losses are associated closely with lost control.

The case study reports on non-manual work control largely reflect those reported earlier on skill. Thus the differences between finance and other sectors (and within it between insurance and banking), or between secretaries and typists, are part and parcel of those described in the previous section. The debate on CAD's effects is also echoed here. This is not surprising, given that prior control or lack of it by different groups was found to be an important explanatory variable for skill consequences. In general, one might expect white-collar groups in non-technical occupations to have less scope for 'claw-back' than manual workers, but this cannot be adduced from available evidence.

Divided control

The comparisons between manual and non-manual work which we have been making demonstrate that, whatever the analytical approach, it is not sufficient to talk of amounts of control wielded by 'managers' and 'workers' without qualification. However, even to identify differences between these two categories of employees lacks perception, unless one then explores the basis of such a division. Clearly such an exploration is beyond this introduction, since it would involve dissections of sector and class – for instance (see Ramsay *et al.* 1991, for a discussion of such issues). None the less, it is possible to exemplify perhaps the most important division, and one which in many respects is masked by concentrating on the manual/white-collar distinction. This is the question of gender, which has already surfaced in our earlier discussion of the social definition of skills.

It has now been systematically established that women's capacities for performing tasks are not readily defined as 'skills', either by management or male-dominated unions (Phillips and Taylor 1980; Coyle 1982; Cavendish 1982; Cockburn 1983, 1985; Game and Pringle 1983; Milkman 1983; Dex 1985; Jenson 1989). Put oversimply (since many of the social processes of gendering of work and people are immensely complex), the segregation and status labelling of tasks tend to be mutually reinforcing, providing a particularly strong example of the way that groups with control are often best placed to reproduce it in the face of change. Cockburn's (1983) investigation of the printing industry is paradigmatic in empirical demonstrations of this process.

This is reinforced by ideologies of male and female capacities to cope with 'technology', so that technical changes are likely to be seen by management and unions as something best controlled by males. Since these ideologies help to shape experience which is identity-reinforcing, they are often internalized and actively promulgated by women themselves (Jenson 1989). This combines with the continued labelling of emergent skills – hence areas of IT in which women are able to assert facility (for example, word processing) are defined as 'lower tech' than other forms of computerized manipulation, for instance.

The explanation of segregation, skill labelling and other workplace disadvantages is variously located in different analyses (Walby 1988). It may be seen as embedded primarily in the processes at work in the labour market itself, or else chiefly in the consequences of women's domestically defined role and its practical impositions (the 'double shift' for instance). The study of white-collar workers by Crompton and Jones (1984) emphasizes not only the 'feminization' of much office work, but also the impact of gender divisions on the response to computerization. They argue that male prospects for promotion are protected not merely by managerial bias in selection, but by the practical possibilities for pursuit of training necessary for career advancement which most women do not share (and many, through self-definition, do not seek). The resulting divisions of opportunity take the 'sting' out of changes, and increase accommodation to deskilling changes by men who can escape them up the career ladder.

Crompton and Jones's study, notwithstanding criticisms of parts of their analysis (for example, on the extent of actual deskilling), provides a combined account of the role of labour market, domestic sphere and ideological constraint in a way that affords an integrated and convincing explanation of responses. More recently Crompton has traced some of the same processes in the banking industry (1989). Importantly, what this discussion also reveals with particularly telling force is the bankruptcy of attempts to define control at task level in a self-contained way.

Whatever happened to flexible specialization?

Those who regard flexible enskilling and responsible autonomy as necessary to realize the potential of IT typically point to cases where management's refusal to adopt the polyvalent option has restricted the scope of the technology and the work system (Buchanan 1985; Buchanan and Boddy 1982; McLoughlin and Clark 1988; Lane 1989). The added costs of training, pay and so forth notwithstanding, they argue that technological innovation is far more effective where autonomous teamwork and/or polyvalence is in operation. For individual employers, though, this may not be such an evident logic – especially when the problems of management control and discipline are anywhere in the foreground.

In these circumstances, the more typical management strategy (if it deserves so grand a label) is to extend skills and task content across work of a similar and limited type. This ensures readier coverage of gaps, and fuller utilization of any 'slack' time, but constitutes job 'enlargement' rather than 'enrichment' in the older human relations terminology. It also intensifies work, by reducing 'porosity' (a term from labour process analysis which refers to the degree of 'slack' in job pressures), and as a form of limited flexibility it combines productivity with relatively manageable and affordable 'human resource' implications (Elger 1989). The combination of increased skill and effort, and particularly of 'responsibility' rather than work pace and method control (for both manual and non-manual work) is highly consistent with this interpretation of management strategy.

As the first sentence of the last paragraph implies, however, 'strategy' is probably too grand a term here; it is more plausible to suggest that this is the approach which seems most readily to hand, especially at a time of technical change and labour weakness, and which best copes with problems arising from pressures generated elsewhere (for example, product design shortcomings; cost competition). This is likely to be reinforced by a consideration of the divisions within management. Campbell and Curry (1987) suggest that lower level management will be inclined to apply IT in a control-intensive fashion, especially where top management pay little attention to labour utilization issues. Such a process would also reinforce the gap-filling enlargement-cum-intensification approach identified above.

In the end, such flexible multiskilling as survives the dissection of recent sceptics (Pollert 1987, Marginson 1989) may well prove to be predominantly of this work-intensifying sort. If job enlargement 'works' for management, which is still hard to disentangle from the public relations imagery that dominates many reports (Ramsay 1985), then it seems more likely to have been through this intensification than by motivating co-operation. Recent case study examples from manufacturing provided by Dawson and Webb (1989), Tailby (1989) and Turnbull (1989) exemplify the pattern well, and it is articulated in more general terms by Elger (1989) as a result of his review of findings to date. The WIRS2 data (Daniel 1987) on increased task range coupled with reduced areas of control reported above, also fit this pattern, especially if increased skill and responsibility are read sceptically in this light. If this interpretation is sustained, the social factors which dictate such a pattern should not be obscured by lamentations about missed opportunities and lost potentials.

CONSULTATION AND INVOLVEMENT

Involvement and democracy at work

The relationship between management-initiated arrangements for involvement and proposals for democratizing the workplace has long been debated, often acrimoniously. The problems arise when in management eyes efforts at communication and even discussion of issues amount to participation in decisions, while employees and their representatives demand a quite different content for a democratically shared process of decision-making.

This contrast has been well-rehearsed in the general literature on worker participation, and the central issues have already been invoked at the start of this introduction. Typically, a management view starts from the presumption that their policies are in the interests of all in the organization. The problem of employee acquiescence is therefore a matter at the heart of management failing to get the message across (of communication, that is) or of employee recalcitrance and irrationality. The latter perception requires that if necessary policies must be enforced, all executive capacities must remain a managerial prerogative. A 'progressive' view of 'human resources' acknowledges that a work-force which has proper explanations provided to it becomes involved in (that is, caught up in/ supportive of) the policy, and a more adventurous outlook might even yield the possibility of employees having a contribution to make to decisions before they are finalized.

The agenda remains management's in all variants of this, however, and the ultimate objective of 'the enterprise' or 'the organization' is the service of profit (or possibly some surrogate) and growth. One further complication is that by 'management' we mean those at the top. There are also problems of conflicts of view and interest within management which may influence the operation of involvement policy, not least because of reactions to the fact that, 'Participation is something the top orders the middle to do for the bottom' (Kanter 1983: 244).

The employee response may be to accept management definitions of reality. If an independent stance is adopted, however, it almost invariably takes the position of a need for industrial democracy. 'Democracy' in turn implies a priority on employee rights rather than profits as the end-goal of the process of participation. It also implies that the process must be vested with power, that employees (directly or through union or other representatives) must be able to exert real influence on policy. Greater autonomy in the work task, even if it should result from a change such as introducing IT, does not fulfil this requirement. Work group claw back of control over aspects of the task organization is also at best partial. The point about influencing investment planning and policy is that this is the level at which the whole framework of work organization is shaped, through the choice of hardware, software, and the very assumptions about employee roles which inform that choice.

In asking questions in this section about consultation programmes, and in the next about trade union involvement and negotiation, it is not just a matter of ascertaining whether these procedures exist to deal with technological change. We also need to know what their content is, to determine whether they are merely involvement or even token exercises, 'soft on power' and fulfilling management notions of participation, or whether real influence on decisions is being exerted from below. In orienting the chapters in this volume towards 'democracy' at work, this collection has required judgements of a similar nature from the contributors on their specialist areas.

Some criteria of democratic influence

Although the available evidence on management practice concerning involvement in technological change is too thin to allow a detailed evaluation, it is worth while specifying a few of the criteria which must be fulfilled for different degrees of influence to be regarded as having been accorded to employees.

The first concerns the extent and detail of *information* provided, and the resources employees have to analyse and respond to this information. Democratic arrangements would require that employees rather than management would set the terms of information provision, and would be able to make their own investigations where they deemed these necessary to make an effective independent judgement.

A second criterion concerns the *constitution* of the consultative process, and the extent to which it permits some form of employee veto or positive input as a right. It will be important to take into account the actual working of decision-making where possible as well: procedural rights may overstate or understate employee influence. An example of overstatement would be where in practice discussion with employees was avoided until the decision became a *fait accompli*, or where management used 'expertise' and monopoly of information to shape employee judgements. Understatement is possible where, say, employee opposition has no constitutional veto, but in practice tacit negotiation or judicious management reconsideration leads to a modification or withdrawal along the lines employees would have wished.

Third, the *timing* of employee involvement plays an important role. This may be reduced to the problem of information being given too late for a meaningful, considered employee response, but it is more systematically analysed as a question of stage of involvement. The gestation of an IT innovation can be divided into numerous phases, many of which will overlap in practice, but to simplify we can identify as broad, simplifying categories: conception of 'problem/ need'; design (strategy) of response; detailed hardware/software design; implementation and debugging; and routine operation.

Fourth, we need to consider the *substantive issues* over which any influence is exerted. Consultation could deal only with system problems, for instance (as a unitarist, managerial view would dictate). It may deal with areas marginal to the change (though not necessarily to employees) such as the precise arrangement, ergonomic, and health and safety implications of new equipment. It could extend further into traditional bargaining areas, such as staffing, grading and pay, and perhaps training. Or it could address equipment choice, and even investment decisions. To some extent the last items by their very nature require involvement at an earlier stage (the others being more a filling in of detail after the change is at least decided on from a production/service provision viewpoint, and so more amenable to a reactive response), but the two dimensions of issues and timing are not identical since, for example, it would be possible to have early involvement without being allowed an input on many topics.

Generally, it can be said that the further on in the process that any consultation takes place, the less scope there is to make radical changes (since organizational momentum will have been gathered behind a proposal, costs will have been incurred that would have to be written off). None the less, this point should be modified by noting that even at the implementation and debugging stage, depending on the information system or type of IT involved, quite significant changes in the work system from the point of view of employee experience of the job may be made. Sometimes these will be informal, and thereby also very difficult for management to monitor and control – hence claw-back may still be important.

Manual employee involvement on IT

'The last time shop-floor participation was mentioned in polite UK society was about 10 years ago.' This is how Caulkin and Large opened their article on employee involvement in CIM (1989). They went on to argue, in a vogue now familiar, that problems with installing automation to good effect were forcing a realization that participation was a desirable thing after all.

In contrasting style, Daniel (1987) opens his chapter on worker and union involvement in technical change matters by referring to the axiomatic assertion by managerial behavioural scientists of the benefits of participation. Daniel's subsequent comments are written, it is worth recalling, by someone who has been a staunch advocate and publicist of the pro-involvement line for many years (see, for example, Daniel and McIntosh 1972). Amidst this unanimity, he observes, 'the only people who are out of step are the practising managers upon whom the implementation of the arrangements for worker involvement depends'. Further, he says:

> The overall pattern which emerged revealed that managers generally operated in a minimally pragmatic fashion. If they could introduce the changes they wanted without having to take account of the views of any other group or individual, they did so. When they consulted or negotiated, it was principally because they were

required to do so, either by the industrial relations institutions at their workplaces, or by resistance to the changes they wanted on the part of workers or their representatives. There was no hint of managerial commitment to worker involvement as a means of improving the form of change or generating enthusiasm for it.

(Daniel 1987: 113)

This conclusion to probably the most authoritative survey evidence on the subject available must scupper all but the most blindly optimistic claims on workplace democracy as concerns IT. Even mild involvement programmes which offer more than token discussion are seemingly rare.

At first sight Daniel's findings may seem to belie the singularly negative cast of his résumé. Informal discussions with individual workers are found in 58 per cent of establishments according to management respondents (who may be thought a poor guide to reality in the circumstances, of course), while informal meetings with work groups take place in 38 per cent of enterprises. Discussion in a consultative committee is reported in 17 per cent, and in a special committee by 11 per cent, (these are both registered as non-union channels). Finally, discussions through union channels are reported with stewards in 39 per cent of enterprises, and with full-time officers in 16 per cent. Consultation increases in incidence as enterprises get larger, and this gradient is especially steep for shop steward discussions. In unionized enterprises, discussions with stewards were reported in 52 per cent of cases, and levels of consultation generally rose as union density increased. All types of consultation were also directly related to lack of support for change.

It is these patterns which lead Daniel to the conclusions we have quoted. As a pluralist, he regards consultations which by-pass the union as potentially token and toothless rather than democratic, and with good cause to go by research on participation more generally. While no forms of consultation on technical change are reported by only 17 per cent of management respondents, manual shop stewards claim that this is rather more common. Moreover, the stewards suggest that consultation of all types is less frequent before the change is made than during implementation, indicating that discussions tend to be held when it is too late to go back on the changes anyway. Finally, as the extracted quotation indicated, managers only undertook these limited exercises when they felt they had to if they were to get acceptance of the changes.

In a subsequent survey of multi-establishment enterprises (Martin

1988b), senior managers confirmed a widespread policy of informal discussions with individuals and/or groups of workers on the introduction of IT in all sectors. Discussion with trade unions in these large enterprises was also common (reported by 77 per cent of senior and 87 per cent of divisional managers), though with the emphasis on management being free to make the final decision. This figure declined for less unionized manual work-forces, such as textiles and clothing or distribution. It is almost certainly union density in larger companies which accounts for the higher level of union consultation in this sample than for the WIRS survey reported by Daniel.

Turning to case study evidence, most of the material which takes account of consultation practice confirms the picture drawn by Daniel. A survey in the electronics industry by Rush and Williams (1984) claimed that 32 per cent of workers were involved at the planning stage, 20 per cent in equipment choice, and 87 per cent at the implementation stage of IT introduction. However, the findings relied on a survey of management, carried out for the National Economic Development Council (NEDC) in the industry, which published an enthusiastic report on the subject itself celebrating management's participative practice. These findings are subjected to scrutiny and rejection by Findlay (Chapter 2, this volume) as a result of far more detailed and reliable research.

In her study of breweries, Davies (1986) reports that in not one of the companies was their any consultation with employees before board decisions on IT were finalized. Similar practices are reported at BL, even in the pre-Edwardes days (Willman and Winch 1984). For manual workers, at least, the wider development of involvement seems far away.

Non-manual involvement on IT changes

On one expectation the pressure from non-manual employees against change might be expected to be less than that for manual workers, with consultation therefore less likely. Alternatively, it might be expected that managers will take a more paternalistically benevolent and empathically sympathetic (for class reasons) view of non-manual employees' concerns, and so be more ready to consult.

Daniel's findings are consistent with the second of these postulations: white-collar workers were markedly more likely to be consulted. Also consistent with this view (as opposed to a third view, that white-collar *unions* are actually more active than their manual counterparts in pushing management), office workers are especially likely to have the matter discussed with them on an individual basis, and are actually less likely to be consulted on a union or joint consultative committee (JCC) basis. The consultations are also at least as likely to be before the change as once it is underway, in contrast to blue-collar reports. The relationship of consultation to union density is also much less marked than for manual workers. Sectorally, union channels of consultation were almost non-existent for white-collar employees outside the nationalized industries (where they were fairly common) and (to a markedly lesser extent) the public services.

The multi-establishment company survey (Martin 1988b) contradicts these findings on the relative frequency of non-manual as against manual union consultation. The levels for non-manual unions are consistently lower, though not greatly so. The most striking figure is for financial services, where discussion with union representatives falls to just 8 per cent of cases (against 47 per cent for non-manual groups overall).

Whether the content of consultations with non-manual employees and representatives was more or less substantial or 'democratic' than for manual workers is a matter for conjecture. We can, however, point to the prevalence of individualized discussions, and the lack of any relationship of non-union based consultation and staffing impact of the changes, to suggest that it seems unlikely that it took great note of 'labour' concerns. Stewards are markedly less likely to report consultation than managers, especially informal, individualist forms (which could reflect poor information or different perceptions over whether the exchanges concerned amounted to 'discussion'). Certainly case studies on white-collar work have often found that paternalism is also autocratic when it comes to matters concerning the provision of the service concerned, notably in the finance sector (Cressey *et al.* 1985, Loveridge *et al.* 1985, Murray 1985, Smith and Wield 1987).

Perhaps the most sustained and ambitious claims for participation policies in office work have been made for user-involvement arrangements in the implementation, and even design, of computerized information systems. Although such involvement is almost universally advocated in the literature, and was reported to be very widely used in a survey of management practice we ourselves conducted, detailed information in the survey showed that the extent and nature of the involvement rapidly dissolved into a minimally significant activity in democratic terms when further detail was elicited (Beirne and Ramsay 1988). In a sequel to that study, Chapter 3 in this volume

examines detailed cases which appeared on the survey evidence to
be particularly *strong* examples of user-involvement. Again the
democratic element of the process is found to be emaciated.

CONFLICTUAL DEMOCRACY: NEGOTIATING TECHNICAL CHANGE

The pluralist school of industrial relations writing, in Britain and the
USA in particular, has long argued that the only secure basis for
democratic influence for employees at work is independent and
effective representation. Given that employee interests differ in
important respects from those of employers according to pluralists,
a system of negotiated compromise is seen as the only condonable
means of settling conflicts. This will allow the concordant pursuit of
shared enterprise objectives, it is argued.

It is not our intention here to plunge into the debate on whether
this pluralistic account overstates or underestimates the extent of
conflict (though such differing assessments clearly do affect the
analysis of where control or co-operation are in evidence, for
instance). We only wish to establish that pretty well every approach
that does not uncritically accept the unitary, managerial image of
technical change (or other workplace issues) is then led to see an
effective trade union and bargaining process as a key feature of work
place democracy. For this reason, an assessment of trade union
capacities to intervene and negotiate technical change forms a major
part of this volume, to which a number of the chapters address
themselves in varying contexts.

Trade union options and strategies

In Britain, it was not until the late 1970s that the unions began to
give serious attention to discovering the best way to negotiate on IT.
A number of possible strategies existed: to leave IT to management
or consultation arrangements and deal only with issues as they arose
in other areas; to leave any negotiation to local levels; to include IT
in with the normal run of collective bargaining; or to treat IT as
special and seek to mount a major initiative to assert union influence
over it. The 'choice' (sometimes made by default) was dictated by
union strength, structure, existing priorities and pressures, union
bargaining culture (particularly the conception of what is an industrial relations/collective bargaining issue and what is not), and by the
implications of IT for the membership and the union itself.

Let us consider each of these optional approaches briefly before going on to look at the pattern of bargaining practice and effect. Leaving IT to management or to consultative procedures (that is, more on managerial terms) seems likely to follow from two union circumstances. One would be weakness, and so an inability to take on IT as an issue, or to hope to get management to bargain. Another would follow from a highly restrictive view of areas appropriate for bargaining, and perhaps a tendency to be reactive and deal with consequences if and when they arise rather than trying to intervene before they appear.

The second option seems more likely where there is a strong tradition of local bargaining, especially if this has engendered a culture of local branch/workplace autonomy. It will also be encouraged if IT is introduced in varied and piecemeal forms, preventing generalizable responses from being easy to formulate and codify.

Resort to normal bargaining above establishment level – that is, involving full-time officers (FTOs) and perhaps the national union more fully – is perhaps likely when the need to codify the introduction of change is apparent from the extent of IT introduction and its likely general effects. However, it may well be that IT is seen as 'just more technical change' (for example, in many manual manufacturing environments where such changes have been fairly constant over the decades), thus not requiring any special treatment. This attitude may well be bolstered by a suspicion of participation and industrial democracy initiatives as more of a threat to union independence and attention to membership needs than a way forward. In each case, many traditional manual unions are likely to fall into this category.

For professional and technical groups, the attitude may be to see IT more as facilitative than problematical, and so a general agreement may be sought in the normal course of bargaining as a safeguard and regulator on certain issues where unions retain a role (the 'bread and butter' areas of pay, grading, staffing and perhaps health and safety, for instance). There may also be a reluctance to challenge management prerogatives, but this time because of a greater legitimation of the management function.

The grand strategy starts with the argument that IT is different, and far more fundamental in its implications for all types of work, from previous technological change. As such, it gives management the potential to rewrite the rules for the whole industrial relations and employment ball game. Alternatively, it may be seen as an opportunity for the unions to take the initiative and do the rewriting themselves. In this format, as David Lea of the TUC (incidentally a co-signatory of the majority Bullock report, and a long-time advocate of industrial democracy proposals within the union movement) argued in 1980: 'The trade union response to technological development is clearly linked to the area of industrial democracy' (quoted by Benson and Lloyd 1983: 166).

Of all the approaches, only this one really requires a 'strategic' approach to the issue by trade unions in order to extend the scope of bargaining, redefine the purpose of IT, and intervene in specific decisions to innovate at the conception and design stage. In 1979 the TUC's *Employment and Technology* report set out to prescribe the conditions necessary for achieving this. Four procedural demands were laid down: for consultation of unions prior to equipment purchase, for effective bargaining machinery on technical change, for disclosure of all relevant information in good time, and for regular joint review and study teams to monitor the effects. To these were added six substantive demands: on employment and output, training, reducing the working week, on benefits to accrue to employees as well as the company, on equipment design including performance monitoring, and on health and safety.

While this checklist raised many of the standard elements of union conceptions of bargaining topics, the framework, and in particular the emphasis on prior discussion and joint determination of changes, went far beyond this. In fact it sought to lever open principles of democratic agreement using IT as a chance to get a foot in the door. Member unions were exhorted to go forth and make New Technology Agreements (NTAs) embodying these.

New Technology Agreements

The fate of NTAs has been traced in some detail, at a survey level especially (Manwaring 1981, Williams and Steward 1985, Batstone and Gourlay 1986). It is not an inspiring story. While agreements mentioning new technology are not uncommon, there is a tendency to conflate these with NTAs proper (Jary 1987). This tends to exaggerate the numbers of such agreements; thus although Labour Research (1983) and Batstone and Gourlay (1986) provide some useful data, the most reliable source is probably Williams and Steward's survey (1985) of NTAs from 1977 to 1983.

Williams and Steward identified 240 NTAs signed in this period, with the incidence peaking in 1980. Most commentators would agree that in the later 1980s full-blown NTAs almost ceased to be initiated (McLoughlin and Clark 1988, Dodgson and Martin 1987), marking the effective death of the strategy, and perhaps with it of the ambitions to impose anything like a union agenda on the future of microelectronics. While the socio-economic and political conditions of the 1980s were far from ideal, it is too easy to place the blame solely on these factors, as Martin (1988a) observes. Further analysis of the pattern casts some additional light on the limitations.

First, it was suggested earlier that white-collar unions might be thought more likely to go for NTAs than would manual unions, partly because of the scope and partly due to the relative novelty of technical change in the office. This seems borne out by the domination of NTAs by four white-collar unions (APEX, ASTMS, NALGO and TASS), accounting for over 90 per cent of the total between them. This pattern is broadly confirmed by Batstone and Gourlay (1986). However, much of the success, if such it be, in achieving NTAs is confined to the public sector also (with local authorities prominent, as NALGO figures suggest). NTAs have been steadfastly refused by management in the banking sector, for instance. Batstone and Gourlay's analysis suggests that it is unions who are strongly placed anyway who have signed NTAs, so it is not clear that the NTA itself was their only avenue.

Batstone and Gourlay also suggest that bargaining range is wider under NTAs than other provisions (and that disagreement over changes is reduced). None the less, few NTAs approach the aspirations embedded in the TUC checklist. While most NTAs do include procedural rights (as opposed to dealing only with specific pieces of equipment, for instance), they are typically limited. Less than one in fifteen in Williams and Steward's survey allowed for any involvement of the unions at the planning stages of an innovation, and almost a third of NTAs laid down no advanced consultation (even at the implementation stage) at all. Two-fifths did state that unions would be involved before selection of equipment.

The degree of control which unions obtained under NTAs also fell short of the effective veto (that is, no implementation without mutual agreement) called for by the TUC. Just over one in ten of the NTAs included such a provision, though a further half of all agreements did stipulate prior negotiation, with management only to proceed after having tried to gain agreement.

Finally, NTAs tended to stick to the traditional issues with which unions felt comfortable, rather than redefining the agenda in the way the TUC wished. The substantive components focused on terms and conditions of employment and job security, usually with health and safety also, but rarely including 'quality of working life' issues on skill, task control and so forth, let alone demands for more extensive joint regulation of management investment strategies and the like. In other words, the industrial democracy aspirations were lost in the pragmatism of the moment, even where unions did take up the NTA option. Moreover, few agreements were joint union exercises as the TUC had proposed, giving management plentiful scope to divide and rule – and this with a type of work organization change that is often peculiarly divisive of the work-force in any case, through its potential demolition of traditional task definitions and demarcations.

The case study evidence of NTAs, and new technology bargaining more generally, tends if anything to reinforce these impressions of weakness. Jary (1987) found that in Ford (UK) the existence of a prior national agreement on change, and the inertial rigidity of existing bargaining arrangements, actually conspired to restrict any scope for effective negotiation, though more success was reported by a more considered approach to the issue in the establishment of a new cable production plant by a single union with a more sophisticated and flexible approach.

In contrast, Price (1988) provides an account of a well-organized white-collar work-force on whose behalf the union had signed an NTA, only to find management disowning the agreement, saying that the changed economic climate made it irrelevant, and introduced an on-line computerized stock-control system without any prior consultation or negotiation. Meanwhile, four cases reported by Moore and Levie (1985), and a further four involving the same researchers (Levie and Moore 1984, Batstone *et al.* 1987) confirm a typically unadventurous and largely conventional approach to bargaining on IT, a theme which will be taken up in the next subsection.

Collective bargaining and IT

The relative failure and seeming decline of New Technology Agreements leaves the weight of union influence with more orthodox channels of negotiation. Since many unions have preferred to tread this road, for reasons suggested earlier, a wider assessment of the extent of joint determination beyond NTAs is called for.

The first background factor, and one likely to be a marked advantage to management at the bargaining table, is that unions and their members are by and large favourably disposed to IT (Daniel 1987), to the extent that the main obstacle to innovation can reasonably be regarded as management initiative and willingness to invest. It is noteworthy that almost the first words out of any union official's mouth when asked to comment on IT will be, 'We are not Luddites' (an unjustified slander on Luddism being committed in the process – see Webster and Robins 1986). Outright union opposition to changes has tended to be confined to industries where the entire existence of unions is threatened, as has been most obviously the case in printing, Willman (1986) has suggested that this kind of disruption tends to be restricted largely to industries with a mature product market (hence competing primarily on cost-efficiency) where 'spot contracting' (that is, shop-floor bargaining) predominates, this obstructing more generalized and broad-ranging attempts to tackle conflicts.

A second factor is the low profile of labour issues, including those relating to the implementation of IT, at the top management decision-making level (Northcott 1986, McLoughlin and Clark 1988, Martin 1988b). This is reflected in the weakness of personnel managers in influencing IT decisions (Millward and Stevens 1986, Daniel 1987, Martin 1988b). Thus while industrial relations issues were said to be 'taken into account' by most corporate workers in the Warwick large company survey, these were very much secondary to technical and production considerations (Martin 1988b).

The third factor, already rehearsed, is the changed climate of the 1980s. Despite the survival of the main institutions of industrial relations, many observers have felt that the limits of discussion of any sort with the unions have been set far more narrowly (Northcott and Rogers 1985, Jones and Rose 1986). Where unions were weak, in many cases management are thought to have taken advantage of this, either compelling their acquiescence or excluding them (Willman and Winch 1984, Martin 1988a, Davies 1986). That this is a change of attitude by management from the 1970s is doubtful; management have always been jealous of their prerogatives (Cressey *et al.* 1985), and technological change (as capital investment) has always been seen as a prominent area where management ideally should be left to make unrestrained decisions. It is more a matter of being able to make this line stick.

In these circumstances, the ability to gain some bargaining leverage (at least in a formal sense) over IT is likely to rely on the union's position in the existing negotiating machinery. Batstone and Gourlay's findings confirm this, showing the levels of the organization at which new technology bargaining operated to be closely concurrent with the pattern for all bargaining. Multi-level bargaining (at shop-floor, establishment and company levels) was found to be the broadest in scope according to shop steward accounts. The public sector and non-manual samples were most likely to report this, along with printing, whereas it was less common in the manufacturing sectors, where only one in ten reported negotiation at all three levels, and just one in four at two levels.

Batstone and Gourlay's findings imply that some bargaining takes place in most workplaces on IT. This does not fit well with the WIRS data reported by Daniel (1987). According to the managers in this survey, change was negotiated with union representatives in only 8 per cent of companies where manual unions were recognized, though the union representatives were consulted in 61 per cent of cases. Where shop stewards were also interviewed, they reported both negotiation and consultation less often than the managers. In the case of changes affecting non-manual workers, managers reported negotiation in 9 per cent and consultation in 44 per cent of cases; stewards were a little more likely than managers to report negotiation, but less likely to report consultation.

The difference between these two sets of findings may well be that Batstone and Gourley were dealing in effect only with the consequences of IT changes, rather than the introduction of the change itself. They also pursued the important question of areas of bargaining, and their figures for negotiation over investment are far more consistent with the overall WIRS result. Their list of areas also includes equipment choice, training, and the traditional areas of union activity: manning, pay and health.

Negotiation over investment is typically rare (except in telecommunications engineering and to a lesser extent for food and drink production workers). Over equipment choice it is somewhat more common, though highly variable by group, being low for all maintenance groups but divulged in over half of all responses from CPSA civil servants and both office and engineering telecom staff. Training hovers around the midway frequency for most groups, and all of health, pay, and especially manning, show very high levels of negotiation. In other words, the unions have retreated or been restricted to their traditional and reactive areas of concern.

A more favourable view of the state of union–management relations on new technology has been offered by Price (1988), based on twelve case studies. In eight of these, he reports that co-operative industrial relations traditions had led to a consultative approach by management, and in these workplaces there was also extensive discussion of technological change which was evaluated favourably by both sides. In the other four, antagonistic relations were reflected in minimal consultation (even in the case where an NTA had been signed, as was described earlier).

However, although union influence was significant in the eight co-operative cases according to his respondents, Price acknowledges that 'none of the workplace union organizations studied here had challenged management's right to set the parameters of the debate about new technology, or posed clear-cut alternatives to management's proposals' (Price 1988: 257). Moreover, it should be noted that his cases were selected to reflect good management practice in information disclosure, or in the white-collar cases particularly strong union organization (Price 1988: 252).

In consequence, it is reasonable to conclude that the process which has predominated is one of defence and damage limitation. There is no sign of the democratic challenge to management over IT, but rather evidence of an 'organized retreat' (Elger 1987). The unions have been unable to amass the kind of resources which would fit them for coping with industrial democracy generally (Lane 1988), and this is reflected in the poverty of union research on IT, and in the failure of any part of the movement to come up with a viable alternative to the failed NTA strategy. As Martin summarizes it: 'One of the striking conclusions . . . is the extent to which management has largely retained discretion over the introduction of new technology and has been able to implement its policies without substantial control from the trade unions (Martin 1988a: 106).

LOOKING FORWARD – AND SIDEWAYS

If we step back from the scrutiny of available research evidence on experience thus far, the obvious question that rises temptingly to the fore is: what does the future of IT hold for workplace democracy? While we will consider the runes we have cast here, we will largely circumnavigate this question for reasons we hope will be convincing.

Before commencing this futurological whitewash, however, we must at least briefly attend to an issue mentioned earlier: that our cited research is largely derived from British experience, and as such is atypical and a poor basis for any conclusive results on workplace democracy and IT.

International comparisons

To what extent, then, does the evidence suggest that the British example might generate unwarranted pessimism? We can consider this as above in terms of comparative evidence on work organization (task, skill and control), and on consultation and negotiation.

It has been claimed that in a number of countries, a far more genuinely *flexible and enskilling* response to automation and computerization has been adopted, leading to a more effective realization of human and technical potential. West Germany, Sweden and Japan are the examples most often cited. Moreover, there is one respect in which the evidence clearly suggests that Britain is a laggard in skill formation, regardless of employer publicity, namely that of training (Coopers & Lybrand 1985, Keep 1987, Senker 1989, Hyman 1988). The former UK Employment Minister, Mr Fowler, recently described the results of a Training Agency survey showing the paucity of vocational training as 'mind-boggling' *Financial Times* 17.11.89). It is hard to take talk of flexible specialization and enskilling seriously when employers have proved so unwilling to invest in their employees, and it is clear that companies in other countries have been far less reluctant.

The nature of training and skilling is not so simple as more or less of each, especially in terms of employee influence and control, however. Smith (1988) has argued that flexible specialization is in many ways a means for companies to attack the craft control of key employees such as maintenance workers. The diffusion of abilities to do these tasks also undermines the work group's bargaining capacity. Of course, this may be seen as diluting control but at least distributing privilege from the elite few, and there is truth in this wry afternote. More serious for all employees' power *vis-à-vis* the employer is the emergence of multiskilling which is company-specific (Lowstedt 1988); unlike a craft, it cannot readily be transferred to another employer. Such skills may be relatively shallow – employees may learn what to do to keep a process in motion but fail to acquire a generalizable understanding of the working principles. In consequence, they may become far more dependent on their employer to maintain their status as skilled, and for pay premiums which may go with the attainment of skills.

This dilemma of dependent skill is in many respects a key feature of the Japanese system. Employees are tied to a firm not necessarily by normative identification so much as by a labour market which is made far more attractive internally than externally by *nenko* (seniority) and cumulative merit pay systems (Batstone 1984, Koike 1987). Workers typically learn about three dozen tasks, limiting the depth of that learning and entailing transfer for the most part between relatively routinized assignments. Thus '"skill" scarcely emerges as a source of workers' autonomous power' (Kumazawa and Yamada 1989).

The generalization of Japanese practices is one of the major forces impelling the business adoption of 'flexible specialization' elsewhere. This raises questions in turn for the kind of multiskilling which might be occurring,and for the new working methods such as teamworking and job redesign which are supposedly the organizational manifestations of flexible specialization. The British experience of this was reviewed earlier, and it was concluded that job enlargement or job rotation was the order of the day rather than any genuine 'enrichment', and that employee control could thereby be seen as reduced rather than increased, as evidenced by the common denominator of work intensification.

However, in our earlier discussion we also observed that many of the German examples appeared to fit this characterization of a 'neo' (rather than 'post') Fordism also. It is possible, then, that additional training takes the form of preparation for this shift rather than a properly 'democratic' one. This suggests the need for more caution in evaluating the German material which Lane (1989) and others (Sorge *et al.* 1982, Nicholas *et al.* 1983) promote with such uncritical enthusiasm.

The Swedish system arguably displays certain differences to the German, British or Japanese examples, in particular as a result of union strength and relative breadth of vision. As a result, the bipartite promotion of semi-autonomous group working which gained momentum in the 1970s (though the union approval for it faltered after a few years) is sometimes seen as creating a more democratic, worker-oriented variant of flexible working. Again, though, the evidence is far from conclusive. Research on the major initiatives in Volvo (most famously, the Kalmar plant) have at least modified notions of a major enrichment of work (Aguren *et al.* 1976, 1985). Berggren (1989) suggests that with a few possible recent exceptions what has been achieved in these experiments amounts to 'flexible Taylorism'.

The record on *representative influence*, whether through unions, works councils or other bodies, on the process of advanced technical change is also more mixed than simple negative characterizations of the British experience may suggest. Certainly the existence of more extensive rights to consultation at least can be cited in Germany, France, Italy or Sweden. The gradual spread of the Scandinavian notion of a more embracing concept than health and safety through 'working environment' legislation has also shifted the formal coverage of employee influence upwards. But the comparative evidence on union influence, while it does not present a uniform picture by any means, does indicate very similar blockages to effective democratic influence over IT to that reviewed for Britain above.

In one comparative study of influence over IT implementation in five European countries, it was clear that the Swedish worker representatives were particularly likely to receive information well in advance of any concrete management moves, and so to be able to consult or negotiate effectively over the changes (Levie and Moore 1984). The combination of participation legislation, established industrial relations practices, co-ordination between local and national union, and a far-sighted development of policy by the national unions on IT, was credited with this relative success.

Elsewhere, results were less favourable. Companies in Italy, Germany and the Netherlands, as well as in Britain, fell into the category of 'late information' (that is, no discussion till long after the project was under substantial development). Management obstructiveness after initial disclosure was, moreover, a feature primarily of Dutch and German examples. The Dutch, and especially the German, cases demonstrate the limits of legal rights to participation since management tended to dispute the interpretation of such rights and to offer the minimum they felt they could get away with, a feature reminiscent of Daniel's observations on Britain. A lack of co-ordination between different levels of representation (a weakness often highlighted by critics of the German system) was also thought to contribute to lack of effectiveness.

In at least one Italian example, the outcome was markedly better, despite the lack of equivalent legislative backing. This is attributed by the researchers to the effectiveness of links between levels of the union, and to the development of an active and accommodative stance of the national union towards technical change. Overall, though, the other Italian cases, and those from Germany, the Netherlands and Britain, are all seen as exhibiting similarly meagre levels of union and worker influence.

Moreover, a comparison of German and French experience (the latter under the relatively recent Auroux legislation of 1982) by Tallard (1988) reaches very similar conclusions about the restrictions on influence, and the effectiveness of legal rights. The picture of poor penetration beyond basic personnel issues (pay, redeployment, job security, grading) and negotiation after management policy is set in Germany is familiar to British observers. The French pattern suggests few enterprise-level agreements on IT, and a generally rather ineffectual industry-level process of bargaining on the subject, resulting only in vague encouragement to firms to consider work organization from an employee as well as a production viewpoint. Again, discussion is at best over the consequences of IT once introduced, and so restricted to a reactive basis.

The days may be past when bullish British accounts of industrial democracy proclaimed the innate superiority of shop steward workplace control in the UK over European models. The reasons for scepticism about many of the alternatives, typically based on some system of statutory works councils, have not dematerialized with the rude demolition of illusions about shop-floor power, however, and we should not be too ready to react with a simple reversal of previous evaluations. Industrial democracy still has few signposts.

Prognoses

We have already indicated our reluctance to make sweeping predictions. In important respects the sceptical view which the evidence seems to us to require when it comes to millenial visions (whether they be 'post-Fordist' *or* 'flexibly specialized'), indicates that we are not inclined to the version of evolutionary optimism which is the main product presently on display in the futurology shop window. Whether the emphasis is on technical determinism, or more circumspectly on potentials and possibilities, the grounds for this sanguine divination seem insubstantial.

At the same time, that pessimistic determinism which depicts an inevitable deskilling and employee powerlessness has been justifiably criticized for an equally selective reading of the evidence. A plausible elaboration might proceed from the argument that we are presently in a transitional phase in which the potential for management control is restricted by the organizational bedding in and debugging, not just of each specific information system but of the use of IT generally. As a result, the co-operation of labour is particularly needed, to plug the gaps and make things work at all – flexibility is a temporary necessity, not the texture of the era it helps to give birth to. As routines tighten and systems become more reliable, so power will shift decisively to management.

This viewpoint is no less plausible than social determinist optimism, driven as it is by the (not unfounded) notion that management will ultimately seek to centralize control if they can. But it supposes a 'transition' followed by a stable new phase, and in this it commits the same probable fallacy as post-Fordism and its equivalents: it posits a 'Fordist' (or 'Taylorist') era which was stable and pervasive. In practice, neither the pervasiveness of such practices – which have never applied in their 'ideal type' form to more than a small fraction of the work-force – nor their fixed and regulated nature has ever existed. Changes of machinery, technique and product were normal features of most manufacturing plants long before IT – which as we noted has led to a dismissive neglect of IT as anything special at all by many union officials. The persistence of breakdowns in programmed systems in the office and on the shop-floor, and the ability of employees to recapture control over such systems in multifarious ways (Cavestro 1989), renews the criticism made by many commentators on Braverman's pessimism concerning Taylorism.

We believe IT, too, will continue to develop and change in its applications for a very long time at the least, so that new and 'transitional' features will continue to crop up at frequent intervals for most workplaces. For this reason, the most definite prediction is that the outcomes of IT innovation for industrial democracy will depend on the interplay of management perceptions, objectives and policies, and employee perceptions, organization and responses (perhaps even strategies, but probably not for the most part). In other words, they will continue to emerge from a dialectic of struggle and control in ways that only actual examples and the derivation of patterns and structural constraints from the collation of those cases can decipher. The chapters in this volume seek to extend this examination of contexts and patterns.

NOTE

1 Detailed studies can be expected to cast more light and to highlight more accurately where change is considerable or nugatory. Surveys can exaggerate in either direction, concealing change where they gather institutional data by masking the shifting content of relations, but paradoxically overstating it where a simple question on more or less skill fails to discriminate along the various dimensions that qualify the conclusions above and below (as in the major surveys on flexibility, for instance – see Pollert 1987, Findlay this volume). None the less, surveys do provide a coverage, and a potential for discerning patterns, that ensure their continued value *alongside and in combination with* detailed studies

REFERENCES

Aguren, S., Hansson, R. and Karlson, K. (1976) *The Volvo Kalmar Plant; The Impact of New Design on Work Organisation*, Stockholm, SAF–LO.
——, Bredbacka, C., Hansson, R., Ihregren, K. and Karlsson, K. (1985) *Volvo Kalmar Revisited*, Stockholm, SAF–LO.

Appelbaum, E. and Albin, P. (1989) 'Computer rationalisation and the transformation of work: lessons from the insurance industry', in S. Wood (ed.), *The Transformation of Work*, London, Unwin Hyman.

Arnold, E. and Senker, P. (1982) 'Designing the future: the implications of CAD for employment and skills in the British engineering industry', EITB Occasional Paper 9.

Baldry, C. and Connolly, A. (1986) 'Drawing the line: Computer Aided Design and the organisation of the drawing office', *New Technology, Work and Employment* 1 (1).

Barras, R. and Swann, J. (1983) *The Adaptation and Impact of Information Technology in UK Local Government*, London, Technical Change Centre.

Batstone, E. (1984) *Working Order*, Oxford, Blackwell.

——, and Gourlay, S. (1986) *Unions, Unemployment and Innovation*, Oxford, Blackwell.

——, ——, Levie, H. and Moore, R. (1987) *New Technology and the Process of Labour Regulation*, Oxford, Clarendon.

Beirne, M. (1991) 'Social paradox and user involvement: a critical study of employee participation in the design of computing systems', Unpublished Ph.D. thesis.

——, and Ramsay, H. (1988) 'Computer redesign and "labour process" theory: towards a critical appraisal', in D. Knights and H. Willmott (eds), *Technology and the Labour Process*, London, Macmillan.

Bell, D. (1973) *The Coming of Post-Industrial Society*, New York, Penguin.

Benson, I. and Lloyd, J. (1983) *New Technology and Industrial Change*, London, Kogan Page.

Berggren, C. (1989) 'New production concepts in final assembly – the Swedish experience', in S. Wood (ed.), *The Transformation of Work?*, London, Unwin Hyman.

Bijker, W., Hughes, J. and Pinch, T. (1989) *The Social Construction of Technological Systems: New Directions in the Sociology and History of Technology*, Boston, Mass., MIT Press.

Blauner, R. (1964) *Alienation and Freedom*, Chicago, University of Chicago Press.

Blumberg, P. (1968) *Industrial Democracy: The Sociology of Participation*, London, Constable.

Braverman, H. (1974) *Labour and Monopoly Capital*, New York, Monthly Review Press.

Bright, J. (1958) *Automation and Management*, Boston, Mass., Harvard University Press.

Buchanan, D. (1985) 'Canned cycles or dancing tools: who's really in control of computer aided machining?', Paper to Aston/UMIST Conference on the Organization and Control of the Labour Process, Manchester.

——, and Boddy, D. (1982) *Organisations in the Computer Age*, Aldershot, Gower.

——, and Huczynski, A. (1985) *Organisational Behaviour: An Introductory Text*, London, Prentice-Hall.

Butler, D. (1989) 'Secretarial skills and office technology', in E. Willis (ed.), *Technology and the Labour Process*, London, Allen & Unwin.

Campbell, A. and Curry, W. (1987) 'Skills and strategy in design engineering', Paper to Aston/UMIST Conference on the Organization and Control of the Labour Process, Manchester.

Carchedi, G. (1984) 'Socialist labour and information technology', *Thesis Eleven*, No. 9.

Caulkin, S. and Large, P. (1989) 'True factory automation must let the people in', *Guardian*, August.

Cavendish, R. (1982) *Women on the Line*, London, Routledge & Kegan Paul.

Cavestro, W. (1989) 'Automation, new technology and work content', in S. Woods (ed.), *The Transformation of Work?*, London, Unwin Hyman.

Child, J. (1985) 'Managerial strategies, new technology and the labour process', in D. Knights, H. Willmott and D. Collinson (eds), *Job Redesign*, Aldershot, Gower.

Clark, J., McLoughlin, I., Rose, H. and King, R. (1988) *The Process of Technological Change: New Technology and Social Choice in the Workplace*, Cambridge, Cambridge University Press.

Cockburn, C. (1983) *Brothers: Male Dominance and Technological Change*, London, Pluto.

——, (1985) *Machinery of Dominance: Women, Men and Technical-Know-how*, London, Pluto.

Cooley, M. (1980) *Architect or Bee?*, Slough, Langley Technical Services.

——, (1981) 'The Taylorisation of intellectual work', in L. Levidow and B. Young (eds), *Science, Technology and the Labour Process* (Vol 1), London, Free Association Books.

Coopers & Lybrand (1985) *A Challenge to Complacency: A Report to the Manpower Services Commission*, London, MSC.

Coyle, A. (1982) 'Sex and skill in the clothing industry', in J. West (ed.), *Work, Women and the Labour Market*, London, Routledge & Kegan Paul.

Cressey, P. and MacInnes, J. (1980) 'Voting for Ford', *Capital and Class*, No. 11.

——, Eldridge, J. and MacInnes, J. (1985) *Just Managing: Authority and Democracy in Industry*, Milton Keynes, Open University Press.

Crompton, R. (1989) 'Women in banking: continuity and change since the Second World War', *Work, Employment and Society* 3 (2).

—— and Jones, G. (1984) *White Collar Proletariat*, London, Macmillan.

Daniel, W. (1987) *Workplace Industrial Relations and Technical Change*, London, Frances Pinter.

—— and McIntosh, M. (1972) *The Right to Manage?*, London, Macdonald.

Dankbaar, B. (1988) 'New production concepts, management strategies and the quality of work', *Work, Employment and Society* 2 (1).

Davies, A. (1986) *Industrial Relations and New Technology*, London, Croom Helm.

Dawson, P. and Webb, J. (1989) 'New production arrangements: the totally flexible cage?' *Work, Employment and Society* 3 (2).

Dex, S. (1985) *The Sexual Division of Work*, Brighton, Wheatsheaf.

Dodgson, M. and Martin, R. (1987) 'Trade union policies or new technology: facing the challenge of the 1980s', *New Technology, Work and Employment* 2 (1).

Dohse, K., Jurgens, U. and Malsch, T. (1985) 'From Fordism to Toyotism? The social organisation of the labour process in the Japanese automobile industry', *Politics and Society* 14 (2).

52   *Information technology and workplace democracy*

Downing, H. (1980) 'Word processors and the oppression of women', in T. Forester (ed.), *The Microelectronics Revolution*, Oxford, Blackwell.

Edwards, P. (1986) *Managing the Factory*, Oxford, Blackwell.

Elger, T. (1987) 'Flexible futures', *Work, Employment and Society* 1 (4).

—— (1989) 'Change and continuity in the labour process: technical innovation and work reorganisation in the 1980s', Work, Employment and Society Conference: A Decade of Change, Durham.

Findlay, P. (1992) 'Electronics: a culture of participation?', Chapter 2, this volume.

Friedman, A. (1977) *Industry and Labour*, London, Macmillan.

Game, A. and Pringle, R. (1983) *Gender at Work*, Sydney, Allen & Unwin.

Gourlay, S. (1987) 'The design of work organisation, or what do work organisers do?', Paper to British Sociological Association Annual Conference, Leeds.

Hyman, R. (1972) *Strikes*, London, Fontana.

—— (1988) 'Flexible specialisation: miracle or myth?', in R. Hyman and W. Streeck (eds), *New Technology and Industrial Relations*, Oxford, Blackwell.

Jary, S. (1987) 'Negotiating technological change?: bargaining power, union resources and workplace organisation', Paper to the BSA Annual Conference, University of Leeds.

Jenson, J. (1989) 'The talents of women, the skills of men', in S. Wood (ed.), *The Transformation of Work?*, Unwin Hyman.

Jones, B. (1982) 'Destruction or redistribution of engineering skills? The case of numerical control', in S. Wood (ed.), *The Degradation of Work*, London, Hutchinson.

—— (1988) 'Work and flexible automation in Britain: a review of developments and possibilities', *Work, Employment and Society* 2 (4).

—— and Rose, M. (1986) 'Redividing labour: factory politics and work reorganisation in the current industrial transition', in K. Purcell, S. Wood, A. Waton and S. Allen (eds), *The Changing Experience of Employment: Restructuring and Recession*, London, Macmillan.

—— and Scott, P. (1987) 'Flexible manufacturing systems in Britain and the USA', *New Technology, Work and Employment* 2 (1).

Kanter, R. (1983) *The Change Masters: Corporate Entrepreneurs at Work*, London, Unwin.

Keep, E. (1987) 'Britain's attempt to create a national vocational educational and training system: a review of progress', *Warwick Papers in Industrial Relations* No. 16, Coventry, IRRU.

Kelly, J. (1978) 'A reappraisal of sociotechnical systems theory', *Human Relations* 31 (12).

—— (1982) *Scientific Management, Job Redesign and Work Performance*, London, Academic Press.

—— (1985) 'Management's redesign of work', in D. Knights, H. Willmott and D. Collinson (eds), *Job Redesign*, Aldershot, Gower.

Koike, K. (1987) *Understanding Industrial Relations in Modern Japan*, London, Macmillan.

Kumazawa and Yamada (1989) 'Jobs and skills under the lifelong employment practice', in S. Wood (ed.), *The Transformation of Work?*, London, Unwin Hyman.

Lane, C. (1988) 'New technology and clerical work', in D. Gallie (ed.), *Employment in Britain*, Oxford, Blackwell.
—— (1989) *Management and Labour in Europe*, Aldershot, Edward Elgar.
Levie, H. and Moore, R. (eds) (1984) *The Control of Frontiers, Workers and New Technology: Disclosure and the Use of Company Information*, Oxford, Oxford University Press.
Loveridge, R., Child, J. and Harvey, J. (1985) *New Technologies in Banking, Retailing and Health Services: The British Case*, Research Report, Aston University, ESRC Work Organization Research Centre.
Lowstedt, J. (1988) 'Prejudices and wishful thinking about computer aided design', *New Technology, Work and Employment*, Vol. 3.
MacInnes, J. (1988) 'New technology in Scotbank: gender, class and work', in R. Hyman and W. Streeck (eds), *New Technology and Industrial Relations*, Oxford, Blackwell.
McLoughlin, I. (1989) 'CAD – the Taylorisation of drawing office work', *New Technology, Work and Employment* 4 (1).
—— and Clark, J. (1988) *Technological Change at Work*, Milton Keynes, Open University Press.
Manwaring, T. (1981) 'Trade union response to new technology', *Industrial Relations Journal* 12 (4).
—— and Wood, S. (1985) 'The ghost in the labour process', in D. Knights, H. Willmott and D. Collinson (eds), *Job Redesign*, Aldershot, Gower.
Marginson, P. (1989) 'Employment flexibility in large companies: change and continuity', *Industrial Relations Journal* 20 (2).
Martin, R. (1988a), 'Technological change and manual work', in D. Gallie (ed.), *Employment in Britain*, Oxford, Blackwell.
—— (1988b) 'The management of industrial relations and new technology', in P. Marginson, P. K. Edwards, R. Martin, J. Purcell and K. Sisson (eds), *Beyond the Workplace*, Oxford, Blackwell.
Marx, K. (1847) The Poverty of Philosophy, Moscow, Progress Publishers (new edn 1973).
Milkman, R. (1983) 'Female factory labour and industrial structures: control and conflict over "women's place" in auto and electrical manufacturing', *Politics and Society* 12 (2).
Millward, N. and Stevens, M. (1986) *British Workplace Industrial Relations 1980–1984*, Aldershot, Gower.
Moore, R. and Levie, H. (1985) 'New technology and the unions', in T. Forester (ed.), *The Information Technology Revolution*, Oxford, Blackwell.
Mumford, E. (1979) 'The design of work: new approaches and new needs', in J. Rijnsdrop (ed.), *Case Studies in Automation Related to the Humanisation of Work*, Oxford, Pergamon.
—— (1983) 'Successful systems design', in H. Otway, and M. Peltu (eds), *New Office Technology: Human and Organisational Aspects*, London, Frances Pinter.
Murray, R. (1985) 'Benetton Britain', *Marxism Today*, November.
Nicholas, I., Warner, M. and Hartmann, G. (1983) 'Automating the shop-floor: applications of CNC in manufacturing in Britain and Germany', *Journal of General Management* 8 (3).
Noble, J. (1979) 'Social choice in machine design', in A. Zimbalist (ed.),

Case Studies in the Labour Process, New York, Monthly Review Press.

Northcott, J. (1986) *Microelectronics in Industry: Promise and Performance*, London, Policy Studies Institute.

—— and Rogers, P. (1985) *Microelectronics in British Industry: The Pattern of Change*, London, Policy Studies Institute.

Pateman, C. (1970) *Participation and Democratic Theory*, Cambridge, Cambridge University Press.

Penn, R. and Scattergood, H. (1985) 'Deskilling or enskilling?: an empirical investigation of recent theories of the labour process', *British Journal of Sociology* 36 (4).

Phillips, A. and Taylor, B. (1980) 'Sex and skill', *Feminist Review*, No. 6.

Pollert, A. (1987) 'The flexible firm: fixation or fact?', *Work, Employment and Society* 2 (3).

Price, R. (1988) 'Information, consultation and the control of new technology', in R. Hyman and W. Streeck (eds), *New Technology and Industrial Relations*, Oxford, Blackwell.

Rajan, A. (1984) *New Technology and Employment in the Financial Services Sector*, Aldershot, Gower.

Ramsay, H. (1982) 'Participation for whom? A critical analysis of worker participation in theory and practice', Ph.D. thesis, University of Durham.

—— (1985) 'What is participation for?: a critical assessment of labour process analyses of job reform', in D. Knights, H. Willmott and D. Collinson (eds), *Job Redesign*, Aldershot, Gower.

—— (1986) 'Industrial democracy and the question of control', in E. Davis and R. Lansbury (eds), *Democracy and Control in the Workplace*, Melbourne, Longman-Cheshire.

Ramsay, H., Baldry, C. and Lockyer, C. (1991) 'Municipal microchips', in C. Smith, D. Knights and H. Willmott (eds), *The White Collar Labour Process*, London, Macmillan.

Rolfe, H. (1986) 'Skill, de-skilling and new technology in the non-manual labour process', *New Technology, Work and Employment* 1 (1).

Rosenbrock, H. (1982) 'Technology policies and options', in N. Bjorn-Andersen, M. Earl, O. Holst and E. Mumford (eds), *Information Society: For Richer, For Poorer*, Amsterdam, North Holland.

Rothwell, S. (1985) 'Supervisors and new technology', in E. Rhodes and D. Wield (eds), *Implementing New Technologies*, Oxford, Blackwell.

Rush, H. and Williams, R. (1984) 'Constitution and change: new technology and manpower in the electronics industry', in M. Warner (ed.), *Microprocessors, Manpower and Society*, Aldershot, Gower.

Senker, P. (1989) 'Technology, work organisation and training: some issues relating to the role of market forces', *New Technology, Work and Employment* 4 (1).

Smith, S. (1988) 'How much change at the store?: the impact of new technologies and labour processes on managers and staff in retail distribution', in D. Knights and H. Willmott (eds), *New Technology and the Labour Process*, London, Macmillan.

—— and Wield, D. (1987) 'New technology and bank work', in L. Harris (ed.), *New Perspectives on the Financial System*, London, Croom Helm.

Sorge, A., Hartmann, G., Warner, M. and Nicholas, I. (1982) *Microelectronics and Manpower*, Aldershot, Gower.

—— and Streeck, W. (1988) 'Industrial relations and technical change: the case for an extended perspective', in R. Hyman and W. Streeck (eds), *New Technology and Industrial Relations*, Oxford, Blackwell.

Storey, J. (1986) 'The phoney war?: new office technology, organisation and control', in D. Knights and H. Willmott (eds), *Managing the Labour Process*, Aldershot, Gower.

Tailby, S. (1989) 'Handling decline in the UK fork lift truck industry', in S. Tailby and C. Whitston (eds), *Manufacturing Change: Industrial Relations and Restructuring*, Oxford, Blackwell.

Tallard, M. (1988) 'Bargaining over new technology: a comparison of France and West Germany', in R. Hyman and W. Streeck (eds), *New Technology and Industrial Relations*, Oxford, Blackwell.

Tongue, C. (1986) 'But what about the workers?', *Computer Guardian*, 24 April.

Trist, E., Higgin, G., Murray, H. and Pollock, A. (1963) *Organisational Choice*, London, Tavistock.

Turnbull, P. (1989) 'Industrial restructuring and labour relations in the automotive components industry', in S. Tailby and C. Whitston (eds), *Manufacturing Change: Industrial Relations and Restructuring*, Oxford, Blackwell.

Wainwright, H. and Francis, A. (1984) 'Office automation – its design, implementation and impact', *Personnel Review* 13 (1).

Walby, S. (1988) *Patriarchy at Work*, Cambridge, Polity.

Webster, F. and Robins, K. (1986) *Information Technology: A Luddite Analysis*, New Jersey, Ablex.

Webster, J. (1986) 'Word processing and the secretarial labour process', in K. Purcell, S. Wood, A. Waton and S. Allen (eds), *The Changing Experience of Employment: Restructurng and Recession*, London, Macmillan.

Wilkinson, B. (1983) *The Shopfloor Politics of New Technology*, London, Heinemann.

Williams, R. and Steward, F. (1985) 'Technology agreements in Great Britain', *Industrial Relations Journal* 16 (3).

Willman, P. (1986) *Technological Change, Collective Bargaining and Industrial Efficiency*, Oxford, Oxford University Press.

—— (1987) *New Technology and Industrial Relations: A Review of the Literature*, Department of Employment Research Paper No. 56, London, Department of Employment.

—— and Winch, G. (1984) *Innovation and Management Control*, Cambridge, Cambridge University Press.

Wood, S. (1989) *The Transformation of Work?*, London, Unwin Hyman.

Wood, S. and Kelly, J. (1982) 'Taylorism, responsible autonomy and management strategy', in S. Wood (ed.), *The Degradation of Work*, London, Hutchinson.

Woodward, J. (1965) *Industrial Organisation: Theory and Practice*, London, Oxford University Press.

Woolley, B. (1986) 'What became of the dream?', *Guardian*, 3 April.

2 Electronics
A 'culture' of participation?

Patricia Findlay

INTRODUCTION

The issue of employee involvement in the electronics industry has been raised in recent discussions, both in Scotland and elsewhere (McCalman 1988, EDC 1983, Morgan and Sayer 1988). On the one hand, much of what has been written focuses on the claim that a large proportion of electronics companies do not recognize trade unions, and consequently there are no adequate channels for the representation of employee interests. On the other hand, the picture of the industry given by both the Scottish Development Agency (now known as Scottish Enterprise) and much of the Scottish media – and based, in particular, on the presence and practices of a number of large American blue chip multinational companies – is one of sophisticated and progressive employee relations policies, which encourage active employee involvement in, and commitment to, the firm. Beaumont (1986) has commented on the existence of a widely held belief that high technology firms are 'overwhelmingly non-union' and 'operate with a management style that has been labelled "sophisticated paternalist"'. In a similar vein, an ACAS commentator, referring to one such high technology firm, went as far as to say that the company in question had achieved 'a revolution in social thinking' with respect to its treatment of employees (quoted in Peach 1983). Clearly, the way in which managers approach the issue of employee representation will affect both the conduct and the state of industrial relations within firms. Attitudes towards recognizing trade unions, their roles and responsibilities inside organizations, the existence of non-union channels of representation, and the content and extent of communication and consultation with the work-force, are all issues in which management are likely to have some degree of choice or influence. Indeed, for some observers, the influence which management can bring to bear on these aspects of industrial relations is crucial (Brown 1986, Bain 1970).

It seems clear then that management have a significant part to play in structuring the system of employee representation within companies. In fact, there is some evidence to indicate that managers themselves are becoming more aware of their role in this area; MacInnes (1987) quotes two surveys, by Edwards and the CBI, which find that employers favour involvement initiatives as a means towards improving the conduct of industrial relations in general. The following discussion will attempt to outline and analyse the issue of employee representation, using a detailed survey of electronics companies in Scotland.[1]

MANAGEMENT, TRADE UNIONS AND EMPLOYEE REPRESENTATION IN THE 1980s

A number of current debates relate closely to the issues to be discussed here. Analyses of the decline in trade union membership in Britain have pointed to the growth of non-unionism, and its consequences for the way in which employee interests are perceived and represented within firms. Beaumont (1988), in his recent analysis of the decline of union organization, argues that while historically British employers have co-operated with trade unions, recent years have witnessed a decline in such co-operation, and moves in the other direction towards a more hostile and openly anti-union stance. Such an approach, he argues, bears more of a resemblance to the recent policies and practices of American employers than to the typical stance of British companies. As evidence of this trend, Beaumont points to the relatively high proportion of non-union establishments among recently created firms. Beaumont is not the only observer to perceive the rise of non-unionism. Bassett has argued that:

> non-unionism is likely to increase or at least to maintain its current share of more than half the workforce. There are now fewer reasons than ever before why an employer starting up should want to include trade unions in the operation.

> (Bassett 1987: 172)

Such discussions have not been confined to Britain. Kochan *et al.* (1984) point out that in recent years, many companies in the USA have publicly been making union avoidance or containment a high priority. In the UK case, however, despite the high visibility and media profile of a number of large non-union firms, there is a need for some caution concerning the general applicability of the non-union thesis as expounded by Beaumont and Bassett. MacInnes (1987) has criticized correctly many of the analyses of the rise of non-unionism for being particular in their coverage and for giving inadequate consideration to the *overall* incidence of non-unionism. Clearly, there is evidence of major sectoral variations in the extent of non-unionism. Further, large-scale survey evidence from the 1980 and 1984 Workplace Industrial Relations surveys (Millward and Stevens 1986) does not wholeheartedly support the rise of non-unionism, either in new establishments or existing establishments.[2]

Partly related to current discussions of non-unionism and the fate of the unions are the debates on 'macho-management' and 'new realism' in British industrial relations. These debates focus on the effects of recession on the industrial relations climate and on the activities of management in particular. The main thrust of these arguments is that management, empowered by the effects of unemployment, the decline in trade union power, and a hostile government attitude towards organized labour, and often threatened by a more competitive international market and the consequent pressure on costs, have adopted a far more offensive stance towards labour, particularly organized labour. Indicative of this stance is claimed to be the bypassing of traditional trade union representational structures in favour of management-based communications and consultative structures. Employees, in their turn, aware of their weakened position in the labour market, are perceived to be 'keeping their heads down' and co-operating with management to a greater degree than previously. (For an example, see Mackay 1986.)

There is, however, considerable evidence to suggest that debates on 'macho-management' and 'new realism' significantly overstate any supposed changes taking place in management–employee relations (Batstone 1984, Edwards 1985). Edwards refers to the findings of a Warwick survey, where two-thirds of employer respondents described their policies in terms of the necessity of gaining the commitment of employees, rather than alienating them with an aggressive management stance. This raises the possibility that managers have adopted a policy of promoting worker commitment to, and co-operation with, management goals. This point is echoed by MacInnes (1987) who, following Bendix (1956), makes the point that management continue to have a vested interest in maintaining good relations with their work-force, if only because most jobs rely to some extent on the exercise of discretion and co-operation by employees.

The contrast between an aggressive stance towards workers and their organizations and a policy of eliciting their commitment is highlighted by Walton (1985) in his discussion of control and commitment in the workplace. Walton argues that the traditional approach of management towards organizing their work-force was based on maximizing control over the work-force both in terms of task-related activities and in terms of employee–representative structures:

> In the traditional approach, there was generally little policy definition with regard to employee voice, unless the workforce was unionised, in which case damage control strategies predominated. With no union, management relied on an open-door policy, attitude surveys and similar devices to learn about employees' concerns.
>
> (Walton 1985: 80).

He argues, however, that the system based on control is under challenge in two ways: from the growing expectations of employees and from the demands of more intense international competition: 'A model that assumes low employee commitment and that is designed to produce reliable if not outstanding performance simply cannot match the standards of excellence set by world class competitors' (Walton 1985: 79).

This is hardly a new argument. Fox (1974) has pointed out that changes in the circumstances facing a firm – for example, increased competition or technical change – may result in attempts to encourage employee co-operation with the aims of management, rather than settling for the 'passive indifference of employees'. Increased competitive pressures are seen to play a similar role by Marginson *et al.* (1986), who argue that these combined with the example of different management styles, in particular, those operating in Japanese firms, have stimulated British management to make changes in working practices which are dependent for their success on securing the active co-operation of the work-force. Correspondingly, Marginson points to the 'growing tendency to talk in terms of "human resource management" rather than "industrial relations" or "personnel management"'.

Such pressures, according to Walton, lead management towards a radically different approach to their labour force based on encouraging employee commitment to the company, thereby stimulating a more productive contribution by way of problem solving, flexible working and related practices. On the issue of employee representation itself,

Walton claims that while a control strategy narrowly restricts the areas on which employee input is allowed and the information employees are permitted to receive to a need to know basis, a commitment strategy encourages employee participation on a much wider range of issues, and with a wider dispersion of business data, to the mutual benefit of both employees and management.

Such arguments concerning the need for employee commitment and co-operation underly many current discussions of management practice, particularly those which concentrate on the encouragement of responsible autonomy and flexible specialization. Often both implicit and explicit in many of these accounts is an emphasis on increased employee participation, either as a response to the problems posed by changing product market demands or to the problems and possibilities of technological change. Employee participation and involvement is often cited as the mechanism by which competitive and technical pressures will be overcome. The earlier work of Batstone (1984) accords partially with Walton's claims. Batstone argues that there does appear to have been a growth in interest on the part of managers in new initiatives in the area of employee involvement, as a response to the need for greater management legitimation, the need to secure co-operation from employees, and the demands of particular types of production systems. Two-thirds of the companies in his survey claimed to have changed their approach to employee relations in the last five years, with the most common change being an attempt to increase employee involvement. However, his later work with Gourlay (Batstone and Gourlay 1986) adds a note of dissent and a plea for a more cautious interpretation. Cressey *et al.* (1985) take this point further by arguing that the effects of recession are more likely to undermine than promote *de facto* involvement, because managers and employers have very different approaches to, and expectations from, employee participation.

It is important to bear in mind the simple fact that management's approach to participation and involvement may be very different from that of employees. Participation is commonly used as an umbrella term to describe a range of policies and procedures which attempt to involve employees in decision-making within organizations. If one considers the discussion of participation in personnel or management textbooks, it is clear that altruistic motives or concerns for equality of influence are unlikely to be the only reasons for promoting participation initiatives:

> Participation is not an end in itself . . . its purpose is to improve the efficiency and effectiveness of the organisation . . . The

interest of employers in participation agreements has, however, declined in recent years as the demands of the recession have turned the attention of industry to more pressing economic problems.

(Employee Relations 1985)

Two points are implied by this quote. First, it is clear that management's desire for participation is related to their perceptions of its potentially beneficial outcomes in profitability terms. Second, it implies that participation will be considered important only in specific circumstances (see also Ramsay 1980). Managers may have a number of reasons for resisting participation initiatives: it may threaten managerial prerogatives and reduce their influence over decision-making; it may slow down the decision-making process whilst simultaneously affecting the quality of decisions if employees are considered inexperienced in the areas of decision-taking; and finally, managers themselves may feel they lack the necesary skills to make participation effective. It would be a mistake, however, to assume that employees automatically support participation initiatives: they may be suspicious of management's motivation towards participation; they may feel they lack the necessary skills to cope with any new practices, and further, they may feel indifferent to participation initiatives at higher levels which concentrate on issues which do not appear of direct relevance.

WHY ELECTRONICS?

Electronics companies provide a useful site for assessing aspects of the debates mentioned earlier. The industry itself is relatively young, originating mainly in the post Second World War period. Consequently, it may feel itself less constrained by more traditional organizational and representational styles in manufacturing. The high proportion of foreign-owned multinational companies in the industry in Scotland, many of which are American-owned blue chip multinationals, is likely to have had significant impact on industrial relations policies and procedures. As has already been indicated, the industry overall has an image of being progressive in its employee relations policies, and is often cited as an example of the 'new orthodoxy' – incorporating a developed human resource strategy and flexible labour utilization. The electronics industry is seen by many (not least by those actually involved in it) as a reflection of the modern environment in which businesses operate: competitive, innovative and flexible, with rapidly changing products and an emphasis on quality and delivery. The rapid rate of product and process change, linked to the fiercely competitive nature of the electronics market international, means that the pressure on companies to maximize the utilization of their labour force is great, and may, on Walton's scenario at least, have spurred such companies on to more radical and innovative policies in the area of employee representation and involvement. Last, and of particular relevance given the relationship between employee relations policies and technical change, the industry is one which produces the technologies which are likely to have an impact on other industries, as well as using them itself.

There is a need, therefore, to put the industry's image to the test, by identifying the dominant trends in its approach to employee representation and participation and using these to allow comparison with other sectors. This necessitates detailed empirical consideration of the extent of institutional procedures for employee input into managerial decision-making. Those procedures for employee participation which are much more closely task related, such as shop-floor participation and job redesign, will not be considered here. These aspects of participation, while of considerable importance in themselves and closely linked to 'higher' level participation, require detailed attention elsewhere.[3] The following analysis will focus on three main issues: first, on the existence of institutional mechanisms for employee representation and participation, both in unionized and non-unionized firms; second, on a variety of mechanisms to encourage employee involvement and enhance communications in the survey firms; and last, on the practice of consultation and participation on issues of technological change.

Before looking at the actual mechanisms for involving employees in decision-making, it is necessary to take into consideration two factors which may significantly affect the approach taken by managers to employee participation: first, the status of the plants studied, in terms of ownership and control, and second, the nature of trade union recognition in the industry.

Ownership and control

Electronics employment in Scotland is dominated, as it is elsewhere, by large corporations, many of which are foreign-owned. The literature on the relationship between subsidiary plants and their parent company is extensive, and no more than a mention of it can be made here (Buckley and Enderwick 1985, Hamill 1986, Marginson *et al.* 1986, McCalman 1988). Much of that literature has concentrated on the degree of autonomy accorded to subsidiary plants over such issues as business decisions and personnel policies, and it is clear that there is a great deal of variation between companies in the degree of centralization and decentralization of decision-making, and hence in the extent of subsidiary management autonomy. Hamill (1986) has argued that there appears to be considerable decentralization of industrial relations decision-making in foreign-owned subsidiaries in Scotland. However, he goes on to make the point that in-depth interviews highlighted a more active parent-company involvement, with decisions with major cost and financial implications normally being centrally controlled, or at least requiring parent-company approval. Hamill found that multinational companies in electronics were more centrally controlled than those in traditional sectors. In my 1990 survey, only two of the plants looked at were stand alone, privately owned establishments. Most of the plants were subsidiaries or divisions of larger companies. Given this, it is necessary to make some attempt to analyse the location of decision-making powers in order to be able to locate the level at which decisions on employee involvement are made.

The twenty-nine subsidiaries in the present survey were asked to what extent the plant was responsible for its own personnel policy, excluding wages and salaries. The responses fell roughly into three groups: 24 per cent of the subsidiaries felt their establishment to be completely autonomous in personnel policy formulation, within an overall constraint of turning in the required profit level to the parent company. The largest group, 55 per cent of subsidiaries, stated that the parent company made no detailed policy input into the personnel function but did issue certain guidelines outlining either the general corporate approach to personnel issues and labour management, or pertaining to specific but limited aspects of personnel policy – for example, pension schemes or company-wide job evaluation schemes. The remaining 21 per cent of subsidiaries felt themselves to be fairly constrained in that a number of detailed policies came directly from the corporate headquarters (or from the central corporate personnel function).

Given, therefore, that around three-quarters of the sample (accounting for a high proportion of employees) had, at minimum, policy guidelines on various personnel issues, it is interesting to enquire whether employee involvement or participation figured prominently in these guidelines. However, on closer inspection, very few companies (only around 20 per cent of all subsidiary companies) claimed to have any guidelines from their parent company relating to the general sphere of employee participation and involvement schemes. Further, within these companies, managers argued that the influence of the parent company was felt more in terms of a general company culture or set of values rather than in terms of any guidelines or directives on specific schemes. Therefore, the data suggests that if any major steps have been taken in the area of participation and involvement, they are unlikely to have been brought about as a direct response to company or corporate level demands. Rather, parent companies have, on the whole, been fairly silent concerning any need for participation.

This finding is significantly different from that of Marginson *et al.* (1986), who state that 84 per cent of Head Office managers in their survey said they had an overall policy/philosophy towards the management of employees, of whom 58 per cent said that the policy was written down in a formal document, copies of which were given to employees in 21 per cent of the enterprises. Their respondents had great difficulty in describing policy in their own words, but some cropped up regularly: fairness, equity, caring, looking after. They further argue that general statements about participation and involvement are translated into specific policies within a significant number of enterprises and divisions. Cressey *et al.* (1985), however, offer an alternative interpretation, arguing that vague and general intentions about employees often result in little in terms of practical management behaviour.

Trade union recognition

Until recently, few commentators disputed the view that the electronics industry constituted something of a black hole for trade unionism in Scotland (Beaumont 1986). The image of the electronics industry as a high-technology, sunrise industry, with low levels of union organization and with a sizeable proportion of very prominent non-union companies pervades most media coverage. Such an image is further reinforced by the state agencies, such as the (former) Scottish Development Agency and Locate in Scotland, and government spokespeople involved in promoting the industry, who place much emphasis on the proportion of non-unionized plants. This image is further sustained by the comments of trade unions themselves, and of organizations sympathetic to their interests (Hargrave 1985, SEAD 1985).

Such an image is not, however, confirmed by the findings of my own research (Findlay 1990), which found that two-thirds of the companies interviewed recognized trade unions for bargaining purposes.[4] Recognition appeared to be related to a number of factors, with country of origin and product sector being the primary ones. Scottish, non-Scottish UK and European-owned firms were very likely to recognize trade unions, whereas American-owned firms were unlikely to do so. Companies in the defence, subcontracting, and industrial and commercial sectors were extremely likely to recognize unions; those in telecommunications and components production were fairly evenly split between companies who recognize and companies who do not; whilst companies in the semiconductors and information systems sectors were extremely unlikely to have conceded trade union recognition. Coincidentally, both the semiconductor and information systems sectors are dominated by American-owned companies. The data does not include enough relevant cases to shed any more light on the respective effects of the two characteristics of the firms.

The strength of union membership is somewhat more complex. Amongst companies who recognize trade unions, levels of union membership are high – higher than for UK manufacturing as a whole.[5] However, when the survey companies are considered as a whole, average union density is low, (due to the presence of a significant number of large, non-union companies), indicating that the electronics industry in Scotland is less well-organized than UK manufacturing industry as a whole.

Union recognition is, therefore, fairly well-established in much of Scottish electronics, and where established, union density is generally strong. However, there is a significant and very visible non-union sector, and there is some evidence to indicate that employment growth may be concentrated in that sector, such that industry density levels are being diluted.[6]

EMPLOYEE REPRESENTATION

This section will concentrate on those companies who have formal mechanisms for employee representation, either through union–management committees or their equivalents in non-union firms. Table 2.1 outlines the various types of group representative bodies.

Just under 90 per cent of companies in the sample had some formal representative channel, with provision for union-based representation in around two-thirds of these. Of the non-union firms interviewed,

Table 2.1 Types of representative forum by company

	%
Shop steward/management committee only	55.8
Non-union employee committee only	22.7
Joint body, including union and non-union reps	6.5
Separate bodies for union and non-union reps	3.2
No formal channels for employee representation	12.8

63 per cent had formal procedures for representation through non-union-based employee representatives.

As a first measure of the effectiveness of these representative bodies, managers were asked whether employee representatives had negotiating rights on these councils or committees. Negotiating rights were taken as a measure, although somewhat crude, in order to ascertain whether, in formal terms, management agreed that employees had a legitimate and acknowledged right to act in a way which may constrain managerial prerogative. It can be argued that the acceptance by managers of a negotiating role for employees is the minimum condition for effective employee participation. Not surprisingly, the research indicates that negotiating rights go hand in hand with trade union recognition, given that with one exception (where shop stewards had representational rights but no negotiating rights) all of the union-based bodies possessed negotiation rights, whilst none of the non-union-based councils or committees had negotiating rights but were simply advisory bodies.

Alternatively, however, it could be argued that employee representative bodies which do not negotiate (and generally are not union based) can be influential in promoting employee participation, without having negotiating rights. Where the consultative or advisory bodies promote active discussion on a wide range of issues, backed up by substantial information disclosure, they may have the potential to encourage high quality employee input, to be listened to and to influence management decision-making. Such a body could, in theory, be as influential as trade-union-based negotiating bodies. Indeed, it may be that management are more inclined to take notice of the opinions of their employees where they feel that they are free from external influences by third parties, in particular trade unions. The presence of trade unions might lead to managers adopting a more defensive stance than would otherwise be the case. In the end, however, the range of influence employees have in these bodies is something which can only be established in detail through comparative case study work. What can be considered for the purpose of this analysis is the range of issues covered by the channels which exist, and the assessment of the extent of employee influence given by the managerial respondents.

It is likely to be the case, as Millward and Stevens (1986) point out, that managers will give a more favourable assessment of consultation and involvement schemes, and of the amount of information made available to workers, than will employees. However, given that this research did not focus specifically on consultation and involvement, it can be argued that management were likely to be more dispassionate about this issue than if they felt themselves being assessed on the relative merits of their schemes for employee involvement alone, compared to those of other companies. In terms of the types of issues covered by participative or consultative mechanisms, responses for both unionized and non-union firms split roughly into two groups: those which covered both company level issues, such as the state of the business *and* shop-floor level issues, and those which covered only shop-floor issues. Of the companies where representation was trade-union-based, 68.4 per cent discussed both company and shop-floor level issues, whilst 31.6 per cent covered only shop-floor issues. Very few companies, either unionized or non-unionized, mentioned discussing higher level information such as investment, business strategy and so on. In the companies with non-union-based forums, there was an even split over the range of issues considered. All of the trade-union-based bodies included wages and conditions in the range of issues covered, while less than half of the non-union companies discussed wages and conditions. For the majority, wages were completely off the agenda – an area in which the company ruled absolutely. It would appear, therefore, that the range of issues covered by trade-union-based bodies is somewhat wider than those covered elsewhere, and trade unions generally have negotiating rights on these issues.

This analysis will not attempt to measure the strength of union influence on specific issues (with the exception of technical change, which will be considered later). Clearly, the ability of unions to bargain with management, the range of issues over which bargaining takes place, and the relatively high levels of union destiny in unionized establishments, indicates that trade unions have some influence over company policies at various levels. (For a fuller consideration of this, see Findlay 1990.) What is particularly interesting for the purpose of this analysis is the way in which non-union-based representative bodies function, - and how far they work to enhance employee participation in decision-making. This is especially the case given the way in which both employers and, to some extent, the government claim that representative or consultative channels which are not union based not only compensate for the lack of employee representation by trade unions, but can actually be more effective because they work on a consensual, non-antagonistic basis.

Given this focus, it is, therefore, interesting to look in some detail at management's assessment of the effectiveness of non-union-based consultation schemes. It is worth bearing in mind that this research concentrated on the opinions and attitudes of management, and that management are far less likely than, for example, trade unions or employees to be critical of company policy. The data give us seven examples of employee works councils in non-union firms. Employee representatives were elected in five companies, either by production area or by the entire work-force, nominated by management in one, and take part on a rota basis in one (with each individual having a turn to attend one meeting approximately every six years!). Around 60 per cent of works councils met monthly, with the remainder splitting between two monthly and three monthly. The number of employees to each representative covered a wide range, from one representative per 15 employees to one per 240 employees.

Those companies who held elections all spoke of the difficulties in persuading employees to become a representative: many employees, and managers for that matter, felt that the role put employees in a contradictory position. Consequently, a majority of these companies had groups of employees who were unrepresented at the time of the interview. As one plant manager pointed out, 'it's a thankless task, as the representatives are between the devil and the deep blue sea . . . it's hard to get people to become representatives as there's no immediate visible payback for being a member of the employee committee'. Another personnel manager stated, 'they're in a no-win situation – if they don't get the answers that the employees want, then they're not popular'.

In terms of the range of issues discussed, four of the non-union companies stated clearly that there was very little interest in the works councils, since they focused on matters of minor importance: Company A's discussions were on car parking, canteen, holiday arrangements and charities; Company B discussed car parking, toilets and plant temperature, while Company C's main issues were canteen and toilets. One plant manager summed up his company's works council by saying: 'it doesn't really have any teeth, or the opportunity to deal with real issues . . . it's just communication really – there's not a lot to talk about when you're not discussing pay and conditions'.

This view of the works council as a communications mechanism and not a negotiating body was echoed elsewhere – other plant managers pointed out that

> a lot of people have the mistaken image that they should be coming up here and talking about wages and negotiating better conditions, but we already have very good conditions and wages, although they may not think so . . . so apart from that we discuss any issue they wish to raise – providing it doesn't interfere with overall company policy.

> There's not a great deal of interest in it – it's only a communications mechanism.

> There's not a lot of enthusiasm for the employee committee, and therefore it doesn't have very wide representation. The majority of people have a pretty poor view of the employee committee, based on the fact that the group tended to be a bitching session, and was seen to be pretty ineffective at doing that. It never got any results.

For these managers, therefore, the main function of the 'representative' body was communication, and in many cases one-way communication at that. Clearly, significant sections of the work-force were disaffected with the operation of the representative body.

The remaining three companies were far less dismissive of their representative bodies, seeing them as useful channels to *inform* employees of company progress and plans; to *consult* employees on matters concerning the company and its work-force; and to *discuss* matters raised by employees through their representatives. For two of these three companies it did not appear, even in the eyes of management, that the councils were in any way powerful. The third company, however, had set up a more sophisticated system of representation, comprising a tiered structure of departmental committees, divisional committees and a central employee committee, with specialist training for representatives. It is worth looking at this company in more detail, since it is the only example of a highly formalized representation system within a non-union company.

In this company, a consultative committee structure had been set up with the establishment of the plant 'to provide a forum at which a free exchange of views on all matters of factory-side interest and the operating efficiency of the total enterprise are discussed'. The lowest level was made up of area or departmental committees, who met monthly with management in charge of that area to discuss local issues and to elect representatives to the Central Employee Committee (with one representative to 150 workers). The CEC met bi-monthly with senior management to discuss any issue raised, and to set up *ad hoc* committees of a specialized nature to carry out specific tasks. In 1979, the structure was revamped, and divisional committees were set up between the area committees and the CEC, staffed by those representatives elected by area to go to the CEC. Furthermore, a full-time chair was established, to be elected by the CEC, to organize the representatives, get involved in higher level grievances, and act as a resource to employees in general.

In 1985, all of the employee representatives on the CEC resigned in a dispute with management. Part of that dispute focused on the consultative structure itself, and employee representatives criticized the CEC for being elitist, objected to the fact that the chair was elected by the CEC and not employees generally, and complained that the remit given to them was too wide. At the time of interviewing, a new structure was about to be set in place, based to a great extent on inputs from employees: the area committees have been abolished, supervisors have been left to deal with issues previously dealt with by the area committee; and all employees will now elect the chair. The main change concerns the CEC; instead of all representatives on the CEC meeting with management, there will be a core group of five employees including the chair who will go to the central meeting with management, and the remaining representatives will attend the meeting in rotation. Further, all representatives will now be trained in one of three specialist areas – wages and salaries, policy, and grievances – by the company, either by members of management or by outside advisers.

According to the personnel director, the company perceived itself as being very similar to a unionized company, with a set of formal channels for the articulation of employee interests. He argued that representatives were given far more information and more of a place in the running of the company than was the case in other non-union companies, and cited examples of large non-union companies who tell employees what they need to know, but will not involve employees in much consultation as such. He also emphasized the fact that the company operated no restrictions on the topics for discussion on the CEC, while these existed in other non-union fora.

On the crucial issue of power, the personnel director stated that while the CEC discussed pay and conditions, it would be false to say that they negotiated with the company, although in the past the company have balloted the work-force on pay deals. What was interesting, however, was his view that as the work-force had moved to a more negotiating stance, the consultative mechanism had ground to a halt:

> My feeling is that employees don't want to get involved in bargaining again, because that destroyed them. And the reality is, of course, that we're part of a corporation, so we don't have a free hand in what we negotiate anyway.

These employees clearly have a more formalized representative structure than do the rest of non-union companies in the sample. Indeed, the willingness of management to adapt the structure to the needs of the representatives appears to show an important degree of concern over the operating of the consultative structure. Despite this, however, the committee seems purely consultative. Attempts by representatives to negotiate with management have simply resulted in decisions being taken by management decree.

These results throw significant doubt on the participatory nature of non-union works councils. Managers seem to regard them as being at most consultative units, or channels of communication. When questioned about their attitudes to trade unionism, many of the managers in non-union companies pointed out that the existence of such lines of representation for employees meant that trade unions were not needed to represent their interests. However, on examining their representative arrangements, the majority of managers could not, and did not, in many cases, attempt to sustain an argument that these representative bodies were powerful. This begs the question: what actual function do these committees perform? If they do not actually represent independent employee interests then perhaps they fulfil a more ideological purpose such that employees at least *feel* they have a say, and thus management decisions are legitimated. However, given the finding that, according to managers at least, many employees were disinterested if not critical of the operations of their works committee or council, this seems unlikely. Alternatively, a commitment to consulting may be effective in ways which are not easily measured – for example, if it makes employees feel that management are at least tackling the issue of consultation or participation, or, as Fox (1974) has argued, if it legitimates management policies to managers themselves. Each of these possibilities were raised by at least some of the respondents in this survey, although it is evident that a more in-depth analysis would be necessary to further clarify the rationale behind such representative fora.

INFORMATION PROVISION

A further issue raised in the discussion of the effectiveness of various forms of representation concerned the provision of information to representative bodies. One report of the Electronics Development Council (EDC 1983) has claimed that 'significant' amounts of information disclosure took place in electronics companies. The Scottish data do not wholly substantiate this. The companies were asked an open question on how much information they gave to their employees on company affairs. Where necessary, respondents were prompted to choose between a great deal of information, a fair amount of information and not much information. The results are shown in Table 2.2.

Table 2.2 Extent of information disclosure by unionization

	Unionized companies (%)	Non-unionized companies (%)
A great deal of information	42	33
A fair amount of information	37	17
Not much information	21	50

The Workplace Industrial Relations Study found that workers or their representatives were less likely to report receiving a lot of information than were managers to report that they give it (Millward and Stevens 1986). Keeping this point in mind, managers in unionized firms felt that the provision of information to representatives was more extensive than appears to be the case with management in non-union companies. Indeed, a number of companies pointed to the presence of trade unions in their plants as the major incentive to giving out information. It must be remembered, however, that few companies stated that they gave out much in the way of higher level strategic information.

COMMUNICATIONS AND EMPLOYEE INVOLVEMENT

This section will be split into two parts. First, companies which had no formal arrangements for employee representation will be discussed. Second, a number of issues relating to the general sphere of communications will be raised in relation to the entire survey group.

For those companies with no formal channels of representation, relations between managers and employees were conducted very much on an individualistic basis. Of the four companies studied, all were American in origin, and three of the four were relatively recent arrivals in Scotland, having located in the period since 1976. In many ways the companies in this category were very similar: they were all non-union, and they all voiced a company commitment to the individual, including a no-redundancy policy (sometimes more implicit than explicit, based on the fact that no one had ever been made redundant). Moreover, all of these companies based their personnel policies on a set of company philosophies or values which were extremely individualistic in nature, and thus many other personnel policies went along similarly individualistic lines – for example, in remuneration, assessment, promotion, training and career development.

In terms of the provision of information, the results were not uniform. Two of the companies believed that they made a serious commitment to providing a wide range of information, while another stated that this information was available should employees wish to obtain it. The fourth company felt it necessary only to give people the information they needed to do their job. One aspect which was uniform to all of them was a commitment that management should be open and responsive to employee opinions. Much onus was placed on management in these companies to act as the communications interface with their subordinates.

In such a situation, it is difficult to assess just how far employees can actually influence management decision-making. It seems likely that certain employees will be able to wield more influence than others, although extensive research on employee attitudes would be needed to answer this question. Any evidence obtained here is purely impressionistic, based on a small number of expressions of discontent by various lower-level managers, on suggestions that the voice of the shop-floor was not really being heard and that individuals found it difficult to put any pressure on management. The focus in these companies on the link between the employee and her/his supervisor or first line manager meant that not only did the employee's direct superior control how much information people received, but they were also crucial in how far employee grievances were considered. Thus, there were major variations between companies in how much particular groups or sections felt their views to be represented.

There are no real channels for constructive criticism. People are 'encouraged' to communicate on an individual level, but individuals can be easily fought off – convinced, if need be, by the argument that they're lucky to have a job, or that they get good wages. That's the rationale behind organizing on an individual basis.

X is a good company to work for, compared to traditional engineering, but there is no avenue for fightback. Open management and employee surveys are just another management legitimation.

These views square with those of Cressey *et al.* (1985) in their study of Comco, another company with an individual approach to representation and communication. They argue that besides consultation integral to the work process, there were few other methods of communication. The plant magazine, information charts and notice boards were passive forms, with few other active routes. The most active involvement on offer outside of the work process was the individual dialogue between worker and supervisor. This form of participation, however, lacked feedback and positive involvement.

With reference to the entire survey group, a number of other issues were raised in the area of management/work-force communication. Companies were asked to list the range of methods they used to communicate with their employees, excluding formal representative channels. The responses are given in Table 2.3.

Table 2.3 Methods of management–employee communication

	Yes (%)	No (%)	DK/NA (%)	WIRS2* All Establish- ments (%)	WIRS2 Private Manufact- uring (%)
Do you use:					
Shop stewards	58	6	36		
Briefing groups	58	42	—	62	58
Meetings with senior/ general management	48	49	3	37	37
Noticeboards	55	19	26		
Company newspaper	29	68	3	34	24
Suggestion schemes	25	33	42	25	15

* *Source:* Millward and Stevens 1986.

We can consider the first three mechanisms for communication in more detail. These are clearly more active forms of communication, involving a two-way process, whereas noticeboards, company newspapers and suggestion schemes are less ambitious and far more passive forms of communication.

Shop stewards

Shop stewards are found to be the most important channel of communication in overall terms. This is not significantly different from the rest of industry, and suggests caution in ascribing to the sector a distinctive or innovative approach to employee relations practices. A number of managers (representing 16 per cent of companies in the sample) expressed satisfaction with the trade unions carrying out this role. On the other hand, however, a larger number (23 per cent) claimed that their companies had made positive efforts to reduce the power of trade unions as the main source of information to employees by giving more responsibility for communicating to management – in particular to first line management. Two main reasons were given for this: first, and most importantly, it was felt that trade unions had become so important in the communications process by default and that it was up to management to regain control of communications. Second, some companies argued that the trade unions were a biased source of information to workers, and that management should work to overcome that bias.

Briefing groups

Table 2.3 indicates that 58 per cent of survey companies used briefing groups. Again, using WIRS data as a comparison, electronics companies do not appear to be significantly different from other establishments, in private manufacturing or overall, in the extent of use of briefing groups. Amongst unionized companies 50 per cent used briefing groups, whilst the figure was 73 per cent amongst non-unionized companies. Clearly, some sort of team-based briefing system is used in a significant number of companies, with the data showing that many companies had recently begun to use briefing groups, and further, that many more intended to do so in the near future. The most common type cited was based on a cascading system, whereby the managing director prepared a 'state of the nation' type of brief, including information on company performance, order intake, shipments, quality, scrap rates, productivity, market forecasts, market share, position of competitors, any changes in progress, personnel issues, etc. This is passed down the management chain, with each level of management adapting the brief to suit the next level receiving it. Theoretically, by the time the brief reaches the supervisor or first line manager responsible for briefing the team or work-group, it should have had a number of additions and subtractions made such that it addresses the issues most relevant to the work-group.

Companies in the survey tended to differ in their approach to briefing groups in so far as some companies see it as simply a method whereby management passes on information to workers free from any outside influence, whilst others see it as a far more rigorous procedure involving two-way communication between management and workers. In companies adopting the latter approach, the meeting works to an agenda, minutes are taken, often the entire factory stops production to hear their briefs, employees are encouraged to raise issues during briefing sessions, and a formal procedure is established whereby a maximum period of time is set within which an employee request or issue has to be dealt with. Companies also differ in how formally structured their briefing group set-up is: how regularly meetings are held, how much notice has to be given for a postponement, the maximum period of postponement, who has to attend, etc. In a significant number of companies, briefing groups were brought in as part of a formal communications programme, involving introductory seminars and training in the required communications and procedural skills, often by outside agencies (for example, the Industrial Society).

Many companies felt that briefing groups had been established to improve communications between management and workers, while (in a number of cases) enhancing the role of the first line supervisor by giving them the responsibility for communicating management information to employees. In unionized companies, a significant proportion of managers used briefing groups as a deliberate method to avoid using shop stewards as the main channel of communication.

> We have actively avoided communicating through shop stewards by encouraging supervisors to have regular briefings with their people.

> We've used briefing groups for 5 or 6 years – we wanted to move away from union-based communications to line communication.

> It's our responsibility and not that of trade unions to communicate with our employees – not all employees are trade union members.

> We think team briefing is a fantastic management tool. It has improved employee relations as people have heard things from management in the way they should hear it, not from trade union representatives with a slightly biased slant on things.

Clearly, briefing groups have been used in these companies in an attempt to weaken trade union influence in information terms. Such attempts have not been without problems, however. One company pointed out that a number of sections of the work-force did not attend briefing meetings because of union resistance, while another spoke of the suspicion of plant trade unions that the briefing meeting could be used by management for propaganda purposes.

On the basis of the survey data, then, it would be difficult to support the view that the majority of companies were satisfied with the results of team briefing. Of the companies who operated a system of briefings, less than 10 per cent claimed that the system worked 'extremely well', although 27 per cent thought briefing groups worked well. Almost half of the companies felt that the groups were very variable in their impact, both across time and from team to team, whilst 18 per cent felt that the groups had fallen into abeyance – though still operating, they were not felt by either management or employees to be achieving very much. The criticisms of briefing in operation were remarkably similar across companies, and fell into three main categories. First, managers came under fire for their role in the briefing system for two reasons: many managers were criticized for failing to make their briefs relevant to their particular work-group, in a number of cases simply reading out the managing director's brief verbatim. Also, it was felt that variability in the operation of the system was strongly related to the efforts of first line managers or supervisors to involve employees, to make them comfortable when discussing grievances with their managers. In part, it appeared that some of these problems were overcome in companies where a training programme was set-up prior to or during briefings.

Perhaps the largest obstacle to successful team briefing, partially but not completely related to the previous point, is that shop-floor employees in many companies showed very little interest in higher-level company matters such as orders, market share, etc. Many managers felt these matters bored employees, and were not tangible enough to be considered directly relevant to their situation. A common complaint concerned finding the right balance between giving important information and making the briefings relevant and interesting to the employees, whilst ensuring that the discussion did not lapse into areas which employees found more directly relevant, such as industrial relations considerations, since these not only proved contentious but were felt to be better dealt with elsewhere. This accords with the findings of Cressey *et al.* (1985) in the Comco case study where they point out that different degrees of enthusiasm existed amongst the work-force, both in relation to corporate matters and to opportunities for involvement, with manufacturing staff being the most difficult to draw into discussions of corporate affairs.

Finally, many managers pointed out that the feedback from briefing groups was extremely variable and in some cases non-existent. In one company, management described the briefing group system as having turned 'not into an answering session, but more into an attempt to stop grapevine information'.

Direct communication via senior management

One interesting comparison with the 1984 Workplace Industrial Relations Survey is in the area of direct communication between senior managers and their employees, where employees are directly involved in communications between themselves and management rather than through their representatives or through receiving documentary information. The results indicate that such communication is more prevalent in electronics than in manufacturing as a whole.

In the Scottish survey, direct management communication was more likely to be found in non-unionized than in unionized firms, although a significant amount of unionized firms also made use of it. It may be that the factors which have led companies to set up briefing groups have also encouraged the use of direct management communication. Further, the use of such direct communication procedures may be related to the concept of 'open management'. This concept, which appears to have become a 'buzz' word in the industry, refers to a culture of openness and involvement, and to new types of management/worker relationships which move away from a 'them and us' attitude. Only 23 per cent of the companies interviewed mentioned 'open management' without prompting, but a further 36 per cent claimed to have a policy of open management when pressed. Further questioning, however, resulted in managers in many companies stating that while an open management policy existed in theory, in practice it was not used very extensively, especially not in a formal grievance sense. One reason for this may have been the difficulty, in companies which had been established for some time, in changing the culture and attitudes of management as well as workers from relationships often characterized by hostility and suspicion to relationships marked by trust and common goals (particularly when very little else appears to have changed). Overall, most of the companies interviewed felt that the various procedures which they operated for communications were effective. A significant proportion (39 per cent), however, felt that while their communications procedures were reasonable, there was much room for improvement.

Upwards communication

Personnel managers were asked what they felt to be the main method used by employees to communicate their opinions and desires to management. Where shop stewards were mentioned as the most important channel of upwards communication, it is not clear whether this took place on an individual basis or through the representative body, although it can be argued that this makes very little substantive difference. In unionized companies, 70 per cent relied on shop stewards, 15 per cent on some sort of supervisor briefing to the group, 10 per cent on the relationship between the individual and the supervisor, and 5 per cent on the works council. Clearly, the communications channel in unionized companies is dominated by shop stewards, in many cases even where some alternative channel for communication exists. Of non-unionized companies, 45 per cent relied on the supervisor/individual link, 37 per cent on the representative body, and just over 9 per cent on briefing groups, with just over 9 per cent unsure. Far more use is made in non-union companies than in union companies of the supervisor/individual link, but this is hardly surprising given that a number of non-union companies had no formal channels for representation or communication. Not all of the non-union companies who had some sort of employee representative body cited this as the main way in which employees made their grievances known.

To summarise: the preceding discussion has indicated that trade unions remain the most common channel for employee representation in the electronics industry in Scotland, although their dominance in this respect is not unchallenged. Taking unionized and non-union companies together, 90 per cent of the survey firms had some formal mechanism for the representation of employee interests. However, where non-union councils or committees operated, management themselves expressed doubts as to the representative nature of these bodies, stressing, rather, their role in communication and consultation. There was no evidence to suggest that managers in these companies acknowledged the existence of separate and potentially conflicting employee interests. Similarly, there was little evidence to suggest that extensive information disclosure took place in the survey firms.

Looking across a range of mechanisms for communication and consultation, the most obvious point to be made concerns the variety of practices being used, often in conjunction with each other. The material did suggest, however, a greater emphasis on management-based rather than union-based channels of communication, although bearing in mind that the shop steward channel still predominated. The next section will attempt to further highlight the nature of employee participation and involvement by considering company approaches to the process of technical change.

EMPLOYEE PARTICIPATION IN TECHNICAL CHANGE

The issue of technical change provides an interesting area in which to examine the extent of employee participation. Batstone and Gourlay (1986) argue that the rationale for looking at the process of introducing new technology, and at the influence which the main groups involved bring to bear on the process, is based on seeing new technology as a critical case. They argue that there may be more scope for changing the patterns of management/worker influence with technical change than with many other issues, yet point out that in many cases management have simply imposed new terms and conditions during the process. They also note that technology is often associated with labour control (although not uniquely), and that the approach taken by employers to its introduction is therefore significant in terms of the power relations within the workplace.

There is little doubt that the electronics industry is, and has been, faced with substantial changes in the goods it produces and the way in which they are produced, especially since electronics companies are often themselves the destination of their own most sophisticated production. The demands of an extremely competitive market have provided the impetus for large-scale investment in research and development, in order to be able to produce goods which are smaller, more powerful and more reliable than their competitors. The market has also dictated that the labour cost element, particularly for companies producing in Europe and the USA, should be reduced in order that firms in high labour cost countries remain competitive against low labour cost, mainly Third World, producers. In consequence, most companies have experienced a significant degree of technical change, and whilst the various product market sectors have been differentially affected, very few producers have experienced no change whatsoever. In fact, technical innovations have extended across virtually all areas of production, resulting in the widespread use of flow soldering and laser welding equipment, automatic insertion and surface mounting equipment for components, robotics and artificial intelligence, computer numerically controlled machine tools, and computer-aided design systems. Warehousing and materials control have also undergone significant change. Many areas of high labour usage have been automated out of existence. Whilst a complete system of computer-aided manufacturing is still a dream even for the largest producers, firms who do not keep up to date with technological developments are unlikely to succeed.

The Electronics Development Council of the NEDC has already given some attention to the issue of employee involvement, particularly in relation to technical change. Its 1983 report claims that

> employee involvement is seen by an increasing number of firms as vital to recovery and future prosperity. Such firms are actively seeking to improve both the degree of consultation on issues important to the firm, and the quality of consultation by improving flows of information.

The EDC research had two main aims. First, it attempted to establish the extent to which the electronics industry engages in open flows of communication and consultation in relation to technical change. This focus stems from the view that the industry's future prosperity is dependent on adapting quickly and efficiently to technological developments – developments which affect both the nature of products and their rate of obsolescence, and partly as a consequence of this, their productive processes. While this is a crucially important point, it must be remembered that technological imperatives are not the sole driving force within the industry, and that an overemphasis on such pressures in electronics production is likely to paint a misleading picture of the environment in which corporate decisions are taken. This overemphasis on technology has even affected electronics companies themselves. As one company in Scotland pointed out, 'we were so overawed with the technology that we lost sight of our marketplace'. However, bearing this in mind, it is clearly the case that technological change is likely to have a direct impact on labour in terms of both employment and skills, and therefore may be an interesting test case on which to assess employee involvement.

The second aim of the research was to identify the costs and benefits of such consultation. This is a far more difficult task. Not only are the outcomes of consultation and communication difficult to cost in any rigorous way, where there is a desire to do so, but further, there appears to be little evidence to suggest that in practice management set up consultation and communications schemes with any clear conception of identifiable costs and benefits in mind. Even where this is the case, any assessment of costs and benefits would require a far more rigorous research approach than is visible in the EDC report, incorporating an examination of the processes leading up to the establishment of participation or consultation schemes, and a far more detailed analysis of their outcomes. The EDC research does not do this, and fails to give an account, in more than very general terms, of the perceived costs and benefits of increasing employee involvement.

The report found that a large majority of companies agreed that employee involvement was central to the efficient introduction of change, especially technical change, and felt that tangible benefits could be obtained in the form of improved industrial relations, increased employee commitment to the firm, greater understanding of the problems of technical change by both the shop-floor and by management, and increased readiness to accept redeployment. In terms of consultation practices, it was found that 90 per cent of companies had 'some form of consultation' during change. This took various forms, such as joint consultative committees, works committees, joint staff union councils, briefing groups and participation meetings. However, no details were given of the extent of usage of each of these forms, nor was any discussion made of the likely power of each, thus making the results difficult to assess in terms of the effectiveness of existing channels. The research concluded from these findings that a 'significant' amount of consultation and disclosure of information is practised by the electronics industry. On the issue of technology agreements, two types were found: one-off agreements specifically related to the introduction of new technology, and procedural agreements incorporating provisions on new technology. It was felt that whilst most employee involvement took place at the implementation stage, that is, the last stage of introduction, new technology agreements led to employees being consulted earlier.

A number of assumptions, both implicit and explicit, permeate the tone of the report. The central assumption made is that the needs of profitability and efficiency in the industry will be best served by actively involving employees through consultation and participation, particularly in the processes of change. The authors make no real distinction between the terms they use, such as participation, consultation and involvement, using them interchangeably. This lack of clarity in their definition inevitably causes some confusion in the interpretation of their results. Their assumption that there is no best model of participation and negotiation serves only to absolve them from differentiating between the various schemes which exist, and from ranking any type better or worse than others. Consequently, one is unable to differentiate between simple communication of information to employees, consultation with employees possessing only advisory powers, and processes whereby employees have some realistic power base from which to affect decision-making. There is no discussion of the problem of power and conflict in relation to consultation and participation, and inevitably the report suffers from its oversimplistic approach. The main underlying concern appears to be assisting the efficient introduction of change, but this fails to acknowledge the potential for conflict over such change.

Further, the report explicitly assumes that 'involving' employees (however defined), will necessarily lead to a greater willingness on their part to adapt to change. However, while there is a substantial amount of evidence to suggest that individuals are more likely to go along with decisions (even difficult ones) where they have had some influence on the making of them, it is clear that this cannot be looked at in isolation from the context in which decisions are reached and changes are taking place. The types of pressures faced by electronics firms at the present time pose many challenges to labour. The industry is faced with intense competitive pressures; its demand cycle is turbulent in many sectors of the industry, with periods of high demand for scarce or new products being followed by periods of extreme overcapacity in many markets. The demands of the market for the latest products at the lowest production cost means that many firms are continually changing or upgrading their production processes, with significant consequences for internal organizational stability and labour management.

Given the extent of these pressures, it is naïve to assume that communicating these changes, however early, and with whatever degree of information disclosure, will necessarily lead to a greater willingness on behalf of employees to adapt to change. Many of these developments have adverse or potentially adverse consequences for labour, in terms of employment, income, skills and job controls, which in concrete terms is likely to lead to disharmony and disruption on their introduction. This is not to argue that employees will necessarily take action to prevent such developments. Many work-forces will be unable to present alternatives to proposed changes, and may, through the dissemination of management information, be convinced of their inevitability for the firm's survival (and conse-quently, their livelihood), which may in fact be 'true', given previous decisions. Other work-forces may be less convinced about the necessity of innovation, but may not be in a position to offer any resistance. The options are wide-ranging. However, what must be acknowledged is that adaptation to technological change is likely to be affected by the conflicting interests of managers and employees and by the power relations existing in the workplace. The EDC report shows no awareness of this. Rather, the entire report focuses on management-oriented participation – that is, 'participation' as a device used to assist management in the pursuit of change. The acceptance of participation as a tool to ease management problems shows no awareness of the potential contradictions in participation or consultation schemes, and no acceptance of employee involvement in decision-making as a legitimate right in itself.

The EDC report claims that there is a need for information and early consultation as this leads to people being committed to the industry, aiding its development. However, this automatic equating of 'involvement' with consensus or commitment fails to confront any of the above issues adequately. As with many previous discussions of employee participation, the consensus-based assumptions take no account of existing differences in interests. By emphasizing 'improving the degree of consultation *on issues important to the firm*' it is clear that in the eyes of the authors of this report the agenda for participa-tion is still defined by management, and this goes unquestioned.

Given the importance of technical change, both in terms of competition and the high levels of investment it requires, it is likely that managers will attach great importance to the issue. The Scottish-based firms confirmed that high levels of technical change had taken place. Technical change in the area of design, manufacture and testing had been introduced by 87 per cent of the companies: of these, 89 per cent had made extensive changes, while 11 per cent had made some changes. Fewer companies, although still a significant amount, had implemented technology for warehousing and stock control: 68 per cent had experienced change, 78 per cent of these significant change, with the remaining 22 per cent experiencing some change. In terms of office technologies, a substantially different picture to that of manufacturing technologies existed, with only 14 per cent of companies having experienced innovation in that area, although in all of this group the degree of change had been substantial. This does not, however, indicate that the office has failed to undergo significant change – rather, it indicates almost the opposite, in that word processors, computerized records and payrolls, and integrated systems were not regarded by the managers interviewed as *new* technology – most had used such technologies for at least five years, and in many cases had been using them far longer.

In order to assess the areas in which employees played a significant role in influencing management decisions on technical change, an open question was asked enquiring about the issues on which employees had a significant input or involvement. The reason for leaving the question open-ended is clear: asking 'do you involve/consult your employees in the introduction of new technology?' is likely to result in more positive replies being received. Thus, given that this research was not solely concerned with new technology, it was felt that a more realistic answer would be received by making no specific reference to technical change. Of the survey companies, only 32 per cent included new technology in their answer. The composition of this group was, however, of particular interest, in that it was dominated by the larger companies. Further, within this group, there was an obvious split on whether or not companies negotiated or consulted with their employees on the introduction of new technology. Of these companies, 70 per cent actually negotiated with employees, and with one exception these were all large, long-established, unionized firms. The remaining 30 per cent stated that while they consulted their employees, there was no right of negotiation on new technology issues.

Further analysis of the procedures surrounding technological development made it clear that few companies (only 6 per cent of the sample) consulted or negotiated with their employees prior to the implementation stage of the process. Thus, planning and choice of equipment were not seen as areas amenable to employee involvement. It is obvious, however, that some consultation with employees is an absolute necessity by the stage of implementation, given their responsibility for the operation of the equipment. Only 6 per cent of companies had any formal agreement on technology with their workforces (or representative body). On an interesting note, one of the companies which had signed a new technology agreement pointed out that 'while the trade unions had sweated blood to get it, it isn't worth the paper it's written on'.

Less formal discussions with a number of respondents indicate possible explanations for the fact that a significant number of companies felt no real need to involve their employees in the processes of change. In most companies, the necessity of introducing new processes was unquestioned, given the perception that the firm's survival in the long term depended on it. While a number of companies did point out that detailed discussion of changes prior to implementation would result in long delays, potentially damaging the firm's competitive position, a significant number had no feeling that technology should be discussed at all, beyond the point necessary to educate operators in its use.

This confirms the general picture presented by Daniel (1987) with respect to worker and trade union involvement in the introduction of technical change, as indicated below:

> Our findings show that, in many instances, there was little or no involvement of workers and their representatives in the introduction of the major changes we studied. The overall pattern which emerged revealed that managers generally operated in a minimally pragmatic fashion. If they could introduce the changes they wanted without having to take account of the views of any other group or individual, they did so. Where they consulted or negotiated, it was principally because they were required to do so, either by the industrial relations institutions at their workplaces, or by resistance to the changes they wanted on the part of workers or their representatives. There was no hint of managerial commitment to worker involvement as a means of improving the form of the change or generating enthusiasm for it.
>
> (Daniel 1987: 113)

Given this, one may have few expectations that the electronics industry would be significantly different, despite its reputation as an innovator in employee relations. On reflection, however, it can be argued that for a number of reasons, the degree of consultation on technical change in this industry might be less than in others. First, given the rapid rate of change affecting much of the industry, technical change may be much more commonplace than elsewhere, and therefore may be less likely to be treated as something out of the ordinary.

Further, many of the discussions of the industrial application of new technologies have related specifically to the introduction of microelectronics-based systems, seeing these as a significant change in type from previous technologies. Given that the switch to micro-electronics on any large scale occurred amongst electronics producers far earlier than in most other sectors, it may be that in the time periods to which the survey related, the changes which had taken place were not of a new type but were extensions of existing technologies, and thus were not considered to be of unique importance, worthy of specific attention and consultation. These arguments are, however, tentative and require further analysis.

Some attempt, however, must be made to account for the differences in results found between the EDC survey and the Scottish survey (Findlay 1990). It may be that the different times in which the surveys were carried out were accompanied by different circumstances facing the industry, and this coloured the responses of the firms. It appears more likely, however, that much of the difference is due to the way in which the questions on technical change and employee involvement were asked. The rationale for choosing an open question has been explained earlier, and it could be argued that the questions asked by the EDC led their respondents into a reply which was perceived to be the correct one. This seems plausible since the researchers failed to follow up with more detailed questions about the actual extent of that involvement. While this would not account entirely for the different survey results, it highlights the EDC's predisposition to favourable images of involvement as an area for further investigation.

CONCLUSION

This chapter has considered a number of issues in the area of employee representation, and highlights two areas of interest: first, the mechanisms for the representation of employee interest in an industry with a sizeable number of non-unionized firms; second, the extent and method of participation on key issues such as technical change. Clearly, trade union recognition in electronics companies in Scotland is well-established, and trade unions remain the dominant channel for the representation of employee interests. This casts some doubt on the relevance of 'macho management' arguments which focus on 'union bashing' or the bypassing of union channels. There was no evidence of widespread attempts to undermine them by companies which recognized trade unions: rather, the dominant managerial viewpoint emphasized gaining the co-operation of workers and their representatives in order to be able to function in highly competitive markets. There were some attempts to forge a more direct link between management and employees through briefing groups in particular, but as pointed out earlier, these had not proved to be an unqualified success in most companies. All-out attacks on union organization were rare. Despite this, however, it is certainly possible that the current 'responsibility' of the trade union movement is not unrelated to their economically weaker position, or, more specifically, to the high visibility of successful non-union companies in the industry. Both management and work-forces in the unionized firms were aware of the comparisons being made between themselves and their peers in the non-union sector, and this was clearly significant in structuring attitudes and expectations.

This brings us to the non-union sector. Non-unionism appears to be the result of a particular corporate philosophy of non-interference by outside agencies, emanating most directly from medium and large US companies. What made the non-union sector different from the unionized sector was the almost complete absence on the part of management of any conception of separate employee interests or of fundamental conflicts of interest between themselves and their employees. Even where employee representative structures had been set up, the dominant ideology was consensual, with room for conflict or grievance only at the margin. The evidence did not indicate that these representative bodies were in any way powerful, and the view of managers was that these channels were not intended to give employees the same formal power as they perceived existed in a unionized company. Much of the evidence from non-union companies suggested that these representative structures neither adequately represented employee interests nor incorporated employees into supporting managerial views. The most likely outcome was a mild indifference, and it can be argued that employee performance and attitude in non-union firms was more influenced by other parts of company manpower policy, such as good conditions, high wages and good benefits, than by the companies' approach to representation. This is not to argue that employees are uninterested in representatives structures, but simply to concede that other factors may be more important in determining their level of satisfaction. Where companies can convince employees that they are looking after them, or at minimum that both the company and its work-force can benefit from a particular set of arrangements, then the need for more rigorous representational channels may be less pressing. This is not a surprising conclusion, and arguably exists in unionized companies as well. From this, it can be tentatively argued that for as long as the majority of employees in non-union companies are relatively satisfied with their situation in comparison with other work-forces, the question of enhanced power for representative channels or indeed of pressure for external representation is unlikely to be confronted. In a number of companies, short-term difficulties have led to increased demands on the representative structure, and to a more favourable recruiting ground for trade unions. The survey did not uncover companies where attempts have been made to significantly change terms and conditions of employment such that questions of representation may have come to the fore, except on an individual level. At present, therefore, it would seem fruitful to analyse management–labour relations in non-union companies more in terms of the internal pillars which promote employee satisfaction than to focus solely on the channels by which collective grievances are resolved.

The evidence indicates that the issue of technical change, despite its importance for management and employees, was not one in which employees were given significant input, for a variety of reasons outlined earlier. In fact, what characterized the survey firms according to their managers was an obvious lack of consultation and involvement, with the possible exception of involvement at the stage of implementation. In this respect, therefore, the electronics industry does not appear to be dissimilar to other sectors in manufacturing.

NOTES

1 The material contained in this chapter is part of the following study: P. Findlay 'What management strategy? Labour utilisation and regulation at Scotland's "leading edge"', D.Phil. thesis, University of Oxford, 1990.
2 Millward and Stevens point out that while they have some limited data that indicates that new establishments are less likely to be unionized, the number of cases involved is too small to make any definitive conclusions. With respect to existing establishments, they argue that there is little evidence of attempts by employers to withdraw recognition from existing trade unions – taking manual and non-manual unions together, 93 per cent of establishments did not change their recognition of trade unions between 1980 and 1984, and of the small minority that did change, more moved towards recognizing unions from 1980 to 1984 than changed in the opposite direction.
3 The issue of participation at task level is dealt with separately. See Findlay 1990.
4 A trade union of some sort was recognized by 65 per cent of companies: 55 per cent of the survey companies recognized unions representing both white- and blue-collar employees, whilst 10 per cent recognized a union(s) for blue-collar employees only. For further details, see Findlay 1989.
5 Looking at unionized companies alone, union density was high: 86 per cent for blue-collar employees, 47 per cent for white-collar employees, and

62 per cent overall. Including all survey companies, union density in the industry was 36 per cent overall, representing 53 per cent of blue-collar employees and 23 per cent of white-collar employees.

6 The results indicated that while similar proportions of unionized and non-unionized firms forecast declining employment, twice as many non-union firms forecast employment growth. In terms of past employment trends, unionized companies were more likely than their non-unionized counterparts to report having reduced employment levels and less likely to report having increased employment levels.

REFERENCES

Bain, G. S. (1970) *The Growth of White Collar Unionism*, Oxford, Clarendon Press.

Bassett, P. (1987) *Strike Free*, London, Macmillan.

Batstone, E. (1984) *Working Order: Workplace Industrial Relations Over Two Decades*, Oxford, Blackwell.

—— and Gourlay, S. (1986) *Unions, Unemployment and Innovation*, Oxford, Blackwell.

Beaumont, P. B. (1986) 'Industrial relations policies in high technology firms', *New Technology, Work and Employment* 1 (2), Autumn.

—— (1988) *The Decline of Trade Union Organisation*, London, Croom Helm.

Bendix, R. (1956) *Work and Authority in Industry*, Berkeley and Los Angeles, University of California Press (quoted in J. MacInnes, 1987).

Brown, W. (1986) 'The changing role of trade unions in the management of labour', *British Journal of Industrial Relations* 24 (2), July.

Buckley, P. and Enderwick, P. (1985) *The Industrial Relations Practices of Foreign Owned Firms in Britain*, London, Macmillan.

Cressey, P., Eldridge, J. and MacInnes, J. (1985) *Just Managing: Authority and Democracy in Industry*, Milton Keynes, Open University Press.

Daniel, W. W. (1987) *Workplace Industrial Relations and Technical Change*, London, Frances Pinter.

Edwards, P. (1985) 'Myth of the macho manager', *Personnel Management*, April.

—— and Scullion, H. (1982) *The Social Organisation of Industrial Conflict*, Oxford, Blackwell.

Electronics Development Council (EDC) (1983) *The Introduction of New Technology*, London, NEDC.

Employee Relations (1985) *Personnel Management in Practice Series: 4*, CCH Editions Limited.

Findlay, P. (1989) 'Trade unionism and employee representation in the Scottish electronics industry', Working Paper 89/9, Department of Business Studies, University of Edinburgh.

—— (1990) 'What management strategy? Labour utilisation and regulation at Scotland's "leading edge"', D.Phil. thesis, University of Oxford.

Fox, A. (1974) *Man Mismanagement*, London, Hutchinson.

Hamill, J. (1986) 'Foreign multinationals: labour and industrial relations effects', IRM/SIBU Conference on Scotland and the Multinationals, Glasgow.

Hargrave, A. (1985) *Silicon Glen*, Edinburgh, Mainstream Publishers.

Industrial Relations Review and Report (1988) *The Challenge for the Unions*, No. 417, 1 June.

Kelly, J. and Heery, E. (1988) Quoted in *The Challenge for the Unions*, No. 417, 1 June (Industrial Relations Review and Report).

Kochan, T., Katz, H. and McKersie, M. (1984) *The Transformation of American Industrial Relations*, New York, Basic Books.

MacInnes, J. (1987) *Thatcherism at work*, Milton Keynes, Open University Press.

—— and Sproull, A. (1986) *Union Recognition in the Electronics Industry in Scotland*, CRIDP Research Report No. 4, University of Glasgow, September.

Mackay, L. (1986) 'The macho manager: it's no myth', *Personnel Management*, January.

Marginson, P., Edwards, P., Martin, R., Purcell, J. and Sisson, K. (1986) 'The management of Industrial Relations in Large Enterprises', Warwick Papers in Industrial Relations, No. 11, August.

McCalman, J. (1988) *The Electronics Industry in Britain: Coping with Change*, London, Routledge.

Millward, N. and Stevens, M. (1986) *British Workplace Industrial Relations 1980–84: The DE/ESRC/PSI/ACAS Surveys*, Aldershot, Gower.

Morgan, K. and Sayer, D. (1988) *Microcircuits of Capital: Sunrise Industry and Uneven Development*, Oxford, Blackwell.

Peach, L. (1983) 'Employee relations in IBM', *Employee Relations* 5 (3).

Ramsay, H. (1980) 'Phantom participation: patterns of power and conflict', *Industrial Relations Journal* 11 (3).

Scottish Education and Action for Development (SEAD) (1985) *Electronics and Development: Scotland and Malaysia in the International Electronics Industry*, Edinburgh, SEAD.

Sproull, A. and MacInnes, J. (1988) 'Trade union recognition, single union agreements and employment change in the electronics industry in Scotland', Glasgow College, Department of Economics, Discussion Paper No. 6, May.

Terry, M. (1986) 'How do we know if shop stewards are getting weaker?', *British Journal of Industrial Relations* 24 (2), July.

Walton, R. E. (1985) 'From control to commitment in the workplace', *Harvard Business Review*, March/April.

3 A creative offensive?

Participative systems design and the question of control

Martin Beirne and Harvie Ramsay

The concept of user-involvement in the development of computing systems has come to the fore in recent years with a profusion of books, articles and conference papers devoted to its potential. The bulk of this literature seldom directly addresses the issue of user decision-making. In most cases considerably diluted meanings prevail, presenting involvement as an instrumental means to combat systems 'noise', to tap the local knowledge of users, or to induce attitudinal changes to foster acceptance of systems rather than resistance. By way of a contrast with this (outwardly at least), an alternative tradition adopts, and claims to substantiate, certain broadly distinctive theories and assumptions about mutually beneficial change. Whereas the first approach concentrates almost exclusively on efficiency objectives, advocates of the second look to establish 'democratic' forms of develpment in addition to workable systems. A few quotes will illustrate:

> The involvement of users in the design process will help to ensure the creation of acceptable and well-functioning organisational structures that users will welcome.
>
> (Mumford 1983: 82)

> the advantages of a participative approach to systems design based on consensus decisions can be said to be the following:
> From management's point of view it is advantageous because the result is an efficient system and a satisfied workforce.
> From the employees' point of view it is advantageous because they are able to create a system that meets their efficiency and job satisfaction needs.
>
> (Mumford 1979: 229)

> Participation by users in the design process is a powerful technique to avoid the isolation of the EDP specialist and the loss of certainty

and control by the users, and to help strike a balance between the specialists need to innovate, and the line managers requirement for stability.

(Land and Hirschheim 1983: 100)

It should be emphasized that these ideas do not float free of any larger analytical system. On the contrary, the intellectual pedigree of the approach lies in the Tavistock/socio-technical tradition of managerial human relations. In a previous publication we set out the major concepts and propositions which tie it specifically to reform initiatives in the wider rubric of 'quality of working life' and work humanization movements (Beirne and Ramsay 1988). Here we intend to follow up some critical points made there concerning the empirical evidence marshalled to vindicate involvement on these terms.

In our review of this area we argued that the claims made for participative design as advancing the democratic rights of employees are founded on a rather flimsy empirical base. Bluntly stated, the image of decentralized design is promoted by a small number of studies whose reliability cannot be accepted by any serious critical assessment. Although great mileage has been made from these the majority tend to be propagandist episodes staged merely to extol the virtues of normative theories and design methodologies rather then research their precise nature and effects in real world situations (Mumford 1980, 1983; Mumford and Henshall 1979). While these studies have undoubtedly played an important role in putting over the case for involvement, they leave room for disagreement on just what has happened and what the results are likely to be. Some of the data presented is highly questionable, or of unknown validity or reliability (see Kraft 1979, and Ives and Olson 1984). To this can be added the fact that much of the work is based on assertion and conjecture rather than rigorous empirical inquiry. This unhappy situation makes it extremely difficult to reach any informed judgement or conclusions whatsoever on the impact or user-involvement on democracy, or for that matter on efficiency. It also means that the factors which enable us to account for the success or failure of particular initiatives, and especially for the opportunities for users to exert some independent influence, remain improperly analysed and understood.

If more secure ground is to be established for an evaluation of user-participation, then more substantive accounts of what actually happens have to be compiled. This requires that detailed questions

Table 3.1 A summary of the systems development process

Step number	Label	Definition and sub-processes
1	Problem recognition	The inadequacies and failures of existing manual or computerized systems are identified and defined.
2	Decision to innovate	Provisional studies are conducted and the initial decision made to change existing systems.
3	Goal setting	Formal objectives and parameters are conceived for planned systems and the feasibility of these determined.
4	Systems analysis	Work procedures are analysed, data collected, and the functional requirements for new systems defined.
5	Equipment selection	Hardware requirements are formulated, suppliers approached, and available equipment reviewed.
6	Detailed programming and design	Systems requirements are translated into detailed plans, codes and programmes.
7	Implementation	New systems are introduced to the organization on a pilot basis, in parallel with existing systems or by a once-and-for-all conversion.
8	Operational adjustment	New systems are tested, modified and declared fully operational.
9	Evaluation	Fine tuning occurs as new systems are evaluated in terms of original goals.

be asked and that key indicators of genuine participation be monitored directly. For instance, sensible evaluation would seem to depend on much closer inspection of the stages of systems conception and implementation at which involvement occurs (see Table 3.1). It is necessary to decide whether user input extends across the gamut of development activities or if, in fact, it is concentrated in the problem areas defined by computing professionals. To this must be added the question of which users are being involved. The meaning attached to the concept is far removed from any valid notion of democracy if it refers to say a senior management group working with data processing (DP) staff to produce systems for regular use by manual or clerical grades. It is also important to draw a distinction between user-influence in decision-making and the exchange of information between users and professionals, and to gauge whether the former is real, or just apparent at first glance, or from management pronouncements. After all, there is no reason to presume that a presence at meetings signals significant influence or discretion on the part of users.

To test some of these contentions, and to open the area for further investigation, we conducted a survey of Scottish companies with computing systems and a postal survey of trade union views and experience of user-involvement. Some of the overall results concerning the scope for genuine participation and the perceived extent of user-influence are summarized in our earlier publication (see Beirne and Ramsay 1988). These will not be reiterated here, but it should be noted that they underline the need for a far more critical and wary evaluation of even outwardly radical involvement experiments. That said, the conclusions drawn from these questionnaires should not be stretched beyond their explanatory power. Although they confirm the complexity of the processes at work and provide preliminary data on the profile of user-involvement, our survey results tell us only what computing managers and union officials report. This in itself is important given the dearth of information on practical experience, but it does not provide sufficient grounds to confirm or refute claims that involvement affords genuine advances in the democratic rights of employees. To extend our research we therefore made additional use of the surveys to pick out what appeared to be bona fide instances of participation for detailed investigation. This gave us the opportunity to examine the extent to which genuine influence is really a feature of user-involvement while avoiding the charge that our studies are biased against favourable outcomes. Any gains or limitations discovered in these cases should accurately reflect the merits or failings of theories of democratic or participative design.

In this chapter we report on four studies conducted by one of the authors between May and October of 1986. These are not intended to provide conclusive proof of the efficacy or otherwise of participative design, but to illuminate the dynamics of user-involvement. However laudable the objective of democratically designed systems may be, achievements must be empirically and impartially assessed, and this we seek to begin to do here.

RESEARCH PROCEDURE

From the returns to our company survey we compiled a list of fifteen likely candidates for case study work. These were selected according to the following criteria:

1 management had a policy in favour of user-involvement in the design and application of computing systems;
2 users were 'always' or 'frequently' consulted when sytems were changed or modified;
3 users were 'always' or 'frequently' involved in the actual design of computing systems;
4 lower managerial, clerical, secretarial or manual employees were currently or had recently been involved as members of a user group in a 'participative design exercise';
5 users had been given the opportunity to sit directly on design teams, to elect their own representatives or to discuss/negotiate any appointments to these groups made by management;
6 lower managerial and white-collar or blue-collar workers had been involved in at least six of the design stages represented in Table 3.1;
7 user department managers and white-collar or blue-collar workers were represented either directly or by union/employee representatives on steering or strategy committees;
8 users or their representatives were supplied with relevant information about computing developments prior to design group meetings;
9 user groups had the power of veto over the plans and recommendations of systems professionals;
10 user groups had discretion in specified areas of decision-making (for example, equipment choice, work organization, etc.);
11 respondents had drawn attention to the merits or drawbacks of user-involvement for industrial democracy.

After some initial difficulties in negotiating access, exploratory interviews were conducted in a sample of eight organizations to check the accuracy of completed questionnaires and to prepare the ground for extended research. Unfortunately, at this stage we discovered that despite our initial selectivity the experience of participation was a good deal more attenuated than many of our respondents believed. Indeed, it turned out that four cases fell seriously short of our criteria. This added to our suspicion that some optimistic academic reports are based on the face-value reading of involvement experiments, and showed that the labels of participative and democratic design are frequently used in a misleading way. Two examples will suffice to indicate the problems and discrepancies unearthed.

First, in the case of a chemical company DP staff told us that clerical and blue-collar workers had elected members of their respective shifts to sit on a design team charged with the task of introducing new process technology to a west of Scotland plant. However, the terms 'elected' and 'appointed' had been confused and conflated in their reply to our postal survey. It transpired that section chiefs had assigned key workers to act as providers of information when directed by systems professionals. In fine irony one respondent declared:

> We [the DP group] might approach a management committee on the first steps of a project and they would elect relevant members from their departments . . . We tend to work with the same people although it really is down to user department managers who they want to appoint.

If this case underscores a potential for terminological confusion, a second indicates how vacuous prima-facie claims for participation can actually be. In the finance division of a large thread makers a new accounting system had ostensibly been installed by joint consultation and shared decision-making. According to their completed questionnaire, selected members of the clerical work-force were involved directly in development efforts, devoting some twelve to sixteen hours per person per week to the project and had autonomy in decisions affecting manpower deployment, workflow and choice of equipment. In addition, the entire user community had the power of a veto over the plans and recommendations of designers. Subsequent interviews with senior managers in both the computing and user departments cast serious doubt on this interpretation. It emerged that a senior accountant had worked closely with the systems development manager to produce the specifications for the system and that these individuals had visited trade fairs and exhibitions to select and purchase all the necessary equipment. Clerical staff played a passive and marginal role in the process. By chance rather than design the software package acquired for the system allowed a choice of screen layout. Individual clerks were merely invited to sit at a terminal and point out their preferences for menus and formats to their head of department and his opposite number in computing. This was the full extent of user-involvement for the bulk of the clerical population.

As a result of these and other discrepancies between the data gleaned from postal questionnaires and preliminary interviews, only four of the cases earmarked for investigation qualified under the criteria set out above. These varied markedly in terms of their sector, industry, market position, ownership, strategy and objectives. Two were from the private sector: a financial services company and a US multinational in information technology. The third was a public sector educational institution and the fourth a trade union. The main research sites were located in Central Scotland and the South of England, and ranged in size from less than fifty to over 2,000 employees. A number of different technologies and applications were involved, including stock control and distribution, office automation and management information systems. At the time of the study, two organizations moved from steps 3 to 7 in Table 3.1: goal setting to implementation. A third had recently introduced a new system and was engaged in a process of revising and re-tuning the resource to accommodate new working practices and procedures. The fourth was at an interim stage where certain systems had been installed as part of an overall programme that was scaled down due to financial restrictions.

Our initial plan for data collection relied heavily on participant observation. However, the scope for direct assessment was limited in practice by existing schedules for development and also by the terms of access agreed with each organization. Two principal means of research were therefore employed. In the first place, information about the situation and history of each establishment and the background to user-involvement was gathered from documents and statistics that were either publicly available or supplied by the organizations themselves. The rest of our material was drawn from in-depth interviews and periodic re-interviews with people who were closely involved in specific programmes and with others who were able to monitor developments carefully. Allowing for slight differences in organization titles, a total of five systems managers and DP professionals, six user-managers, eight users and two trades union representatives were interviewed. The questions asked of respondents were left open-ended to encourage them to express their own attitudes and opinions and to enable us to build up a picture of the circumstances at large in each organization.

THE SAMPLE OF ORGANIZATIONS

To set the scene for the main discussion and core deliberations of this chapter, we now turn to a brief description of the case study organizations and the arrangements installed for user-participation.

TCL – a financial services company

Trust Credit and Leasing (TCL) is a highly successful hire purchase and leasing finance house and a wholly owned subsidiary of a major bank. It operates through a number of functional centres which service a large network of area offices. Prior to 1986 computing power in the company was based on large, rather dated and totally stand-alone systems. These were out of favour with employees who were unhappy at the amount of duplication involved in re-keying customer information (names, addresses, financial data, etc.) for products logged on different systems. For their part, management were concerned with the inefficiency of existing procedures, with repetition, but also with the cash-flow problem of chasing credit arrears through different customer files. By the autumn of 1985 senior management had decided that a redevelopment programme was in order, and DP staff had set out to formulate appropriate methods for dovetailing systems to avoid any duplication of design and programming efforts.

The subsequent structure of design procedures and the whole approach to the provision of new systems was influenced by two factors. First, the company was engaged in a rolling programme of rationalization initiated when the parent organization acquired 100 per cent ownership. The major strategy here was to cut out all existing low margin business. As a result, the computing project was linked to a broader process of streamlining the range of services currently offered. Second, environmental changes impinged on the plans for reorganization, producing a shift in market focus towards lending to the personal sector. The investment in new systems coincided with major decisions on this front, and development activities were soon organized for the centralization of commercial business in Central Scotland (the locus of our research) and personal sector business in London. These changes led to some job loss, but also to grading improvements for 'key' personnel. The Banking, Insurance and Finance Union (BIFU), the only union in the company, was not involved in systems design or implementation and campaigned against the adverse effects of rationalization.

The development process began with a review of existing package systems. This showed that the available software was too narrow for the job in hand and that TCL requirements would be satisfied by a combination of off-the-shelf and bespoke (in-house) applications. An 'umbrella' package was then acquired from a major software house on the grounds that this had appropriate facilities for an integrated customer information system, loans and on-line collection systems, and tools that could be harnessed to meet the company's specialist needs. Once the systems and areas of application had been selected, a feasibility study was conducted by DP staff to prepare the ground for user-participation. This involved consultation with company directors to find out their views and elicit their support for a two-phase programme. In the event, a management consultant was hired, partly to appease the concern expressed by various directors about the validity of user-involvement.

With approval at high level, designers embarked on the first stage of the involvement plan which covered systems planning and analysis, detailed programming and implementation. The main feature of this was the creation of a user group that was responsible for designing acceptance test procedures, ensuring that specifications catered for peripheral work activities and that adequate training materials were available for ground-level staff. This group was composed of users representing the principal divisions in the company – corporate and personal finance – who worked as a team supported by systems analysts. The users' role in the project was full-time, based mainly on a six-month secondment from 'normal' duties. Outside of the formal team sessions, users were paired-off with systems analysts to define the data and prepare the specifications for a specific part of the development exercise. At reconvened team meetings the partners in each project would present their results in the form of a structured walk-through, and try to secure the approval of their colleagues by way of a formal phased sign-off procedure.

The second part of the involvement plan was formulated in recognition of a strong tradition of branch autonomy. The stated intention was to delegate a measure of responsibility for the systems changeover to selected branch and area managers in each region. To facilitate this, a procedure was devised to circulate design documents for approval. Managers were expected to check the functional specifications contained in these and to register their agreement or any reservations, again through a phased sign-off process. The results of this exercise would then be collated along with the findings of a similar survey of divisional chiefs before the final report was produced for approval by the board of directors.

The TTU – Technicians' Trade Union

Our second study took place at the head office of an industrial and TUC-affiliated trade union with a membership of just over 20,000. Like many other unions, the TTU had learned from experience that a flexible and effective administration was vital for survival in the face of declining financial resources, shorter membership rolls, and industrial change. Officials argued that more extensive membership communication systems were required to establish wider participation and secure a higher level of commitment to industrial objectives. This, together with the widening scope and increasing complexity of union affairs, produced a strong measure of support for computerization within the organization.

Serious work on the introduction of computers began in 1979 when the Finance and General Purposes Committee agreed in principle that systems should be developed for membership records, dues collection and finance. At this stage a working party was established in line with the union's general policy of joint consultation and participation between management and workers on new technology. This group consisted of national officers (management representatives), department specialists from Membership and Finance, potential users, and APEX shop stewards from the national officer and clerical 'shops' within the office. The terms of reference for the group specified that members should fully assess union requirements, examine different makes, models and types of computer, submit proposals for the purchase of appropriate systems, and oversee their introduction and use. A further important objective was to increase the job satisfaction of staff as far as possible and to avoid creating tedious and highly repetitive work with new systems.

From the spring of 1980 and for a period of two years the working party met frequently, often at the request of individual members who would circulate memoranda proposing a date, time and agenda for discussion. In the first instance, work systems were analysed and described in detail. Consultations with specialist advisers, software design and equipment decisions, and finance and training provisions were then all made and recommended jointly by the group. The resultant submission was ratified by the General Council towards the end of 1981, and appropriate expenditure was authorized for a series of networked terminals in the Records and Employment Department, together with a stand-alone work-station for accounting purposes.

Following the introduction of these systems the working party was suspended. A basic pattern of computing had been established and this functioned on a par with the original specifications for the next three years. Although a modest expansion of systems occurred within the respective departments, this was due to specific initiatives from national officers that gained the support of the Deputy General Secretary. These plans were hatched in response to 'bugs' and problems in particular areas and were essentially a means of fire-fighting to maintain the viability of the computing operation. However, by 1984 demands on the system had reached a point where slight modifications and amendments were subject to ever-decreasing returns. The main problem was a bottleneck for the use of the Records database. Non-Records staff were hampered in their efforts to draw information by the lack of terminals, and the limited capacity of the existing processor often resulted in 'collapse' when new data was integrated into the central files. At the same time, users were beginning to think of using computing power for other purposes. Office staff were pressing for a word processing facility, the research officer wanted direct access to the subscription database for analytical work on salary and employment surveys, while the journal editor was looking for on-line screen editing. To accommodate these demands and explore the options for expansion a new working party was established.

This reconstituted user group included representatives from all the areas covered in the earlier exercise with the addition of a lay member of the union who was interested in the development of networks and the provision of computer-based services to members. By August 1984 the working party had agreed to recommend a phased plan of expansion that would upgrade existing systems and integrate new research and word processing applications in the first instance. This would be followed by enhanced systems in Finance and the supply of personal computers and modems to regional branches. These proposals were commended to the Finance and General Purposes Committee in July of 1984. However, financial restrictions at this time meant that only immediate needs for additional power, terminals and printers were met. The working party continued to formulate options and cost piecemeal additions to the computing resource, but the overall programme had yet to be implemented when we studied the situation in 1986.

National Invigilation – bureau for issuing academic awards

National Invigilation is an educational examination board. It employs around thirty permanent staff with an additional complement of approximately 100 temporary clerical and secretarial grades. The bureau was established by Act of Parliament to conduct examinations and award certificates, either directly or on behalf of any other accredited examining body. The operation is financed by contributions from education authorities.

In 1981 a review committee of appropriate local authorities approved in principle the creation of a computer resource that would enable the bureau to dispense with external computing services for exam processing. A systems manager was subsequently appointed, meeting rooms were converted into a computer hall, and equipment finally installed after a process of competitive tendering. By November 1982 the acceptance trials for the new system were complete and work had commenced on testing the programmes and routines required for processing the examinations scheduled for 1983. Our own research took place three years after the initiation of the system by which time attention was focused on updating and refining the resource to cope with changes to the work system occasioned by an independent review of examination arrangements.

From the outset, users were to be involved in development efforts. The organization sanctioned staff consultation on a wide range of topics as indicated in the annual report for 1982:

> [National Invigilation] places considerable value on consultation and keeps members of staff informed on matters affecting them as employees and on the various factors affecting the responsibilities, developments, activities and performance of the [organisation]. This is achieved through formal and informal meetings. Staff representatives are consulted regularly on a wide range of matters affecting their current and future interests.

With regard to new technology, these principles were translated into a series of guidelines on job security and health and safety that were negotiated with NALGO, the union recognized for collective bargaining purposes. They were also important for the system of collaboration that emerged between DP professionals, user-department managers and their staff. The union was not involved directly in this, although it was kept informed and consulted on matters covered by existing agreements.

Once the decision had been taken to tender for equipment, a design group from computer and user-department management was set up to work out the requirements and oversee the introduction and fine tuning of the system. This was the main forum for discussion where a senior administrative officer and two administrative officers from the Procedures (administration) division met weekly with the head of Computing to provide information, but also to propose amendments and argue for and against specific developments. Administrative assistants and clerical officers were expected to express their opinions either collectively or individually to their immediate superiors who would then channel their input into design group meetings. In addition, some administrative assistants had formal lines of communication to a systems analyst and these were used on a daily basis to clarify procedures, notify problems and highlight any concern about 'bugs' or protocols. At an informal level, debate within the user-department was open and often quite vigorous. Indeed, many of the ideas for the system came first and foremost from discussions between administrative and clerical officers. Having said that, the design group had the final decision on how the computing department would handle a particular job.

The Multicom Corporation – a multinational in information technology

Our final case involved a manufacturing subsidiary of a US multi-national company. This produced 'small computers', had an extensive and highly sophisticated range of capital equipment, and employed in excess of 2,000 people.

Over the years Multicom has acquired a reputation as a good employer with above-average wage rates and generous pension schemes, describing itself as both benevolent and 'people oriented'. As with many US companies it fosters a strong corporate image among employees and articulates a philosophy of individual growth and fulfilment through the pursuit of work goals and objectives. This is exemplified by its strong sense of informal work-force involvement in the organization of plant operations, and also by its non-union format. Team activities are at a premium here and much effort is expanded on 'people building' schemes that encourage commitment and wide competence across task and functional boundaries. With regard to computing and production technologies, group working or user-involvement has been widely used as a means of improving the user-perceived quality of final systems. The basic framework for this has been laid down by corporate headquarters and followed for a great variety of applications with changes mainly at the margin to suit local situations.

This corporate umbrella for involvement depicts a process of top-down design through a structure of steering groups and committees. The main body is dubbed the Strategy Committee and consists of senior management grades from Finance and Information Systems together with the 'Prime Clients', the managers with overall respon-sibility for the functions affected by systems development. A project director is appointed from this group by the site manager and he, in turn, identifies the 'Owners' of the system. These are usually first line managers who take on full time development roles and control the details and progress of the project.

The Owners are responsible for providing the applications sanctioned by the Strategy Committee. They operate with a staff of around 10 to 15 full-time white-collar grades who interface directly with systems analysts and co-ordinate the input of their colleagues in operational and manufacturing departments. During our own research at Multicom we looked at this in a development section engaged in the production of inventory, shipping and materials-management applications as part of a continuous flow manufacturing ('Just-in-Time') system. In this case, the Owner of these applications delegated the bulk of the planning and design work to eleven full-time agents or developers who led and collaborated with small teams of systems analysts and likely users to sort out the fine details and formal specifications. Although these individuals fulfilled a development role they were aligned to user-departments rather than Information Systems. Most of them had a background in either procurement or production control. If user managers or shop-floor workers had any problems or doubts about systems development then they were the point of contact rather than computing professionals. In this capacity, as guardians of user requirements, the developers invited key users to define their needs to computing staff, organized 'walk-through' meetings and monthly reviews for line managers, acted as catalysts for development efforts and negotiated different technical possibilities with the designers on the project who had their own reporting lines to the head of Information Systems. In addition, they organized 'exit' or sign-off meetings for senior functional managers at various stages of development defined by the corporate standards. These specify certain grades of sign-off which dictate whether and to what extent the procedures associated with subsequent stages can proceed.

DISCUSSION: A SUMMARY OF RESEARCH RESULTS AND CONCLUSIONS

Having set out the context and mechanics of user-involvement we now look at the actual experience of design, and examine what each distinctive set of arrangements meant in terms of content and outcome. It is worth noting in advance that the reality of each situation was found, on the face of it, to be somewhat different to optimistic academic theories of mutually beneficial change. Things were not nearly so straightforward as some authors imply. Each scheme stirred up a lot of dust but when this finally settled authority relations were virtually intact.

The management of user-involvement

Virtually all of the managerial and computing grades interviewed in the case studies were unreservedly positive in their assessment of user-involvement. Some discussed setbacks and teething troubles, but it was clear that all of these respondents had confidence in the principle of involvement as they saw it. They felt that their own schemes had made an impact on decision-making and the quality of their development projects, and that experiments with participation invariably yielded dividends for all concerned.

However, despite this widespread and often undiluted praise, it became clear that management never conducted any proper evaluation of the actual mechanics of user-involvement or constructed any systematic way of assessing whether and to what extent the results of their projects were due to the particular forms of participation employed. Of course, there were yardsticks for developing the systems themselves, usually budgetary restrictions and certainly operational guidelines. Yet in judging the importance of user-involvement as a vehicle for reaching a satisfactory outcome and for meeting such terms of reference, managers relied on rough estimates or conjecture. Most referred vaguely to the merits of communication between departments or, when pressed, made a statement to the effect that their system was ahead of schedule or would have taken longer to produce had there been less of a dialogue with users. For instance, at Multicom one executive referred to the experience of some other organizations who had taken delivery of systems and installed them without user-collaboration only to face the costs of failure and debugging at a later date. Perceptual measures of this order tend to exhibit a 'halo effect', and certainly as far as this research is concerned it can be expected that management interpretations in at least three cases were influenced by the fact that the authority figures who sanctioned these investigations were also the architects and promoters of the respective schemes.

Despite the dearth of hard measurement, there was a strong sense in which the process of involvement in each of our study organizations was highly product-oriented. The overwhelming picture which emerged was that systems effectiveness was the ultimate, if not the only, priority and that other outcomes were strictly peripheral. Apart from the TTU, it would perhaps be surprising for these organizations if this were not the driving force, at least from a management viewpoint. None the less, this gives us a rather different slant on the idea of mutually beneficial change or 'joint optimization'. It appeared that any gains that were mooted for employees in terms of satisfaction or influence were attractive extras or 'spin-offs' that were welcome so long as value was added to the development process and the imperatives of business were honoured.

At Multicom and TCL the main preoccupation was clearly with efficiency and profitability, with frugal management of the time and resources devoted to applications development and the installation of systems that 'produced the goods' as far as management was concerned. Success in this sense served as the bottom line. It was perceived as the primary criterion and basis for determining whether involvement would continue or be surpassed in certain areas and applications by more conventional design methods. To Multicom management involvement was one small part of the corporate concept of information systems (IS) excellence. User-involvement intertwined neatly with their philosophy on 'quality circles' and other employee integration and commitment schemes (that is, management thinking on how the 'human resource' should be handled) and gave computing professionals a 'broader than normal view' of work procedures. As one department manager put it:

> The motivation [for user-involvement] is not one of democracy. This will probably be an output from it, but its motivation is business efficiency . . . As a consequence of involvement, yes! The enthusiasm we get from relatively low levels is encouraging because I think it's challenging, they are being creative.

At National Invigilation the emphasis was also on integration, on getting the right message across to users and tapping their knowledge on matters directly related to programming and protocol development activities. What did come across strongly, however, was that managers saw involvement as a natural extension of their broader problem-solving arrangements. Our interviewees frequently pointed to the small size of their organization and to the informality that was introduced into the design exercise as a result of this. They repeatedly drew attention to the importance of friendships and co-operative relationships within user-departments and between administrative and computing grades in the organization. The head of the Procedures (administration) department was confident that his assistant administrative officers and clerical staff could adjust to their new system, and sort out the details of the computing operation through informal discussions at the workplace and beyond: 'Clerical Officers talk amongst themselves all the time . . . It's a learning experience for them as well and this very often brings about suggestions and reactions which we take on board.' The computing manager also stressed the importance of personal relationships: 'They know at the end of the day I'll give them what they want.'

By way of a contrast with our three other cases, TTU management sought to justify their involvement exercise on the basis of maximum job satisfaction and discretion for users in addition to the 'hard benefits' for their computing resource. The Deputy General Secretary endorsed the accepted view in our research that staff expertise was mobilized to ensure that systems were effective and productive. However, he also expressed a rather detailed commitment to user interests and a sensitivity to moral arguments for involvement:

> Irrespective of whether they [the clerical grades] were interested or not [in computers] they still have a right to know what is going on.

This, again, was a reflection of the broader context of relations between management and work-force in the organization. After all, a trade union could hardly be seen to ignore the views and concerns of its own staff or even afford to treat them differently from its clients for fear of action by APEX (the clerical union) on grounds of hypocrisy.

In addition to personality factors and contextualizing patterns of industrial relations, involvement in our case studies was heavily influenced by the structural, market and work organization problems that management sought to control. When looking at the organizations, it was clear that the problems of the British economy, and in Multicom's case the problems of the global economy, had left their mark. Change and turbulence had caused management to reappraise their priorities, to instigate or review plans for computerization and to formulate, extend or continue to refine arrangements for user-involvement. Of course, the pressures and constraints differed in each case but the respective schemes were suitably adjusted to cope with fluid situations and changing environments.

For the TTU the pace of technological development was restricted by a tight financial situation, though this in itself heightened the requirement for the improvements in labour productivity which the technology was supposed to bring. If financial resources were to be increased, staff would have to deal with an expansion of membership communication and service systems that might help to recruit new members or encourage existing card-holders to pay higher dues. Those involved in the Working Party eventually recognized this problem and developed an incremental strategy for change which had knock-on effects for the quality of industrial relations in the organization and for the progressive development of union products and resources. In this way employees who had experienced an intensification of work, and had pressed for systems to relieve the pressures they were facing, came to accept changes in task routines and adopt a regulatory role as far as developments in work organization were concerned. The involvement exercise at National Invigilation had a somewhat similar effect in that staff internalized demands for an improvement in labour productivity that resulted from a change in the rules governing examinations. In this case involvement was credited not only with producing an adjustment to new systems and procedures, but also with an acceptance of the workload created by the transformation.

With Multicom and TCL a different set of pressures had similar results. In each case the introduction of involvement had been located within a structural adaptation to new business environments. It was set against a need for rationalization and for a different kind of labour utilization based on greater flexibility and expertise. TCL managers were quite open in stating that their scheme was an integral part of a considered strategy for dealing with reorganization and cost-cutting problems in the wake of their acquisition by the parent organization. The company had recently announced a major redundancy package with branch closures and a revision of work systems at their functional centres. This had made staff rather suspicious of management plans for computerization and added to their general concern about the impact of technology on jobs and career prospects. User-involvement was perceived by management as a means of allaying these fears, but also as a mechanism to secure the compliance and co-operation of the work-force in the transition to new work systems and procedures.

For Multicom the key problem was its sectoral position in a highly competitive and changing industry. Caught between pinched profits, the budgetary constraints on customers and intense price competition (especially in market segments penetrated by Far Eastern producers), corporate management had introduced product development and cost-cutting exercises across their global operations. For the manufacturing plant we examined this meant controls on production expenditure and staffing, despite ongoing plant expansion and systems development programmes aimed at reducing stock levels and costs and improving performance. For some employees these initiatives were of concern, not for their possible impact on employment levels – most had faith in the company's commitment to its work-force – but because they could see their work-load increasing over time. Although as producers of technology they had a generalized perception of the implications of capital restructuring for labour productivity, this in itself was not sufficient to alleviate their fears on this score. However, the interview material from this study gave a strong sense that the experience of involvement had actually brought home to users the message that particular development projects augured well for their own work situation. It had reinforced their broad inclinations by giving them a practical demonstration. In various discussions, white-collar respondents who had worked on development projects marvelled at the sophistication of the technology and virtually became evangelists for the new systems.

Hierarchy and authority

Our conclusion that user-involvement was managed towards precise goals in the case study organizations would seem to suggest that leadership roles were important for the status of the discussions and for the extent to which they escaped from considerations of hierarchy and authority. In this section we present a body of evidence which lends weight to this contention, which indicates that involvement was *not* free from hierarchy but was set within traditional patterns of authority relations and infused with a management orientation which rendered it far more limited than some authors contend.

Since our research was located in the most favoured rather than the most typical cases it was inevitable that at least some elements of employee participation would be found. However, with the exception of the TTU, only a small proportion of each work-force had actually experienced any sustained involvement in design activities. Percentage figures were difficult to compile as our managerial respondents were usually vague when it came to the precise numbers of staff per phase of development. What did emerge quite clearly from the interviews at Multicom, TCL and National Invigilation was that the extent of involvement varied markedly across the process, and that only very small groups of core users had experienced prolonged periods of working on each project. The vast majority of participants in these cases had provided their input at specific stages – notably problem recognition, systems analysis, implementation and operational adjustment. In this way the statement that each organization had made to us indicating that shop-floor workers had been involved in at least six specified stages concealed peaks and troughs for particular groups that coincided with the pattern established by our earlier postal survey (see Figure 3.1 (a)). It seems that while our case study organizations had a greater spread of involvement,

(a) Phased and controlled involvement

Percentage figures for staff grades involved per stage of development in a total of 92 schemes.

Stage of development (see Table 3.1)

	1	2	3	4	5	6	7	8	9
Senior management	55.4	65.3	60.3	9.1	32.2	2.5	17.4	9.9	46.3
Middle/lower management	56.2	34.7	33.1	43.8	18.2	15.7	58.7	56.2	51.2
Computer professionals	54.5	48.8	54.5	69.4	66.1	69.4	67.8	64.5	55.4
White-collar staff	27.3	3.3	5.8	28.1	3.3	11.6	47.9	45.5	22.3
Manual employees	6.6	–	0.8	2.5	–	–	9.1	6.6	1.7

(b) Tiered involvement with multiple groups

Stage of development (see Table 3.1)

	1	2	3	4	5	6	7	8	9
Senior management		SPT							SPT
Middle/lower management		Steering/Mgt UIC					Steering/Mgt UIC		
Computer professional				Information Systems/DP Team					
White-collar staff	UICs			UICs			UICs		
Manual employees	UICs						UICs		

Figure 3.1 The pattern of participative design
Key: SPT = Strategic Planning Team; Steering = Steering Committee; Mgt UIC = Management User-involvement Committee; UIC = White-collar/Manual-worker User-involvement Committee.

their experiments actually concentrated on certain stages in a fashion similar to that of ostensibly less-extensive schemes.

In addition to these fluctuations across the systems 'life cycle', there was strong evidence of a multi-team approach to user-involvement with extensive tiering along conventional lines of authority. The projects at Multicom and TCL were of particular interest in that each was characterized by a large network of groups based on coalitions of users from similar grades in the organizational hierarchy. The time that each group devoted to systems development, the steps at which their involvement occurred, and the influence they exerted varied with their members' decision-making capacity within the enterprise. In this sense, involvement entailed a division of labour of the form illustrated in Figure 3.1 (b).

This model shows that the position of each group was determined by different definitions of competence and authority. Senior executives initially formed Strategic Planning Teams (SPTs) with high levels of discretion but short spans of participation, dealing mainly with the priorities and direction of each development. At TCL this group was composed solely of divisional directors, while at Multicom functional managers sat on the most senior and influential committee along with the project manager. Beneath this level of strategic decision-making there existed a multiplicity of management teams ranging from quite senior standing committees responsible for steering, planning and budgeting decisions to junior advisory councils and work groups that were convened for a specific purpose at a particular stage of development. Computing professionals were involved in all of these, but again the hierarchy within the computing (DP or Information Systems) department had a bearing on the level of interaction with users. At TCL high-ranking computing staff sat on the equivalent of a steering committee that established the terms of involvement for the entire work-force, including middle level managers. In the Multicom project the head of Information Systems was a member of the strategic planning group, while the senior grades in the systems development departments were responsible for organizing user contributions. In addition to programmer teams and groupings within the computing departments, systems analysts and designers worked mainly with lower managerial and shop-floor users on *ad hoc* user-involvement committees (UICs) which were assembled during the four key stages mentioned above. Only a minority of the individuals in these were considered core users. The bulk of lower managerial and shop-floor participants had only a fleeting association with systems development.

Significantly, the influence of these user-involvement committees was not greatly affected by their composition. The decision-making capacity of core users was much the same as that of participants of a similar grade who had been involved at only one or two stages. This was true for both management employees and for shop-floor staff. The main constraining factor in each case was the dispersion of authority within the organization. Those at the top of the hierarchy had to be convinced that involvement was worthwhile, and that practical measures were constructive and meaningful in both an operational and financial sense. In the case of TCL the architects of the project had to actively sell it to divisional directors in the first instance. The progress that was eventually made at this stage was contingent upon an action plan which specified the amount and kind of involvement required and the control measures that would be installed to ensure that the process was productive. Our respondents in the DP department were quite clear that the act of appointing an external consultant with experience of running involvement schemes was instrumental in gaining approval. The decision to select the majority of participants from supervisory and management, rather than clerical levels, was also considered important.

As a consequence of the highly structured and controlled approach to involvement at Multicom and TCL, team member roles were tightly defined. In addition to group segmentation by stage and task in the systems 'life cycle', individuals within particular groups were often assigned work in different areas of the total project. For instance, at TCL group meetings tended to be convened when the users who had been paired-off with systems analysts were ready to present a 'solution' to their allotted portion of the systems specifications. At Multicom the systems development departments co-ordinated the activities of a multiplicity of small UICs where single individuals, or perhaps two individuals working together, would be assisted by a developer to translate their experience of a particular and predefined section of the work process to a systems analyst. In both cases the performance of individuals and groups was monitored to ensure that pre-specified objectives were realized. This was achieved by regular assessment of the standards of communication and discipline within groups, and by the isolation of 'good' users: those who were single-minded in the pursuit of systems goals and who were core user material.

The control of UICs was also realized via the review procedures that were installed for checking and assessing their output prior to its incorporation in formal design documents and specifications. At Multicom and TCL, phase sign-off procedures were strictly the preserve of management and steering committees. Lower management and shop-floor groups often had to prepare formal submissions, conduct walk-throughs, and gain approval for their conclusions from those on the next level of the involvement heirarchy. User veto in this sense meant management control of their subordinates' activities. As one Multicom executive put it: 'User management calls the tune. It's me that defines the need subject to resource constraints.'

Managers in the Procedures department at National Invigilation engaged in a similar, though much less formal process of regulating the input of ground level users. Although the smaller size of this organization made high levels of informal work-force involvement more feasible, as a general rule assistant administrative officers and clerical grades were not eligible to direct their proposals or comments at computing professionals unless they had been finalized through normal channels of communication to their superiors, who in this case were the core users in the design exercise. As with Multicom and TCL, user managers conceived of user-involvement within the limits of established hierarchical relationships.

Our overall impression from the case study material is that user-involvement had more to do with conformity than actual or potential autonomy. The projects at Multicom, TCL and National Invigilation depended on sets of organization rules that determined the boundaries for innovation, both in terms of hard technology and also in terms of the permissible social relations for its production. This was most obvious at Multicom where the framework for involvement was established at corporate level and used throughout the organization. The image created here was of an open and forward-looking company that was determined to consult its work-force on the most crucial questions of work organization. However, in practice the scope for autonomy at lower levels was restricted by the requirements for strong leadership, narrow terms of reference, and the selection of teams by executive sponsors. User-influence was also marginalized by the nature and amount of information made available to UICs and to the wider user community. The main source of data in this case was the systems developer who would provide information relevant to a particular task, or perhaps disclose some wider details in the course of group discussions. Since some developers were not entirely clear themselves about the overall direction of projects and about related business issues, shop-floor workers had few insights into the choices that lay before management.

A further sign of the lack of authority vested in our case study UICs is that the personal as opposed to the efficiency related benefits mentioned for users were usually trivial. Barring their contributions to the productivity of technology, our respondents could only point to minor changes in systems and work procedures as evidence of users exerting their influence for their own personal or sectional ends. DP managers at TCL pointed to a selection of different menus displayed on various terminals, while other respondents, including some at the TTU, gave the attachment of acoustic hoods to printers as an example.

Clearly, on this evidence, user-involvement does not dramatically alter the decision-making capacity of shop-floor workers. If anything our research shows that formalized involvement can potentially contain and condition the activities of those who already exert influence and discretion in respect of their work. The vast majority of our managerial respondents were concerned not with the creation of representative groups, but rather with tapping the knowledge and expertise that individuals had acquired by virtue of their strategic position in the work process. As one Multicom executive stated: 'We don't go round everyone and ask them what they want. . . . These are people experienced in operational procedures . . . experts in the inadequacies of the current system.'

It was an added bonus if potential participants had influence on the shop-floor, if their opinions carried weight with other users, or if they were especially receptive to management blandishments or the 'company line'. However, the interview material from each of our studies strongly suggests that participants' skill levels were sufficient to command much higher returns in terms of influence and outcomes, and that these could have been realized had their attention been directed beyond user-involvement, perhaps by trade unionists to collective bargaining or in-house forums established by negotiated agreements. Of course, this line of argument probably reflects some *post hoc* rationalization, and certainly exaggerates any potential that actually existed. Trade unions had no part in the schemes at TCL or National Invigilation, and on-site representatives knew very little if anything about them, some showing scant regard for their existence. Moreover, the structuring of involvement created its own problems of co-ordination and timing, and this gave some users an opportunity to exploit the process for sectional gain. For instance, at National Invigilation a number of participants were using involvement arrangements to 'fight for their corner' to moderate the pace of on-line developments:

> Involvement has given us the ability to cope, to stave off develop-ment plans. . . . It's not that we are consciously trying to slow down the introduction of new methods, but we have to be convinced that they will help the work without risk to our priorities.

Having said all this, the TTU case does indicate that trade unionists can give direction to an involvement exercise, and that developments at this level are complementary to established industrial relations activities.

The TTU project has rarely figured in this section largely because it proved the exception. Management here seemed to trust the abilities of supervisors and ordinary staff. They were involved throughout the systems development process and contributed to a working party – a single team that had numerous representatives from each grade in the organization hierarchy. Many of these were elected by their colleagues in the user departments. Shop stewards were involved as a matter of course and, since employees were all members of APEX, 'shop' meetings were often used to sort out the details of collective action within the working party. The authority of shop-floor staff in the design process included calling meetings, conducting negotiations with consultants over the details of programmes, assessing work-loads, allocating tasks, and deciding on procedures for operating equipment. As far as˙ drawbacks are concerned, there was a feeling among clerical respondents that they lacked basic technical knowledge about the process of computerization and that although they had power to interrogate computing experts and choose from alternative systems, a training programme would have enabled them to accept less on faith alone.

Employee reactions

Evaluations of the impact of user-involvement differed between managers and shop-floor employees. The former enthused about their respective schemes and tended to project an image of generalized gain, including higher levels of job satisfaction and discretion for those at the lower end of the hierarchy. The latter themselves were more reserved, although the majority seemed to agree with the official response that participative design is more desirable and effective for organizations than traditional, technocentric forms of systems development. There was strong support among white-collar, clerical and manual grades for the idea of a more consultative approach to the introduction of new technology, and approval for the way in which some authority figures had used their schemes to encourage contributions and promote an atmosphere of informal co-operation. There was also a feeling that executives had gone to some trouble to create the process, that a lot of money had been spent, and that the promoters of some schemes had been courageous in taking a leap in the dark. The view here was that 'other' organizations imposed technology on their work-force and that management had gone to some lengths to promote goodwill.

Significantly, the most positive appraisal came from the TTU where staff regarded the project not as a novel or innovative means of introducing technology, but as just another aspect of good industrial relations. By contrast with the reactions of executives in the other case studies, the Deputy General Secretary was rather surprised by our interest in their arrangements. None the less, shop-floor staff were extremely enthusiastic: 'It was a real solid project. Nobody's point of view was ever dismissed. . . . People were listened to. The fact they were on the secretarial staff didn't make any difference whatsoever.'

We met quite a different reaction in the other three cases, where involvement was not demanded or even expected but rather was put forward by management. While the users at Multicom, TCL and National Invigilation were happy in some respects, they were quick to point out the limitations and shortcomings of their respective schemes. Continually in interviews they cautioned about over-estimating the extent of their independent influence, and warned against confusing the accommodation of employee views with their ability to meet management aims. A small number even expressed some disbelief that management had made claims or had hinted that they were able to make decisions 'off their own back', or had autonomy to choose freely between available options.

There was considerable agreement among users in these cases that they merely had the power to offer suggestions. In discussing the reasons for this we were told more than once that users had the opportunity but not the experience to make changes. They could speak openly but they lacked the training, the confidence, and the basic information to change systems. This attitude undoubtedly reflected a certain reverence for the technical skills of computing professionals. However, it also encapsulated the notion that users could be trusted with more influence and information, and could adopt more constructive roles if either of these were forthcoming.

Some of our respondents were convinced that project managers or systems professionals filtered out their influence and devalued their recommendations by imposing quite arbitrary standards of worth or value to the organization. Beyond the concrete realities of technical feasibility there seemed to be a sense in which management acted to protect existing patterns of work and authority relations, allowing change only at the margins and under tight controls. The attitude in two cases tended to be paternalistic, that of a wise and strict father who knew what was best and expected passive trust in his judgement. A sample of quotes will illustrate:

> They listen possibly, but action depends on their view.

> If we come up with a request which is sensible and reasonable and certainly one which has obvious benefits to the organisation, to the way in which we do things, then we would get it.

The most emphatic comment by respondents was that their understanding and appreciation of automated systems had significantly increased. We had numerous replies to the effect that involvement was a means to comprehend, rather than question, management strategies and objectives. Many of these were half-hearted attempts to impress management, and were clearly for our own consumption as researchers introduced to the work situation by authority figures who had promoted, or were involved in design activities. However, a large number of interviewees were honest and forthright in their opinions and the picture they painted of participative design was not as a forum for users to express their concerns or realize their own desires, but as a vehicle for encouraging them to come to grips with new technology and with procedures for operating it efficiently. At National Invigilation an Assistant Administrative Officer told us:

> Involvement helps us to understand the full complexity and even the unreasonableness of some of the things that we have been asking for.

In this case the respondent felt that she had more of a say-so than previously, but this manifested itself in greater worry about her personal responsibility for meeting management objectives and for effective systems development. She never conceived of participative design as a channel for employee interests, or as anything other than a management-directed process geared to producing an economically efficient system.

It should be noted that this particular response was exceptional, at some remove from the majority of replies in this category. Most came from users at TCL and Multicom who were relatively satisfied with their situation and open in their identification with company aims. Having said that, there was a sense in which the tractability of some of the employees in these organizations came neither from an acceptance of management ideology nor satisfaction with user-involvement. Commitment here was based on the much broader calculation of what management offered in terms of pay and benefits, job security and promotion. The most blatant example of this occurred at TCL. After a long and glowing discourse on the process, one user pointed out that he had been promoted shortly after being seconded, and proudly declared that he was now ahead of his colleagues who were in the game for the same reason.

Finally, at National Invigilation, where the system was in place some time before our research, users indicated that costs had been incurred by way of routinization and deskilling. Clerical officers had apparently lost an element of discretion from their work which had been counterbalanced for full-time staff by the addition of a supervisory role over temporary employees who were faced mainly with repetitive tasks around the new system. We had no contact with these temporary grades, and so there was no chance to gauge their impressions of participative design. It is impossible, in any case, to judge whether this particular outcome would have occurred had involvement been greater than it actually was. None the less, the notion that a period of participative design may be followed by a longer period of routinized work does beg further questions as to whether user-involvement measures up to the mutual benefits thesis.

CONCLUSIONS

To state that user-involvement redefines, or even raises, new possibilities in social relations does not solve the fundamental question of the precise relations currently being established in many organizations. The profile of involvement schemes and the factors that prove decisive in shaping outcomes have rarely been explored. In fact, attention has been narrowly focused on a small number of so-called success stories, and this has been due largely to the enthusiasm of promoters of participative design, most notably Enid Mumford. Despite this emphasis, and by way of a contrast with the glowing reports that have been produced and reproduced from these studies, our own research indicates that even the 'best' schemes fall short of the ideal of mutually beneficial change.

The findings from our studies paint a far more complex picture of the practice of user-involvement than is usually presented in the literature, and cast serious doubt on the easy assumption that it constitutes a potent force in transforming authority relations. Clearly, when set against the standards and seductive arguments advanced by Mumford and other advocates of participation, our case study schemes were not unambiguously successful. They were highly contingent on the setting, on the intentions and philosophy of management, and also on the reactions of users themselves.

Although some participants were given more of a say in their work situation, the changes that occurred can hardly be described in terms of democratization. Indeed, the majority of promoters and managers of participative design that were interviewed could rarely be expected to conceive of the process in these terms. Having said that, there were signs, especially from the TTU, that involvement need not be a trivial matter. None the less, the main impression from this research is that the claims made for industrial democracy and increased autonomy from user-involvement cannot be justified from the available evidence.

NOTE

Thanks are due in large measure to our contacts in business organizations and trade unions in Central Scotland and London. This project would have foundered at an early stage had these people not given so freely of their time and effort.

REFERENCES

Beirne, M. and Ramsay, H. (1988) 'Computer redesign and "labour process" theory: towards a critical appraisal', in D. Knights and H. Willmott (eds), *New Technology and the Labour Process*, London, Macmillan.

Ives, B. and Olson, M. (1984) 'User involvement and MIS success: a review of research', *Management Science* 30 (5).

Kraft, P. (1979) 'Challenging the Mumford democrats at Derby works', *Computing* 2, August.

Land, F. and Hirschheim, R. (1983) 'Participative systems design: rationale, tools and techniqiues', *Journal of Applied Systems Analysis*, Vol. 10.

Mumford, E. (1979) 'Consensus systems design; an evaluation of this approach', in N. Szyperski and E. Grochla (eds), *The Design and Implementation of Computer Based Information Systems*, New York, Sijthoff & Noordoff.

—— (1980) 'The participative design of clerical information systems: two case studies', in N. Bjorn-Anderson, B. Hedberg, D. Mercer, E. Mumford and A. Sole (eds), *The Impact of Systems Change in Organisations*, New York, Sijthoff & Noordoff.

—— (1981) 'Participative systems design: structure and method', *Systems, Objectives and Solutions*, Vol. 1, Part 1.

—— (1983) 'Successful systems design', in H. Otway and M. Peltu (eds), *New Office Technology: Human and Organisational Aspects*, London, Frances Pinter.

—— and Henshall, D. (1979) *A Participative Approach to Computer Systems Design*, London, Associated Business Press.

4 The intelligent office and the locus of control

Peter Bain and Chris Baldry

INTRODUCTION: THE NATURE OF THE WORKPLACE

Although the term 'workplace' is widely used in industrial sociology and related behavioural sciences, it is actually used in two distinct ways. There is the abstract use of the word to denote the concept of any place where work is done, analogous to other concepts such as 'the home', and second a more specific usage referring to the actual physical surroundings, the built work environment. In this latter sense we have come to associate it with certain types or classifications of building or structure – the factory, the office, the mine, the shop. This is where labour power is sold, bought and put to work.

While in recent years great attention has been given to the development of the electronic office and the effects of computerization on the labour process, health and safety and the organization of work, the characteristics of its location, as a *variable* in work organization and behaviour, have been under-examined. Similarly, whilst it has been rightly argued that the technology employed – both hardware and software – cannot be regarded as 'neutral' because it has been consciously designed to carry out specific functions in the real world and incorporates a definite view of the role of the user, similar strictures have not been applied to the design of the buildings which house these activities.

Yet clearly the two parties to the employment relationship are likely to view and experience the workplace in fundamentally different ways. In the economics of capitalism, the workplace has a dual role in the process of capital accumulation. First as fixed capital, where buildings are used to facilitate the process of production. Here, as with production technology, its costs of construction and maintenance are spread over the historical production period as an overhead and, like the machines it houses, the building as productive capital depreciates in value.

Second, buildings are property – investments in their own right. Due to the upward appreciation of their site values (for, as Mark Twain remarked about land, 'they've stopped making it'), the factory, and more particularly the office block, as *property*, appreciates in value. Thus, at those times when the circulation of rents and other forms of finance capital is faster than that of surplus value accruing from production, it can be of more worth to a corporation to leave the building empty and simply see it as a financial store of wealth.

While bearing this point in mind, if we start to examine what workplaces are used for in the sphere of production, an initial response would probably refer to the necessity to house the productive technology and the accompanying need to integrate the work associated with its use. Walker has reminded us however that: 'Although the association of tasks and workgroups in close proximity is often physically necessary for carrying out the collective project, one cannot assume that work tasks carried out side by side have strong technical connections' (Walker 1985: 174).

Marglin (1976) pointed out that at the commencement of industrialism the early factories used the same technology as was then in use in the home – hand looms and spinning machines. It was not technological necessity that caused the early capitalists to bring workers together in one location, under one roof, but the necessity of increasing surplus value. The separation of 'home' and 'work' into two distinct concepts symptomized the beginning of industrial discipline. The factory as workplace gave the employer *control* over the amount of effort of the workers; he could specify the length of time that was to be worked for a given wage in ways that were not possible under the putting-out system. This concentration of labour power in the new workplaces then facilitated the development of the detailed division of labour and accompanying technological developments.

A similar process can be seen in the development of the office as a distinct work location. Early office functions were dispersed throughout the city and carried out from the houses of merchants or from coffee houses; for example, the early banks and even trading companies such as the East India Company operated from private houses until the 1720s and 1730s (Cowan *et al.* 1969). Given the under-capitalization of the office until the second half of this century, it is clear that the creation of the office as a work location was even less driven by technological necessity. Indeed, as Braverman (1974) was the first to point out, the elaboration of the processes of control of the manual labour process created an equivalent office function to process the paper information which measures, evaluates and remunerates productive labour.

Clearly control over the labour process lies at the heart of the creation of the 'workplace' as a distinct location to which we travel to spend our 'sold' time, and from which we travel to spend our 'free' time. This is likely to be an essential component of any employee view of the workplace, but there will also be other factors involved, through the way that the workplace operates to enable or constrict social relations. Urry has reminded us that spatio-temporal location is one of the ways that individuals come to gain and reinforce various identities for themselves in society and quotes Webber:

> the physical place becomes an extension of one's ego. . . . One's conception of himself [*sic*] and of his place in society is thus subtly merged with his conception of the spatially limited territory of limited social interaction.
>
> (Urry 1985: 31)

Or, put another way, *where* we are and who we interact with at particular times form part of *who* we are. Workplace conversational usage such as 'the lads on the shop-floor', 'the girls in the typing pool', 'them in the office', define identities by both location and social group. Turner (1971: 74) explored ways in which job roles, no matter how low down in the organizational hierarchy, convey a certain sense of 'life-space' or self-definition which includes immediate territory in the workplace, and for the newcomer

> it is an early priority for him [*sic*] to learn the cues which signal territorial boundaries, and the specific local conventions which divide the topography of the factory or the office into socially meaningful areas.
>
> (Turner 1971: 50)

There are two important aspects of this sense of territory. The first is the way in which control over territory is directly related to the hierarchical organization; in Turner's words 'Hierarchical organizations contain a hierarchy of territories' (Turner 1971: 70). The supervisor feels she has the right of intervention in the territories of each of her word processor operators, the office manager feels he can intervene in the territory of each of his supervisors (even though, as Turner found, senior figures in the hierarchy may make a show of deferring to a subordinate and ask for permission to make a tour). The hierarchical allocation of territory extends to the artefacts

within the building and how they are allocated. In classic bureau-
cracies, such as the civil service, hierarchical position may be finely
designated by size of room, size of desk, and whether or not a
hatstand is standard issue, and even in apparently less hierarchical
structures woe betide the probationary teacher who unwittingly sits
in the wrong chair in the staffroom!

This last example of the way in which certain key artefacts – a
person's chair or desk for example – are treated as if they were
that worker's individual property seems to reflect the second
characteristic – namely, the importance of having some sort of
personal control over one's immediate territory, such as the arrangement of office furniture or even just the top of the desk. This can
serve to maximize what Baldamus called 'traction' (Baldamus 1961);
by suiting the environment to individual characteristics (the height of
a chair, the level of heat or lighting) it is possible to create the basis
for smooth work rhythms which 'pull' the worker along and thus
provide relative satisfactions in a work situation (such as repetitive
data entry) which may be fundamentally unpleasant. Or, localized
control may simply be desired in order to create a sense of 'self-
definition'. The humorous posters and postcards from abroad that
surround many a secretary's desk are a good example of this: they
mark out that space as 'hers' and tell us (and are meant to tell us)
something about her as a person. (The same principle applies to the
varied artefacts that adorn the walls of university lecturers' offices.)

In this attempt to identify how buildings interact with the social
organization of work, we can therefore suggest that first of all work
buildings encapsulate the necessity for control that lies within the
employment relationship. Buildings define the boundaries of major
areas of social territory and thus, within the building, the allocation
of territory will itself reflect the hierarchical structures of authority
which govern the labour process. However, within this top-down
control structure there seems to co-exist a strong need on the part of
individuals in the organization to assert some degree of localized
control over their immediate working environment.

We can envisage a situation where the demand for such localized
control over the working environment may run counter to the
dictates of the control structures of the labour process. In such
circumstances, localized control may be limited or minimized either
organizationally (a prohibition on fixing posters, or using fanheaters),
or structurally through the design of the built environment – it may
not be possible to alter the level of air ventilation, or the offices may
be configured so that there is no external wall with openable

windows. The building thus comes both to reflect and constrain the boundaries of control.

MANAGEMENT VIEWS OF WORK BUILDINGS

Managers too will gain their own identity from this combination of group and location, only for them the group is likely to be corporate and the location seen as expressing aspects of the corporate identity. A study of how twenty-two leading UK companies managed their offices (Wilson 1985) found five different perceptions of the role of the companies' buildings:

1 a container – of minimal significance to performance, with expenditure kept to a minimum;
2 a prestige symbol – the key factor being exterior appearance rather than interior working conditions;
3 a vehicle for industrial relations – a healthy work environment plus employee facilities (for example, recreational) to show care and concern for the work-force;
4 an instrument of efficiency – with high expenditure on the work environment based on 'value for money' rather than staff welfare;
5 an inspirational force – an appreciation of a building's functional and symbolic role, followed through in management and design.

The major difference between management and employee views of the work building is that management are likely to feel in control of both layout and utilization. As with the take-up of technology, we can distinguish between the reasons for initial choice of a building and factors that govern how it is used following occupancy. The first are what McLoughlin and Clark (1988), in the context of technological change, have called strategic reasons. In the case of a building these are likely to include geographical location in relation to markets and transport, the amount of floor space, the cost of rental, adequacy of power supply, etc. Once chosen, there will then be operational factors that govern how long-term strategic goals are met, and these are likely to depend on the priorities of the particular labour process and the type and amount of control over production deemed desirable and necessary by management.

Until very recently, the physical and structural characteristics of buildings – their size for example, or appearance (their prestige value for the company) – were seen to affect strategic choices only. In operational terms the building was a given, the operational *variables* were the ways in which work and technology could be organized within its shell. This view was apparently supported by several of the classic foundation stones of management education. While the early industrial psychologists spent a great deal of time examining optimum levels of light and heating, the popularization of Human Relations in the 1930s led to a rejection of phsyical environmental factors in employee performance in favour of a focus on the structure of internal social relations (Rose 1988). The much reported Hawthorne Effect was, after all, based on the observation that changes in the physical environment did not noticeably affect work groups' productivity compared to the more powerful social pressures of being constantly monitored. Then from the 1940s, with the spread of flow-line technology into the new light industries, emphasis was put on the interaction between group and technology, all within a neutral built environment.

This neglect of the built environment in subsequent debate in most social science and management literature is perhaps why architects, when they think of actual, rather than corporate, users, tend to use individualist psychological views of the employee. This focuses attention on the ways in which environmental factors might affect the employee's motivation, drawing on post-war contributors such as Herzberg, who saw the working environment as one possible 'hygiene' factor which could cause dissatisfaction but would not positively motivate employee performance.

Now however, just as there is much more awareness of choice in the design of technology, companies are being presented with buildings that offer them increased variable control over aspects such as heating, lighting, ventilation and security. If an uncritical approach to work buildings ever had any validity, the advent of these 'intelligent buildings' has killed it off.

THE INTELLIGENT OFFICE

An intelligent building (henceforth IB) has a high level of internal office automation (PCs, text-processors, local area networks, etc.), and also operates as part of an external telecommunications network (via fax, telex, wide area networks, external databases, etc.). These two features in themselves do not make the building 'intelligent' however; for this label to have any meaning we would expect the building to display some capacity for autonomous control over its own functioning. Thus, IBs have, as their defining feature, auto-mated building control systems in which a central computer controls the provision of services such as heating, lighting, ventilation, water, security, and fire. Such buildings, it is claimed, offer the prospect of virtually unlimited IT expansion into the foreseeable future, substantial savings on operating, maintenance and labour costs, and the provision of a safe, healthy and comfortable working environment.

Sometimes the architects' vision of the potential of the IB would almost do credit to Isaac Asimov or Ray Bradbury. Thus a member of the Richard Rodgers Partnership waxes eloquently (if anthropomorphically) on the IB of the future:

> Look up at a spectrum-washed envelope whose surface is a map of its instantaneous performance, stealing energy from the air with an iridescent shrug, rippling its photogrids as a cloud runs across the sun; a wall which, as the night chill falls, fluffs up its feathers and turning white on its north face and blue on the south, closes its eyes but not without remembering to pump a little glow down to the nightporter, clear a view-patch for the lovers on the south side of level 22 and to turn 12 per cent silver just before dawn.

(Davies 1988)

Such fancies apart, intelligent buildings, which combine both strategic advantages and an enhanced ability to control operational costs, will seem extremely attractive to corporate management but will they prove so attractive to those working within their smoked glass confines? To structure lighting and heating to the times and density of human occupancy may seem economically admirable but raises a fundamental question about the consequences for office workers of removing their ability to control their local working environment.

Offices and IT

The creation of the intelligent office must be seen as a fusion of two parallel but interconnected developments. The late 1980s saw both an expansion and growth in the construction and development of office premises, and an increase in the take-up of information technology and its integration into electronic communication networks.

The constant pressure on organizations from imposed financial constraints or competitors, makes the installation of complete IT systems in new or refitted offices an increasingly attractive proposition. The fact that the business applications of the technology also offer unprecedented opportunities to measure, monitor and control the output of the seemingly ever-growing ranks (and proportional 'weight') of their white-collar employees, represents another inducement to employers, even if this potential for control is at present underutilized.

The application of IT, however, can run up against the problem of the structure of existing buildings, with cabling requirements in particular rendering many offices technologically redundant (including some built in the 1970s). Harnett (1988) estimated that within three or four years at least 50 per cent of firms would be faced with a total redesign, and this would continue to fuel the search for new or more appropriate premises.

It is in this context of the need for new offices capable of accommodating state-of-the-art IT systems that the attractions of the intelligent building become apparent and, at the same time, appear to offer even more opportunities for occupiers to make substantial cost savings. It is perhaps no coincidence that despite the broad term 'intelligent building' being in use by architects and building design specialists, virtually all existing IBs are in reality office complexes. Hence, our specific concern is with the intelligent office.

The corporate occupants of the new offices are typically large organizations – often from banking and finance, the public sector, or transnational corporations. For example, tenants of what are claimed to be the two most 'intelligent' office buildings in Glasgow include three government departments, two financial institutions, three transnationals, and one media company. Recently constructed custom-built IBs in the city include the headquarters of Coats Viyella and Britoil.

Under the pressure of technological change – generated by competitive or financial constraints – it has become more and more difficult for employers to regard their office as a mere container. The rapidly expanding range of IT applications has necessitated greater cohesion between the more image/prestige-oriented views of top management responsible for strategic, medium/long-term decision-making, and the efficiency/welfarist concerns of lower-level management centred upon running things on a day-to-day basis.

⟨ One reflection of this recognition of the need for a more integrated approach has been the advent of 'facilities management' responsible for co-ordinating all efforts related to planning, designing and managing buildings and their systems, equipment and furniture. This remit could include responsibility for general maintenance, heating and air treatment, lighting, security, fire precautions, and internal fixtures and fittings. The emergence of this discipline seems to reflect a shift in management thinking about the workplace building, away from a shell for work operations towards something much more interactive:

> [facilities management] . . . has a wider and more responsible role of transforming an organisation's building, or its stock of buildings, from an overhead into a company resource . . . [for] where once office work was for the most part stable and unchanging, the equipment base low, and the amount of capital invested in each office worker minuscule [compared to blue-collar counterparts], there is change on all fronts.
>
> (Wilson 1987)

What these developments mean in terms of building utilization can best be illustrated by looking at four examples of IBs – two in this country (one custom-built and one speculative-built), one in Japan, and one in the USA. The information has been obtained from a variety of architectural and building design journals and thus, if anything, errs in its generally uncritical acclaim for such technical developments.

Rank-Xerox, Marlow

Following their decision to invest heavily in computerization, Rank-Xerox closed a number of their buildings in the London area and, in 1987, concentrated operations in a new international headquarters designed to meet their technological requirements for up to thirty years ahead. The building accommodates about 1,000 people on four floors designed around a number of courtyards, with office automation and communications systems involving 3,700 miles of internal cabling (Greig 1988). Offices can be both open plan and enclosed, the configuration being changed by mobile partitions, whilst movable metal floor tiles give access to underfloor service sockets, thus facilitating equipment relocation. Acoustic separation between offices is provided by loudspeakers generating white noise so as to distort hearing of distant speech (Greig 1988).

The CCMS (Central Control and Monitoring System) covers energy management, access and fire, and monitors the temperature in the building's fourteen zones, outside temperature, relative humidity, air velocity and pressure. Only if the outside temperature falls below 13°C does the heating system come into operation, otherwise the heat generated by lights, equipment and people is sufficient. Although the occupiers of each office area can control local heat pumps, they cannot override the centralized zone control, in short, the area can be made cooler but not warmer. The performance of the environmental equipment is continuously monitored, and anything unusual, defective, or changed in status is logged; the current situation in any room, zone, or floor can be displayed. In the event of an alarm, the fire control system, based on smoke sensors, rings the fire brigade, pages members of staff responsible for evacuation, displays the plan of the area affected, and turns external video cameras on it. Security measures include TV cameras and movement sensors, while entry to the underground car-park is only accessible by magnetic cards and every entry is logged with name and time.

Northgate, Glasgow

The first phase of the Northgate development in Glasgow opened in 1987 at a cost of £20 million, and was claimed by its developers, DCI Ltd, to be one of the most advanced office buildings in Britain and the product of years of intensive research. In this case also, flexibility of office layout is attained by utilizing movable partitions and by linking all cabling straight into an underfloor grid which it is claimed allows work-stations to be located 'literally anywhere' irrespective of the number of VDUs, telephones and power requirements.

The BEMS (Building Energy Management System) computer controls a hot and cold air treatment system which, it is claimed, can heat and cool open-plan or partitioned areas down to 3 square metres, whilst ducting for specialized air-conditioning needs is incorporated in the building. Lighting is controlled by movement sensors (lights only come on if someone moves), and is overridden by daylight sensor cells to prevent lights coming on when natural light levels are deemed adquate. Security is maintained by means of computer monitoring of camera scans, silent alarms, and when lighting is activated by movement. In the event of fire, the system automatically calls the fire brigade, and in the event of power failure, a stand-by generator provides emergency back-up.

The developers claim that utilizing such systems offers a potential 80 per cent saving on lighting costs, 50 per cent on heating and ventilation, at least 50 per cent on fitting-out and wiring costs, and 90.4 per cent on water. The developers' inducement to potential tenants, then, is not only to provide an environment enabling the use of IT systems for business applications, with boundless flexibility in configuration and location, but also substantial financial benefits arising from the building's technology.

NTT TWINS Building, Tokyo

NTT – Japan's Telecom agency – accommodates 2,600 employees in its 14-storey showpiece 'intelligent' TWINS building in Tokyo (TWINS representing 'Towards Information Network Systems'). Although NTT is heavily involved in IT research and development, not all of the building-related technologies available have been installed in its headquarters, the emphasis in Japan as a whole being more on using a building to promote 'intelligent productivity' (Evans 1988). However, NTT has incorporated computer-based control systems and other features of the IB. As well as vertical shafts dedicated to power or office automation on each floor, there are cable racks and ducts to cater for additional equipment, and the building also has satellite links. Offices are open plan – but noisy or heat-dissipating equipment can be partitioned off.

Electricity, water, sewage, air-conditioning, lifts, and lighting are controlled by computer, as are fire detection and security. The entire building relies solely on the heat produced from the IT equipment, and hot water is provided by solar panels on the roof. Air-conditioning operates in winter and summer, but in spring and autumn the motorized windows can be dropped to provide ventilation. Blinds can be manually controlled, but perimeter lights are controlled to daylight intensity (uplighters and task lights have been installed at work-stations). The employee's ID card is used for clocking on and off, logging on to terminals, general security checks, and paying restaurant bills.

Bonneville Power Administration, Oregon

The US government General Services Administration (GSA) financed the 7-storey Bonneville Power Administration headquarters in Portland, Oregon as the federal government's prototype 'advanced technology' office building, and it was ready for occupancy by the 2,100 employees in April 1987. As well as encompassing building system efficiency, low maintenance costs, security and fire safety, it also aims to reduce relocation costs by 75 per cent by installing flooring for ease of access to power and distribution services. Estimating a 30 per cent relocation of office employees each year, the company previously lost 600 work days annually due to this cause alone.

The main function of the computerized Building Automated System is to obtain maximum efficiency and longevity from heating, ventilation, and air-conditioning systems. Heating is supplied by using reclaimed heat from computers, lights, people and solar gain, and lights go out if no movement is sensed for five minutes. The offices are open plan, so employees working outside regular hours access the computer by telephone to turn on lights in their immediate area. An uninterruptible power supply is provided only for life-safety systems and for the mainframe.

Fire-sprinklers are located above ceilings, and the security system incorporates eighteen TV cameras. Employee key-cards are used to gain entry, and name and assigned floor location are displayed and recorded at the guard desk. At night, the card-operated elevators will only take users to their designated floor. The entire building control system can be monitored and controlled from hundreds of miles away over conventional telephone lines, and 'This capability will become increasingly important as the agency reduces its number of employees' (Wright 1988).

LOCAL CONTROL AND 'USER-INVOLVEMENT'

It can be seen from the details contained in the above examples that a common feature of IBs consists of a shift in the locus of control over the immediate working environment away from employees (who may not even be able to turn on a light switch, much less open a window) and even departmental managers and into 'specialist hands' – facilities management, the building's computer systems management, or the developers of multi-tenanted premises. This becomes even clearer if we summarize, in tabular form, what knowledge is publicly available about these four examples (see Table 4.1).

If we examine the managerial rationale which lies behind these control mechanisms, we can perhaps see why such buildings, while undoubtedly creating working environments which are *visually* pleasing, in practice deny the occupants much chance of participating in the way such environments *work*. A recent survey of 'user experiences' (by which it is meant corporate users) of computerized building management systems ('Building management systems' 1989) concluded that the user-organizations derived three main benefits: (a) energy costs went down; (b) labour utilization was more efficient; and (c) there was an improved internal environment. There is an assumption in much of the official developmental literature that

Table 4.1 Locus of control

	Rank-Xerox	Northgate	NTT (Japan)	GSA (USA)
Heating	centralized	centralized	centralized	centralized
Cooling	localized	centralized	centralized	centralized
Ventilation	centralized	centralized	centralized	centralized
Lighting	centralized	centralized	mixed	mixed
Fire	centralized	centralized	centralized	centralized
Security	centralized	centralized	centralized	centralized
Noise	centralized	not known	not known	not known
Maintenance	centralized	centralized	centralized	centralized
Can individual:				
Open window	no	no	motorized control in spring/autumn	no
See natural light	not known	no	not known	no

Note: 'Centralized' indicates controls pre-set centrally which determine employees' conditions, but over which they exert no control.

these three areas are mutually supportive. Thus, at Northgate, for example, the energy control system is supposed

> to ensure that energy conservation and operational efficiency of building services are at optimum performance levels and at the same time to achieve minimum bottom-line costs . . . a researched work environment – to achieve healthy, happy staff with attendant improved staff efficiency and increased work productivity.
>
> (DCI Ltd 1988)

At Bonneville Power, the GSA sees a pleasanter environment having definite economic benefits: the agency estimates that the cost of all building operations and equipment maintenance ranges from $4 to $6 per square foot per year, but employee salaries equate to $180 to $300. 'Thus, even a one or two day disruption of an employee's work area has a significant effect on productivity' (Wright 1988).

However, a combination of rising energy costs and an increasing environmental concern has given energy-saving a priority over other goals and made it very much a 'motherhood' concept, impossible to criticize and boosted by repeated governmental exhortations. For management it is likely to seem a more immediate route to economic saving than the more circuitous one of creating pleasant working conditions, and this increasing emphasis on energy saving may actually have negative implications for the quality of the working environment. For example, while ASHRAE – the American Society of Heating Refrigeration and Air Conditioning Engineers – recently decided to increase the recommended rate of fresh air supply, it was actually *reduced* from 10 to 2.5 litres per second per person in the mid 1970s in the interests of fuel economy following the oil crisis. The example of the Northgate building demonstrates how this contradiction works in the IB. The developers of the building state of their energy management system:

> Management control is the primary function of BEMS and in order for management to control, information in an understandable form is needed. The technology incorporated in Northgate II within the BEMS will produce a whole range of definable specific control parameters and targets.

> (DCI Ltd 1988)

'Control' is used here in the conventional sense of economic control over costs but we can see that these 'definable specific control parameters and targets' to be determined by management mean that the end-users – the vast majority of those who work in the premises – play a totally passive role. If control levels are set by management then the ability of staff to influence environmental conditions is either totally removed or greatly reduced. For example, here is what DCI (1988) say about 'lighting control': 'The ABUSE of lighting by people in their working environment is well known and it accounts for significant proportions of electrical power wastage. We have removed that potential' (emphasis in original).

Similar strictures have been applied to ensure centralized control over heating and cooling the office but, for optimum effective working of the building, the developers see it as desirable that potential tenants: 'must be educated as to how such buildings can work for their occupiers to meet the prime objectives of reduced annual occupation costs and increased business efficiency' (DCI Ltd 1988).

Statements like these indicate that, in the UK at any rate, despite the undoubted good intentions of those architects who have latched on to ideas of 'user-involvement' in design, construction and post-occupancy evaluation, there is often not much clarity about whether the 'users' are the organization for which the office was built, individual workers, or something in between. As Rubin has pointed out there is an assumption in building design (as with the evaluation of IT systems) that individuals in the management hierarchy can readily speak for all users. Furthermore, potential conflict between the organization's objectives and outlook and those of employees is often ignored in favour of the belief that: 'a "value free" determination of organisational activities is possible resulting in technically-based objective decisions suitable for all circumstances (Rubin 1988).

Evidence for the above is given by documented instances of engineers paying lip service to localized user-control but with technical systems actually structured around other priorities. From here the office worker can be viewed as an alien intruder, disrupting energy-efficient office systems. Thus we find a case where management's response to employees' desire to open windows was to reduce the room temperature as a deterrent (Byatt 1989). Perhaps the most cynical response to the desire of office workers to exert greater control over their working environment has been the provision of dummy control switches. These 'controls' – fitted to thermostats, ionizers, etc. – are purely decorative but are provided in order to try to delude employees into believing that they can influence environmental conditions (for examples, see Wilson and Hedge 1987, Leaman 1989).

A similar clash of economic and environmental goals is evidenced where computer-controlled fire evacuation systems have enabled a reduction to be made in the number of fire-escapes, with a corresponding increase in lettable office space (Greig 1987). In 1988 an horrendous fire occurred in a 62-storey Los Angeles office block. There was no sprinkler system (apparently a common feature where there is heavy use of IT equipment) and the computer-controlled doors which were supposed to close remained open, enabling the flames to spread up the stair-well from the 12th to the 16th floors. In addition, the lifts, instead of automatically returning to the ground floor as they had been programmed to do, carried on operating. The only fatality was a maintenance man who was delivered to the inferno on the 12th floor (Gregerson 1989).

THE SICK BUILDING SYNDROME

Another possible reason why the incorporation of economic priorities into the control systems of the IB may run counter to an improved internal environment is suggested by the coincidence of some of the main characteristics of IBs with those thought to be associated with sick building syndrome.

The sick building syndrome (SBS) is recognized by the World Health Orangization (WHO) as occurring where a cluster of work-related symptoms of unknown cause are significantly more prevalent amongst the occupants of certain buildings in comparison with others. The typical symptoms listed by the WHO include: eye/nose/throat irritation; sensation of dry mucous membranes and skin; skin rash; mental fatigue; headaches, high frequency of airway infections and coughs; nausea, dizziness; hoarseness, wheezing, itching and unspecified hypersensitivity (quoted in HSE 1988). It should be noted that this excludes attributable causes of illness such as legionnaires' disease which are not regarded as examples of the SBS.

In this country the Health and Safety Executive recently estimated that 30 per cent of newly built or remodelled buildings evidenced 'excess illness amongst the staff', with up to 85 per cent of employees affected (HSE 1988). In Canada it has been estimated that there are 1,800 such buildings, containing 250,000 sufferers (Centre for Building Diagnostics 1988), whilst in the USA one company has been called in to diagnose and clean up 233 buildings in five years. The scale of the problem is evidently substantial.

The typical building exhibiting the symptoms possesses the following characteristics; it is air-conditioned, has tinted and sealed windows, is open plan, has a high use of carpets and modern synthetic furnishing materials, and a high reliance on artificial lighting. Factors that may contribute to SBS symptoms are thought to include inadequate ventilation and/or fresh air supply, unsuitable lighting, critical levels of high/low temperature and humidity, and airborne pollutants and contaminants. However, as indicated earlier, no definitive diagnosis has emerged so far. Indeed, one leading authority – discussing the general problem of the conditions being created in such examples of the new generation of buildings as the very large-scale developments at Kings Cross – has admitted: 'These are unknown areas where our body of knowledge is incomplete' (O'Sullivan, quoted in Guest 1989).

The Centre for Building Diagnostics (CBD 1988) for example, points out that the rate of introduction of office automation and new machinery often requires different environmental conditions for different activities, and that attention also has to be paid to 'combined stressors . . . which independently do not exceed acceptable limits'. They also make the point that:

> Adopting code limits for setting control systems is also inadequate because there are no 'typical' users, activities or exterior environments. In defining the typical user, present codes and standards are intended to provide satisfactory conditions for 80% of the occupancy. It is not clear what is to be expected of the remaining 20%.
> (CBD 1988)

The conclusions drawn by some building designers examining the spread of SBS and its incidence in buildings of recent construction (although it is not confined to these), has been to reject rigid 'top-down' models of environmental control systems to which those who work there are expected to adjust, and to advocate varying degrees of localized control over the working environment.

It is clear from this review of some of the evidence in the architectural and building design literature that, first, the IB is a development that is likely to characterize the office environment of the 1990s. Second, despite the recognition that a healthy and pleasant workplace may be directly correlated with the degree of localized control available to employees, the new building control systems, constructed around and incorporating economic priorities, often deliberately decrease employee control over the built environment and may actually create an environment that is not simply unpleasant but unhealthy. If this possibility is added to the knowledge we now have about the health and safety implications of intensive IT usage, we are faced with a potentially extremely unpleasant workplace.

THE GLASGOW STUDY

In the summer of 1989 we conducted a small pilot study which compared two recently opened new offices in Glasgow – one a newly constructed office development advertised as being among the most advanced 'intelligent' buildings in the UK, the other a completely refitted Victorian building, with capacity for IT expansion but containing few of the features of the 'intelligent' building. The two major companies in our survey were, quite coincidentally, subsidiaries of the same major Scottish banking group, the company in the 'intelligent office' being in the field of credit card operations ('CredCard') and the other company, in the older building, dealing with international financial transactions ('GlobalFund'). The nature of the work in the two locations and the information technology utilized were a very similar mix of data entry, file adjustment, telecoms and word processing. All CredCard's employees had been brought into the new unit from a variety of other jobs within the banking group and, including the manager, had not worked together before. In contrast, the majority of GlobalFund's staff had transferred to their offices from some fairly cramped and decrepit premises elsewhere in the city. We constructed a sample to represent all the major operational areas in each organization and the major grading distinctions. Around 15 per cent of CredCard's employees were interviewed from both management and staff, and approximately 10 per cent of the staff of GlobalFund were interviewed using the same questionnaire.

At Globalfund the architects had utilized the Victorian origins of the building to create a fairly spacious set of offices with a substantial feel to them. The company occupied the whole of the fourth floor of the building, which had been built around an inner atrium to maximize natural light penetration. The gutting of the building had largely done away with internal partitions, creating large connecting areas of open space. There were only three enclosed offices: one for the senior manager, the others used for conference and meeting rooms. The remaining managerial working areas were delineated by movable acoustic screens. All the working areas had large, openable windows onto the atrium, and the major area also had windows onto the street on the other side; there was no air-conditioning system. Cabling for the wide range of IT equipment was via the ceiling with vertical columns to bring the cabling down to work-stations clustered in 'islands'. Access to the offices involved passing through an outer doorway, passing a porter at a desk in the atrium who released a security door giving access to the stair and lift area and then passing though another electronically locked door, openable by keying in the right combination or by Globalfund reception. An additional glass-sided lift ran up inside the atrium.

At Credcard the offices were again originally designed to be entirely open plan but Credcard managers had demanded their own closed offices and these had been created along the edges of the work-space. Other closed areas consisted of a meeting room, a coffee area and a specially constructed telecoms room to house the telecommunications equipment which Credcard used for data transmission. Two of the opposing walls of the rectangular work-space were comprised of sealed, tinted windows. Cabling was provided via a raised floor which in theory offered users a ducting grid with a range of outlet points to work-stations which were also grouped in an 'island' configuration. Lighting was governed by movement sensors, coming on when anyone entered the room, and heating ventilation and security were controlled from a central building management system which remained in the hands of a subsidiary of the building's developers and was applied not only to Credcard but to all the other tenants of the building. Entry to the building involved passing a security barrier adjacent to the central control room, then passing through an inner door in Credcard's section of the building, then again through an electronically locked security door into the offices themselves. Instead of conventional air-conditioning, the developers of the building had opted for an air-treatment system where external air was passed over heat-exchanging coils.

Despite about 80 per cent of staff in both locations being members of the Banking, Insurance and Finance Union (BIFU) or the Manufacturing Science and Finance Union (MSFU) there was little evidence of any employee participation in the matter of working environment and conditions. While some respondents mentioned occasional section meetings at which it was possible to raise questions relating to their work, all building facilities and office equipment had been selected by management, with no employee or trade union involvement. This is probably a reflection of the fairly rigid hierarchical structure of banking employment.

We first asked all managers and employees in the sample which aspects of the new building they liked most, and the overwhelming majority in both locations mentioned those associated with their appearance – they were new, clean, bright, spacious, open plan. Lighting, working space and office furniture were all rated quite/very good by large majorities in both establishments, as was noise level at CredCard.

When asked what they disliked most (if anything) *every* CredCard respondent – the occupants of the 'intelligent' building – nominated the heating and air-treatment system, and rated temperature and ventilation 'quite bad' or 'very bad'. Whilst the heating and air-treatment system also scored fairly highly in the GlobalFund list of dislikes (six out of seven managers and six out of sixteen employees) and a small majority of employees rated ventilation 'quite/very bad', the level of dissatisfaction was much lower than at CredCard. Typical comments from Credcard staff were: 'When it's cold outside, it's cold inside; when it's hot outside, it's hot inside', 'they can't seem to do anything about it', and even 'I dread coming in'. Blame was apportioned by the staff fairly equally between lack of an air-conditioning system and the role played by the large amount of windows in creating a 'greenhouse effect', despite blinds installed by the company. One assistant supervisor said 'It was 93 last Monday, in winter it's freezing, and in the afternoons it's unbearable as the sun heats up the building'.

At Globalfund the comments seemed contradictory, with several employees stating that what they liked best about the office was the ability to open a window and get some fresh air, while others (including most managers) complained about general stuffiness and the lack of air-conditioning. The clue is given by a credit clerk who remarked, 'It's very warm and airless. We're beside windows but they open into the atrium and we're not allowed to open them – I don't know why'. This would seem to indicate the presence of an organizational constraint on local control even where the built environment made such control possible.

Not surprisingly, when asked what were the three most important features which make an office a pleasant place in which to work, comfortable temperature and good ventilation scored highly in both locations.

When asked about any experience of 'persistent or above average ailments' in possible relationship to the building, over 40 per cent of employees in both buildings mentioned headaches, and mental fatigue/tiredness affected 33 per cent of Credcard respondents and 25 per cent of those from Globalfund. Colds and sore throats were reported by smaller numbers in both buildings, but only at Credcard was dry skin put forward as a complaint, as were sore eyes by those employees who wore contact lenses, which they said were affected by the dry atmosphere. Because of the relatively short time they had been in the buildings, most managers were unable to answer a question regarding the incidence of sickness, absenteeism and turn-over, but one CredCard manager stated that his impression was that more people suffered headaches due to the office temperature and another that colds seemed to be more common and to spread among the staff more readily.

In both locations the complaints seem to be the result of a three-way interaction between the physiology of the operators, the technology of the work, and the technology of the building, and this interaction was taking place within a structure of work organization which demanded long periods of IT use for a high percentage of the staff. Many of the complaints were all too familar from other studies of IT workplaces. 'At the end of the day I have difficulty focusing driving home or reading the rail noticeboard', said one of the credit control staff at Credcard who worked with a VDU for seven hours a day. The importance of the right relationship between the work technology and the built environment is now well chronicled – the importance of blinds and suffused lighting to minimize reflected glare on the screens, for example – but in neither location did the arrangements seem to accord with best practice here, although anti-glare filters had been fitted to the screens at Credcard. However the fact that IT use was not entirely to blame for all complaints is suggested by responses from some supervisors who only used VDUs for an hour or so in a day and yet complained of headaches, dry skin and an increase in the number of colds.

The link between the built environment and the work technology is most clearly demonstrated by the complaints of sore eyes by those VDU workers at Credcard who wore contact lenses. Two factors seem to be at work here: the dry air in the Credcard office, and the fact that VDUs create an electrostatic field in front of them which carries a stream of dust particles away from the screen towards the eyes of the operator. It is recommended that the relative humidity (RH) of an office with a high level of IT use should be maintained above 40 per cent to reduce the strength of this field and minimize the evaporation of protective liquid from the surface of the eyes (Lane 1988).

One possible area of concern of which Credcard employees seemed unaware was that regarding fire alarms and prevention. Mention has already been made of developers' claims of reduced maintenance and security manpower requirements when computerized building management systems are employed. For this reason and the previously mentioned problems of water drenching electronic equipment, no fire sprinklers are installed in the Credcard building. Sensors alert the centralized computer in the event of smoke being detected and the computer phones the fire brigade. The only on-site prevention was in the Credcard telecoms room which had been specially constructed by the company and where not only was the sensitive telecommunications equipment protected from fire by a halon gas system, but was also kept at a correct temperature by its own air-conditioning system, again specially installed by Credcard – a luxury which the employees had to do without!

We asked the respondents in both locations how the new buildings compared to previous offices they had worked in. A substantial majority of GlobalFund respondents of all grades stated they preferred the new office, but whilst this was the unanimous view of Credcard managers, only just over half of Credcard employees shared it. When asked to rate the new building's 'user-friendliness' (that is, an overall assessment of the extent to which it seemed to have been designed and built to suit the requirements of people) on a scale between 1 = very low and 5 = very high, GlobalFund's employees' average rating was 3.4, compared to 2.9 at CredCard. When again asked to compare this with their previous workplace, a majority of CredCard employees were of the opinion that their control over the environment had decreased, but only one GlobalFund respondent took this view.

On the question of localized control, our visits to Credcard threw up some practical examples of the drawbacks of automated systems.

The Credcard manager mentioned ruefully that if he had a meeting in his office, especially after hours when not many people were moving about, the lights had a nasty habit of shutting off, forcing him to leap up and wave his arms under the sensors, somewhat to the alarm of his visitors. He also pointed out that there was no way of turning the lights off during working hours. On visiting the offices ourselves during the summer heat wave of 1989, we found the electronic combination-lock high-security doors tied open with string in a vain attempt to improve the ventilation: a good example of employees constructing their own localized environmental controls to override the central system!

Overall, with the exception of noise levels, our respondents' experience of the 'intelligent' building compared badly as a workplace in every respect with the more conventional structure.

CONCLUSIONS

Earlier we suggested that substantial evidence was available to indicate that a significant number of organizations would move to new offices over the next few years, primarily because of the need to accommodate new equipment. It seems to be the case that organizations moving to new or re-fitted offices are increasingly taking the opportunity to adopt an office systems approach to work organization – that is, by installing or moving towards complete integrated business systems. In our own research we found that CredCard had adopted and updated an existing parent company system so that every aspect of work in the office was now carried out electronically. GlobalFund, on the other hand, initially made fairly minor adjustments when they moved office but within 2–3 years plan to have gone over completely to an integrated electronic system.

The conclusions of this chapter are that, just as we cannot view information technology as a purely neutral technical system, so we should not be lured into regarding the high technology building as such either. The way the intelligent building operates is as much a reflection of social relationships as the work organization within its walls. Power relationships decide what systems are installed and for what reasons, what levels of light and temperature are deemed 'suitable' or 'adequate', and of course a particular view of the users – whether they are to play an active or passive role – is inevitably incorporated into the system design.

Developers of the IB of course dangle the prospect of considerable savings through 'energy efficient' facilities. At the time of our study the landlords of the CredCard IB took in around £1.5 million per annum in rental, and approximately 13 per cent of this (£200,000) was a service charge for building facilities. These facilities – ventilation, temperature, security – are, as previously described, set by the centralized BMS under the landlord's control. What this means is that the requests of those working in the building for more air or higher temperatures cut directly into the landlord's profit levels and so the potential for a conflict of interest is apparent.

It is clear also that the reliance in IBs on such building management systems creates yet another hierarchy of control in which the key question is *who* instructs the computer to boost the heat or cool things down. The individual worker can go to his/her supervisor, the supervisor can go to the section manager, the section manager to the general manager who then presumably has to request the controllers of the BMS to modify their settings. In the case of CredCard the comments quoted seem to indicate that even this level was not able to obtain the necessary changes. It is clear that a major source of dissatisfaction (and possibly ill-health) was the inability of end users to modify their environmental situation.

Davies has forcefully criticized the direction in which IB design has been moving:

> So far, buildings only seem able to provide automated, rather than user-responsive, control over a fairly restricted range of environmental factors; to provide access to a rather formal and managerially centred information system which heavily constrains user autonomy and flexibility. On both counts such conventionally intelligent systems are often seen by workers or users to be an overt manifestation of traditional managerial authority, whose environmental or information edicts emanating from on high are simply reflected in the systems' monitoring and control functions . . . [and] in no sense appear to be neutral to their users. Rather they become a serious invasion of privacy, providing possibilities for continuous but discreet surveillance at a distance.
>
> (Davies 1988: 54)

We are under no illusions that these developments replace some sort of Golden Age of office employment where high levels of local environment control were the norm. However we do feel that we can demonstrate that what *small* areas of control office workers once had are being eliminated. A Harris poll conducted in seven UK cities showed that 60 per cent thought that they did not have sufficient control over their environment and that 70 per cent wanted more control (Rantell 1989). As more and more technology enters the world of the office worker, invading not only the organization of work but also the environmental conditions under which it is performed, then we should perhaps expect an increasing challenge to the assumption that office workers will be content to let control of these issues be determined by a technocracy of 'experts' in alliance with management.

In addition, as we have suggested, the issue for the work-force might not be confined to feeling a total lack of control over their working environment but could include concern over symptoms associated with the SBS which, when combined with the effects on health and well-being of prolonged IT work, can create quite an unpleasant cocktail of working conditions. The claims put forward by the developers of IBs, that they deliver reduced absenteeism and a generally more healthy working environment, would on the basis of this intitial comparison seem difficult to sustain.

REFERENCES

Atkin, B. (1988) 'Progress towards intelligent buildings', in B. Atkin (ed.), *Intelligent Buildings*, London, Kogan Page.

Baldamus, W. (1961) *Efficiency and Effort: An Analysis of Industrial Administration*, London, Tavistock.

Braverman, H. (1974) *Labour and Monopoly Capital*, New York, Monthly Review Press.

'Building management systems – user experience', *Facilities*, July 1989.

Byatt, R. (1989) 'LEO + EED + BRE = £', *Premises Management*, July/August.

Centre for Building Diagnostics (CBD) (1988), *A Trivial Pursuit in Architecture? – The Impact of Advanced Technology on Total Building Performance*, Dundee CBD (Scotland).

Cowan, P., Fine, D., Ireland, J., Jordan, C., Mercer, D. and Sears, A. (1969) *The Office: A Facet of Urban Growth*, London, Heinemann.

Davies, M. (1988) 'Design for new technology', in B. Atkin (ed.), *Intelligent Buildings*, London, Kogan Page.

DCI Ltd (1988) *DCI's New Intelligent Office Development: Glasgow*, Developments Commercial and Industrial Ltd, 27 October 1988.

Evans, B. (1988) 'Focus on telecoms: smart office for Japan', *Architects Journal*, 21 December.

Gregerson, J. (1988) 'How L.A.'s worst high rise fire spread', *Building Design & Construction*, February.

Gregory, G. and Urry J. (eds) (1985) *Social Relations and Spatial Structures*, Basingstoke, Macmillan.

Greig, J. (1987) 'Integrated Building Technology is here', *Architects Journal*, 25 November.

—— (1988) 'Xerox: model for copying', *Architects Journal*, 20 April.

Guest, P. (1989) 'Profile: Pat O'Sullivan', *Building*, 21 April.

Harnett, J. (1988) 'Where do we go from here?', *Office Environment*, October.

Health and Safety Executive (HSE) (1988) *Sick Building Syndrome – A Review*, London, HSE.

Lane, J. (1988) 'Developments in workstation technology and the impact on building design', in B. Atkin (ed.), *Intelligent Buildings*, London, Kogan Page.

Leaman, A. (1989) 'Creating healthy buildings', in *Proceedings of the Developing Healthy Buildings Summer School*, Building Performance Studies Unit, University of Strathclyde.

McLoughlin, I. and Clark, J. (1988) *Technological Change at Work*, Milton Keynes, Open University Press.

Marglin, S. (1976) 'What do bosses do?' in A. Gorz (ed.) *The Division of Labour*, Brighton, Harvester.

Powell, J. A. (1988) 'Towards the integrated environment for intelligent buildings', in B. Atkin (ed.), *Intelligent Buildings*, London, Kogan Page.

Rantell, K. (1989) 'One man's crusade against sick buildings', *Glasgow Herald*, 6 September.

'Remedies for sick building syndrome', *Building Design and Construction*, April 1988.

Rose, M. (1988) *Industrial Behaviour* (2nd edn), London, Penguin.

Rubin, A. (1988) 'What building users want', in B. Atkin (ed.), *Intelligent Buildings*, London, Kogan Page.

Tong, D. (1989) 'Intelligent and healthy buildings', in *Proceedings of the Designing for Environmental Quality Conference*, Birmingham, September.

Turner, B. (1971) *Exploring the Industrial Subculture*, London, Macmillan.

Urry, J. (1985) 'Social relations, Space & Time', in G. Gregory and J. Urry (eds), *Social Relations and Spatial Structures*, Basingstoke, Macmillan.

Walker, R. (1985) 'Class, division of labour, and employment in space', in G. Gregory and J. Urry (eds), *Social Relations and Spatial Structures*, Basingstoke, Macmillan.

Wilson, S. (1985) *Premises of Excellence: How Successful Companies Manage Their Offices*, London, Building Use Studies.

—— (1987) 'Making offices work', *Management Today*, October.

—— and Hedge, A. (1987) *The Office Environment Survey: A Study of Sick Building Syndrome*, London, Building Use Studies.

Wright, G. (1988) 'Federal building showcases advanced technology', *Building Design & Construction*, September.

5 Computerizing the council

IT, jobs and employee influence in a local authority

Harvie Ramsay, Chris Baldry, Anne Connolly and Cliff Lockyer

Although the literature on the consequences of introducing information technology (IT) has burgeoned immensely in the last few years,
there remains remarkably little written on the public sector, and in
particular on the administrative services of national and local government (Lane 1988). Yet there are several good reasons for regarding
this as a particularly important area. Not least of these is the importance of this sector in sheer size terms, historically and currently. In
the UK, central government administration accounted for 4.9 per
cent of total employment in 1951, while local government employment encompassed 6.1 per cent of the total. By 1976 these proportions were 8.1 per cent and 12.1 per cent respectively, thus amounting
in combined terms to over one in five of the UK work-force
(Gardiner 1981). By the end of the 1980s, total public administration
amounted to 1.9 million employees, or 8.7 per cent of the work-force,
with a further 1.7 million in education and 1.4 million in health. Some
of these latter groups are included in local government employment,
which amounted to 2.97 million in 1989.[1]

A second reason for paying particular attention to local authority
administration concerns the potential importance of the technologies
which come under the IT heading to the labour processes and
organizational structures in the office environment, of which this
sector forms a major part. The office was always likely to see the
most radical changes as a result of the implementation of IT
applications. Apart from the photocopier and the typewriter, technical change had been slow until the arrival of the mainframe computer
or central processing unit. Productivity had been relatively stagnant,
and administrative costs were progressively rising as a proportion of
total costs in most organizations.

Third, the public sector was especially vulnerable even within the
area of administration, given the high proportion of labour costs (47

per cent of all costs nationally), and the high proportion of Administrative, Professional, Technical and Clerical (APT&C) within this
(reported as 43 per cent generally, but 57 per cent in the region we
studied). Government cuts and cash limits were creating greater
pressure for savings than in most parts of the private sector, and to
save on costs using IT meant avoiding the more politically difficult
task of cutting services. There were countervailing pressures on
public administration, however, and we will come to these later.

A fourth, and more academic, reason concerns the efforts to
comprehend state employment and state employees in work, labour
market and stratification analyses. The dilemmas created by this
sector may help to explain why many prefer to stick to more
straightforward studies of private sector employment. The issues here
are addressed in greater detail in Ramsay *et al.* (1991), a discussion
which is drawn on below where appropriate.

In this chapter, we will consider evidence drawn from a three-year
study of the introduction of IT into a major local authority, referred
to as Caledonian Regional Council (CRC). For comparative purposes we will also make considerable use of a parallel study in two
overlapping authorities in Australia, referred to below as Wallaby
City Council (WCC) and Kangaroo State Government (KSG).[2] The
reason for covering both these Australian authorities (apart from
opportunity) was that the division of functions between them means
that each carries out some of the functions for which CRC takes
responsibility under the UK system. The populations covered are
comparable (the city being the dominant population centre in the
state), though KSG covers a geographical area several times greater
than the UK, while CRC is far larger than WCC in this respect. The
latter factor also allows a bracketing of the spatial variable, if this
should prove a major factor.

We will consider a number of linked dimensions of the introduction
of IT in these settings, including management strategy, trade union
approach, the content and initial operation of a New Technology
Agreement, and the reported changes in employee job content and
control. The implications of these for workplace democracy will be
discussed in the final section.

MANAGEMENT STRATEGY FOR IT APPLICATION

As IT burst onto the organizational scene, it was accompanied by
extravagant claims for its productive potential (Baldry 1988). Word
processors were to generate up to sixfold increases in throughput,

allowing swingeing reductions in the number of typists. Electronic mail and other networking, direct filing, decision support systems and other applications were also expected to cut a swathe through office employment. Of course, these expectations were rarely realized (Immel 1985), and on occasion productivity has actually fallen, while the increased task possibilities arising from IT have often seen increases in employment, especially in information service organizations, including those within public administration.

A number of factors reinforce this limitation on the technical capacity of IT, apart from the difficulties of debugging hardware and software systems. One is that secretarial and other non-manual work often involves a far wider range of tasks than the new equipment can perform. More important still in most contexts are forms of organizational inhibition. These include user resistance or lack of training, a lack of management capacity to integrate the new systems effectively in the wider setting of work arrangements in the office, disjunctures between local and top management plans and initiatives, micro-political manoeuvring over the introduction and application of IT, and so forth. These considerations all encourage a more gradual and considered introduction of IT than those perspectives (optimistic or fearful) which view the adoption of microprocessor applications as unproblematical for management.

Policy variants

When it comes to formulating a management policy on the introduction of IT (that is, going beyond those situations particularly evident in the late 1970s and early 1980s, where purchase was left entirely to local and *ad hoc* initiative dependent on available funds), two contrasting ideal-type strategic approaches can be identified. The first, 'Policy A', encourages local departmental expenditure and experimentation, allowing constant updating and maximum use of the equipment before it becomes obsolete. This decentralized control arrangement faces the problem of a lack of an industry standard to make systems in the organization compatible and facilitate networking once that becomes possible. This explains the attractions of the 'old blue' policy in many organizations, taking up IBM-tied systems despite their relative cost and effectiveness, and constraining local purchases to this standard. The weakness of IBM in providing cross-system compatibility for networking purposes somewhat sabotaged even this weak integrative option during the 1980s, allowing specialist competitors a growing foothold, though latterly by 'cloning' to IBM standards and building on this.

The alternative approach, 'Policy B', places far more emphasis on evaluating options and reaching a single, considered, and co-ordinated decision on system adoption for the entire organization from the outset rather than retrospectively. This view may also take a more sceptical approach to the value of IT *per se*, reasoning that techno-logical innovation often performs far below specification unless carefully planned (an argument for which there is much support on the office equipment front as we have seen, and one reinforced by the bug-ridden experiences of the previous generation of mainframe hardware and software). One technique which may be popular in such settings is the establishment of an experimental or pilot project to evaluate the systems and allow for initial debugging.

Such a cautious approach, we would venture, will be found to be more likely where the organization is centralized, and where finances are tightly controlled and perhaps also limited in general availability. In addition, as we have analysed elsewhere (Ramsay *et al.* 1991), large public sector organizations have a very characteristic trajectory of technological change. They were very often among the earliest users of mainframes for large batch processing of payrolls, tax or rate assessment and revenue. The second stage in the change path (commencing around the end of the 1970s) typically saw the intro-duction of micro and mini computers and the gradual spread of distributed processing, often for department-specific technical tasks (engineering calculations in Roads departments for example), with office automation only making an appearance in the early to mid-1980s. This sequence inevitably gives considerable internal power to the already established central Computer Services department, whose first reaction was to extend the old 'batch processing', based system, rather than to develop distributed processing, with the emergent systems design likely to remain a centralized 'spoke' configuration adaptation of the batch approach to information flows.

Even where this had to be discarded in the face of the versatility of stand-alone PCs, Computer Services were often able to stamp their authority on subsequent IT systems (including word processing) via their presence on internal vetting committees, on the grounds of ensuring internal compatibility. This attempt to retain a grip on all things computer-based often went to the extent of Computer Services designing, writing and testing systems software in-house (a lengthy and often less than successful process), despite the existence of proven commercial software on the market.

Local authority policies in practice

It seems reasonable to conjecture that budgetary and bureaucratic factors are likely to make public sector organizations more likely to fit the Policy B model, and there are signs of this in several authorities.[3] In the Australian cases, there was evidence of rather more widespread introduction of IT (word processors and specialist equipment in draughting and mapping in particular) in the early 1980s, but an evaluation pilot was afoot in the premier's office of KSG, and moves were underway there and in WCC to co-ordinate introduction more closely.

This is not the whole story, however, since different constraints and approaches may characterize different types of department within an organization. This difference will be elaborated later, but for now a likely difference between technical departments and others may be noted, where in the former budgets often allow space for autonomous equipment purchase and selection is likely to be on a specialized and more experimental basis than elsewhere. The meaning of and control over such equipment to employees in such departments is also likely to be quite different to experience elsewhere. This distinction seems valid in CRC, as will be discussed later, and from observation holds true in the Australian examples also.

In CRC, the union expectation when they achieved a New Technology Agreement was that this would give them at least some measure of control over an expected flood of equipment. In the event, the latter part of this expectaticn proved wrong (we discuss the first part later), since the rate of introduction over the following two years was remarkably slow. Instead, CRC appeared to adopt a Policy B approach, proceeding cautiously whilst evaluating IT potential like KSG, through participation in a pilot study of office automation. This was organized by the Local Authorities' Management Services and Computer Committee (LAMSAC) in Department of Trade and Industry Offices in a sample of authorities, forming part of a wider programme also operating in selected private sector locations. The extended application of a particular manufacturer's equipment at concessionary rates was expected to lead to further orders for compatible equipment in later phases of introduction (as, indeed, it did). Because of the resulting restrictions on new equipment purchase, which were tightest on word processing, most of the examples of IT which we were able to study in

CRC were stand-alone micros used for other tasks, and mainframe terminals.

A strongly centralized committee structure was established in CRC to control and supervise the adoption of systems, with a highly bureaucratic and very slow process of approval through what was labelled the Computer And Office Technology (CAOT) application procedure for projects. For large systems this was a high-powered committee including the Chief Executive, the Director of Manpower Services, the Director of Finance, and the Director of Computer Services, who collectively exercised powers of total veto. For smaller projects, vetting was usually left to someone in Computer Services, which had the logical virtue of encouraging compatibility and expendability for longer-run effectiveness but also acted as a delaying tactic and maintained Computer Services' control over developments.

A similar, highly centralized system had emerged in KSG, again seemingly reflecting the power of the old central data processing department which resisted the demands from other departments to decentralize networks. Extensive computer bureau services were constructed at the centre to keep activity and advice 'in-house'. WCC was rather less tightly organized, with a computer liaison group that included representatives of the various departments, reportedly allowing horse-trading and in some respects weakening the power of the central computing facility. It should be added that even in CRC the micros which were in place in particular had escaped close central control, and conformed to no systems plan at that time.

Centralization did facilitate the subsequent uniform adoption of the new system, spreading out from the original experiments. One implication of this kind of arrangement is that once a strategy of introduction is agreed, change may be very rapid indeed. After a couple of years of evaluation, CRC had invited suppliers to tender for setting up compatible systems for the first two phases of an office automation programme, with 250 work-stations planned to be intro-duced within a year of the end of our study. Preferential co-ordinated equipment purchase contracts were also sought in KSG, with man-agers being allowed to step outside this only at their own risk and with good justification. Again, in WCC control was rather looser, due partly to the balance of internal organizational politics, and co-ordination was at the time of interviews rather less in evidence, though the rate of equipment application was much higher than in CRC due to the latter's restraint on purchase.

Unions, council politics and management style

The management strategy towards introduction was also influenced by the position of the labour movement within the organization. In all local authorities, union membership among office staff tends to be far higher than for any equivalent group in the private sector, and this acts as a potential constraint on management behaviour. Most such bodies in both Australia and Britain have formalized and centralized collective bargaining arrangements, with some provision for consultation on areas of change affecting employees being typical also. The emphasis on workplace bargaining is limited in both countries in the local authority non-manual sector, but workplace organization is probably weaker overall in Australia, partly due to the industrial relations system (that is, the focus on federal or state arbitration tribunal awards as the primary means of settlement) and partly to the far more fragmented union structure of which we will say a little more later.

The cautious rate of advance in CRC relative to the two Australian cases is probably attributable in part to the more cohesive union organization under the British union for the sector, NALGO, though later discussion will qualify the extent of this influence. Another factor which is interesting to consider is the effect of the political complexion of the local council. In CRC and WCC there was Labour Party domination, while in KSG a party well to the right of centre and known for its hostility to the unions prevailed at the time of the study. Since in any council the elected members are formally supreme, and are served rather than directed by the administrative apparatus, it could be thought that political leanings might substantially sway management policy. On the other hand, the resource limitations (time and information), and the temporary tenure of elected positions, may be expected to leave continuity and expertise firmly in the hands of the permanent management staff.

The balance of the case study evidence pointed to the latter factor as the most influential. Management in each case saw the potential for intervention from elected councillors, especially if their policies were starkly anti-union or involved severe job cuts. This created some caution and restraint, a pattern also reported by Barras and Swann (1983), who found that Labour-run councils were more likely to try and avoid contradicting council policies of job creation, while Conservative councils were more likely to push for cost-cutting exercises and reduce job security. Within such limits, however, there was felt by the local authority managers interviewed to be fairly untrammelled room for manoeuvre.

Thus management at KSG did not seem to be any less consultative or considerate of labour issues than those in WCC (which was not saying a great deal in practice), while in CRC, too, managers reported little 'interference' from councillors in personnel issues. Formal consultative procedures appear to be relatively common in the public service sector in the UK and Australia, but this seems to be more a matter of adopting 'good practice' as preached to other employers, and working with a unionized staff and centrally administered personnel system, which further encourages acceptance of a rule-governed relationship with employee organizations.

Service or profit?

A final question concerning management approaches in local authority settings concerns the prioritization of objectives which the application of IT can serve. Crudely, there are two contrasting approaches: those which emphasize productivity and efficiency as a means to cut costs and, perhaps, jobs; and those which emphasize the need to preserve employment, but to use the equipment to improve the service to the public. The ethos of the public service sector, officially embraced by both management and unions, would stress the latter option.

In a time of financial pressures, however, that philosophy is a useful line of employment defence for the union but a potential obstacle for management. The accompanying intensification from the state (in both countries) of the contrary ethos of management as an exercise in efficiency, and of the need to emulate private sector management values, might also be expected to shift the emphasis of local government administrators onto cost savings and thereby to sharpen differences between the two sides of the negotiating table.

Our interviews with management, in Australia as well as in Scotland, found them largely still expressing primary commitment to the service objective of IT innovation, however. In CRC, examples were given of how the Roads department could make faster and more detailed calculations on such matters as traffic flows and the effects of improvement plans, or how Education could now make statistical projections of demographic trends and their implications for future school rolls. In WCC, similar examples were given, such as a reduction in the time taken to process applications for planning permission, or the ability to offer more information to clients. While this was clearly sometimes a matter of giving the more legitimate response, it seemed to be broadly borne out by the buoyancy of employment levels.

It may be, therefore, that despite contemporary pressures, there are still significant differences between public and private sectors in this respect. Whether this is a transitional feature during the early years of IT (since evidence on private sector introduction does not produce strong evidence of job cuts either for the most part), or a more enduring contrast, remains to be seen. Certainly, union fears of job loss had been substantial, and in CRC had impelled the signing of the New Technology Agreement (NTA), together with the union interest in the monitoring of its operation which we were to undertake. Similar concerns and interested co-operation in the study was encountered in the Australian settings. We will now turn to an analysis of the unions' strategy and its effectiveness.

UNION STRATEGY AND THE NEW TECHNOLOGY AGREEMENT

In 1979, after lengthy deliberation on the best way for unions to respond to the challenge of IT, the British TUC proposed the New Technology Agreement as the most effective way forward. As is detailed in other contributions to this volume, the NTA was an attempt to wrest the initiative from management, and to use the radical changes promised by IT to lever open new areas of management decision-making for influence by the unions. Its brave ambitions have not been realized, however, and as those other discussions demonstrate, the NTA seed has generally fallen on barren ground.

Such NTAs as were signed in the UK were found by Williams and Steward (1985) to be almost entirely in the province of white-collar unions, with NALGO the third most likely union to be involved in their promulgation. As has been noted already, there is likely to be a willingness of management in the public service sector to conform to best formal practice in industrial relations, and so the door may well be more easily pushed open in the local authorities than elsewhere.

The potentially effective and so disruptive impact of union resistance to office automation in British local authorities, with high membership densities in a single union giving a strong basis for banning equipment, also impels a willingness to reach formal agreement. In the Australian context, in WCC several unions competed for an overlapping membership; here, management were noticeably less inclined to negotiate and consult on IT, let alone sign a formal agreement.[4] In KSG, there were only two unions, with less rivalry over constituencies and developing co-ordination of efforts, and management had taken note of this; despite the political complexion of the state government, markedly more progress had been made on agreeing to consultation. The Australian interviews were carried out in the aftermath of a significant upsurge in public attention to the question of participation in new technology, and in particular of an important 'technological change' judgement in the Federal Arbitration Commission, which effectively extended union rights in this area (Deery and Plowman 1991, Markey 1987). Management in the two public authorities had responded to this with guarantees to discuss each item, though they admitted this intention had not been fulfilled as the number of items swelled.

In the UK, NALGO had established a record of examining the issue of IT closely for purposes of official policy formulation. A New Technology Working Party was formed in 1979 and issued negotiating guidelines in 1980, followed in 1981 by a fairly detailed review of the employment questions involved (NALGO 1980, 1981). The former document included a model agreement close to the principles laid down by the TUC, including full advance disclosure and consultation, a *status quo* provision, maintenance of employment levels (that is, not merely a no-redundancy provision), training and equal opportunity components. The latter exposition displayed a sensitive appraisal of the particular threat to office jobs, and the uneven gender impact that this could also be expected to have. Extended discussion of health and safety and retraining issues, and a review of international experience were also included. The cases for a democratic approach between labour and management, and for an approach in terms of broad social welfare rather than narrow efficiency considerations, were made forcibly. Similarly, most of the Australian unions interviewed had conducted studies and had begun to prepare policy statements, though for the most part this was less advanced than NALGO's national-level preparation.

There is only limited evidence of these principles showing through in the particular NTA signed between NALGO and CRC. The Agreement was signed as part of a service conditions package, and this may have left its mark as we shall discuss in a moment. The NTA covers all forms of IT affecting any APT&C staff, and provides for redeployment at protected salary in the event of displacement, but does not specify no loss of posts. The formulation on the last is rather for no compulsory redundancy (implicitly allowing both natural wastage and voluntary redundancy). The clauses on health and safety matters and on training are noticeably vague, beyond the acceptance of the right to information of health and safety representatives. Advance consultation on each new system, including effects on job content and staffing levels, is supported by a *status quo* clause in the event of failure to agree. Equal treatment issues are notable by their absence.

In 1985 NALGO undertook a national survey of their local government branches on the subject of new technology.[5] They found 52 per cent of branches responding had negotiated or were negotiating an NTA (though the total number of agreements registered at head office suggests a definite bias to respond to the survey by branches with NTAs). Employer resistance had led to 28 per cent of branches trying and failing to do so, however, with a good many authorities unwilling to make a firm commitment to consult.

Of the NTAs which had been signed, 96 per cent guaranteed advance information to the union, 79 per cent provided for union involvement at the planning stage on new equipment, and 64 per cent had a *status quo* clause. Over three-quarters (78 per cent) had a no compulsory redundancies clause, though only 36 per cent had achieved a promise of no reduction in staffing levels. Health and safety safeguards were agreed in 87 per cent of agreements, and training/retraining was covered by 97 per cent.

A subsequent analysis (in 1986) of NTAs recorded at NALGO head office broadly confirmed most of these patterns on consultation, advance information provision, training and so forth, though only 10 per cent were found to specify no job loss, while over half used the much weaker formulation blocking only compulsory redundancy or even promising only to 'make every effort' to avoid redundancies. Only 18 per cent of agreements made any reference to equal opportunities, and then in very vague terms. A *status quo* clause was found in only 36 per cent of agreements, and although 92 per cent required exhaustion of consultation and negotiation procedures first, in the majority management could eventually exercise a prerogative to impose the equipment.

The patterns suggested by NALGO's own figures confirm the strengths and limitations detected in the CRC agreement. Traditional union concerns are catered for, along with good formal provision being made for consultation. But little headway was detectable in laying the groundwork for a more proactive union role, or in tackling issues like work content and job satisfaction, or gender inequalities.

To some extent, this dilution of the original intentions of NTAs can be seen as part of the general failure of the TUC proposals, though it also has some aspects peculiar to the type of union and context involved. NTAs in general were not only limited in coverage, but failed almost entirely to fulfil the aspiration of taking the initiative and exercising effective democratic control over the innovation process. Some reasons for this may be found in the deficiencies of orthodox union negotiating strategy, such as: a lack of union resources to sustain the challenge to managerial definitions; a tendency to focus on employment rather than job or collective control issues; a short- rather than long-term perspective on techno-logical change; and a tendency to overestimate or underestimate the scale of the changes (promoting fatalism or nonchalance respec-tively). Most agreements tended to treat the 'bread and butter' ground of jobs, wages, and conditions – areas with which the unions felt most at home.

Other factors weighing heavily on the realization of NTA ambi-tions were environmental: the collapse of the tripartism which had bred the TUC aspirations; the severity of recession, overwhelming union capacities to do more than try to slow the tide of job and control loss, forcing them to neglect more ambitious issues; and the attendant management resistance in the 1980s to a democratization which would invade their powers of decision-making. There was a ready opportunity for employers to conceal IT job losses amidst general contraction and restructuring, and so evade any agreed protection for jobs if they wished.

In respect of these weaknesses rooted in the economic conditions, NALGO was better placed than most other unions in the UK in the early 1980s. Despite cash limits imposed by Westminster on local government, employment levels held up, and the attack on union rights in most authorities was at worst a muted version of that in many other locations. This helps to explain the impressive coverage of NALGO's efforts, of course, and this success should not be underestimated. None the less, we have seen that the NTAs signed remained well short of the model in content.

At least some of the explanation for this, it can be suggested, may be found in more immediate features of the union and its situation. First, the union represented a very broad range of staff with quite diverse task roles and occupational identities, who thus faced quite varied possible effects from IT (and actual effects – see p. 167 for elaboration). Unlike a craft union, it was hard for them to specify what work would be affected in what ways and this difference was reflected in a broad distinction in bargaining strategy that is apparent in an examination of those locations that negotiated NTAs in the early to mid-1980s.

NTAs typically include both procedural and substantive elements but the precise mix depends on the situation in which the union finds itself. A craft or technical union with members concentrated in a few specific locations (for example, drawing/design offices) may be faced with the introduction of a functionally specific system (such as CAD) which could be used (in the sense that they will be trained to use it) by most of its members in the company. Here the typical agreement will probably be highly substantive in content, including guarantees on universal training and perhaps some kind of IT premium for users (Baldry and Connolly 1986).

For a large white-collar union like NALGO, organizing across all grades, the priorities will tend to be different. Only some of its members are likely initially to be direct IT users, and the types of IT systems and items of equipment encountered by them will both present considerable variety – word processors, PCs, terminals, telecoms – and will be non-funtionally specific (that is, the same item can be found in different departments but be used for very different purposes). Clearly, here, there is going to be no single 'moment' of change represented by the introduction of a given system: change, once begun, is a long-term process in which systems get added to, modified, and expanded. Under these circumstances, it is logical for the union to go for a broad 'enabling' agreement, laying down jointly agreed rules for the future introduction of any item of IT in any location in the organization and with fairly general (but some might say weak) guarantees on employment, grading and health and safety.

Many of the substantive gains sought by a union like NALGO, then, can be expected to take the form of a general improvement in conditions (for example, a reduction in working hours) for everyone, as a 'sweetener' for accepting the new technology. A good example is CRC's service and conditions package negotiated at the same time as, and seen as part of, the NTA. Improvements for IT users alone would have given the bulk of the membership nothing from the agreement, and separated IT users from the rest. Management will often go along with these general demands, as they neither create IT 'elites' (as IT premiums can do), nor fuel any potential fires of hostility towards technological change. However, because a reduction in working time can be a more immediate issue to the bulk of the membership than the new technology itself (the prospect of which might seem vague and distant to many) it was often the case that these elements were more keenly pursued than guarantees over IT use.

A second reason for the distance of actually negotiated agreements from the union's model was that the local branch did not really know quite what to expect. The stereotypes of the time led them to anticipate a flood of equipment and consequent job cuts, though, and this they were tensing themselves to face. Separate approval of each item offered a delaying tactic (though in practice it caused much frustration for management, for staff seeing equipment awaiting clearance for months, and for union officials, trying to keep tabs on things).

When the flood did not materialize, it was difficult to reorient the approach to tackle questions of job content. Questions of regrading were pursued, but with limited success (only 16 per cent of locations reported any kind of regrading exercise). Even health and safety, a comfortable priority for most unions, seemed to attract little attention – though our survey (reported later) revealed that members found this a major area of problems with the new equipment. This, too, may be a matter of union coverage: the problems were likely to affect those with long exposure to routine tasks, not more senior and technical staff whose use of IT was likely to be very different. As NALGO is unusual in having many of its leading representatives drawn from the more senior ranks (Nicholson *et al.* 1981, Terry 1982, Ramsay *et al.* 1991), their experience of IT may have shaped their perception of the issues significantly.

Another factor compounded this, namely that the NTA was tangled up with a general agreement on conditions of service as mentioned earlier. The reason for this strategy by the union reflected the bargaining structure of local government. This was highly centralized, and left almost no space for local negotiation on matters of substance. But management were prepared to bend the rules if they could get an agreement on IT, so the new technology issue presented a golden opportunity which local officials were perhaps not prepared to miss, even at the cost of some diversion from the refining of the NTA itself.

The operation of the agreement predictably exhibited its strengths and weaknesses. The union requirement for continuous notification seemed to be a victory, but in reality it was a bureaucratic response restricted in effectiveness. In practice, management rarely consulted the union, let alone the membership, on any detail concerning equipment, and as we have argued formal notification did not enable either side to undertake proper evaluation and negotiation in advance. As a result, 'blacking' of the equipment by the union remained common. One-third of CRC locations reported that management were 'uncooperative' over the introduction of IT, with most disputes focusing on regrading disagreements. The constructive content of exchanges between the union and management as a result of the NTA were thus minimal, and could scarcely be called participative.

For comparison, the Australian survey, in a context without an agreement in WCC, found no prior discussion of the introduction of equipment with union representatives at all. Some advance discussion with staff themselves had taken place in 48 per cent of locations, however. Such an arrangement does not seem likely to allow much influence to employees beyond details of implementation, though, and in this respect at least the NALGO agreement did place greater limits on management action. On the other hand, it did not involve those who would have to use the equipment at all.

In KSG some consultation was reported by both sides, but the unions complained that it was becoming patchy, and management argued that the system was too time-consuming to follow to the letter. A new arrangement was being sought, but this was complicated by the state government's move to outlaw union recognition agreements. This had not only created hostility in the labour movement, but had put the unions on their mettle to prove their relevance to a membership which was no longer guaranteed. It should be noted that in several other states in Australia with different political complexions, more elaborate Technology Implementation Agreements (TIAs) had been negotiated.

IT AND WORK CONTENT

Although the main union fears in advance of IT concerned jobs, in CRC there was little sign of employment loss in the reports from the locations. The results appeared to be typical of the early stages of automation, with many user locations needing additional staff to carry out expanding functions, and the systems insufficiently bedded in and debugged to permit significant rationalization. In the Australian authorities, too, the unions reported few if any job losses and that the organizations were generally unlikely to sack people. Each of the unions interviewed in Australia reported that this made for an apathetic response by many of their members to attempts to campaign on IT.

Given this relative calm on the employment front, whether eventually it proves to have been a 'phoney war' prelude or not, attention might be expected to shift to aspects of work experience and control. However, the extent to which this happens depends on union structure and membership pressure. We have already suggested that the bargaining system, and other aspects of union representation, were not particularly conducive to a sensitivity to work-level issues, particularly in the UK situation.

Since the union in the UK was therefore unlikely to seek out problems and initiate campaigns, the membership response to work content and related issues became the main potential source of further issues to be taken up. This requires us to examine the reported experience and attitude of the work-force to the introduction of IT. For information on this, we will draw on our survey of workplace representatives in CRC, and on interviews with those involved in the office automation pilot (OAP) project. This will be supplemented by NALGO's own national survey on the working of new technology bargaining, and where possible by the parallel Australian interviews and survey.

The volume and pressure of work

An increase in workload was reported from over half of the CRC locations, and by more than two-thirds of those covered in the NALGO national survey and in the Australian survey. This was echoed by widespread reports of increased work pace in CRC, though only a third of locations in the Australian study indicated this. These changes were in any case not necessarily experienced as greater pressure, due to other aspects of the perception of working with the new equipment reported below. Rather, in some cases at least, the increased throughput was celebrated as an achievement, and attributed to the facilities provided by the new equipment – for keying, error correction, editing and work organization generally on word processors, for instance.

In CRC, this came through especially strongly in the interviews on the OAP. Work control, variety, and also the novelty of the equipment, combined to make the outcome an improvement in the eyes of most, especially those moving from the typing pool, and perhaps rather less (though still noticeably) for secretarial and committee clerk staff. The contrast to Webster (1986) and Butler (1989), who suggest that secretaries will gain more than ordinary typists, is worth noting. The special conditions which applied in the Project may have affected this.

Training, grading and promotion

In the majority of departments in CRC, only a minority of employees used – or were trained to use – the new equipment. This had the effect of dividing the work-force, or at least of creating (or reinforcing) relative advantage for some employees. Similarly, in the Australian survey it was reported from 69 per cent of locations that only a few were offered training.

The quality of the training was strongly criticized by the Australian unions interviewed, and also by those involved in the OAP in Scotland, but one result had been that operators found themselves taking on a training function for others, which enhanced the responsibility and variety of their jobs. On the other hand, there was some resentment that this and other increases in skill they felt had occurred had not been recognized through any regrading. After a considerable period of dispute (during which the equipment was boycotted), just two increments had been granted to secretarial staff, for instance, and this was seen as a poor reflection of their job changes and personal contribution to increased productivity.

Regrading was found to be strongly resisted by management in our study of CRC, with numerous disputes arising between NALGO and the council over this matter. In WCC a policy of no allowance for a shift to word processing was being maintained, though in KSG some allowance was said by management to be normal. Most NALGO representatives reported further that little or no increase in promotion opportunities had flowed from the introduction of IT, a judgement echoed by their Australian counterparts. However, NALGO's national survey found 57 per cent of branches reported some regrading (though unfortunately the proportion of employees involved is not specified). The regrading was negotiated through specific machinery set up to deal with the introduction of IT rather than through conventional grading appeals machinery in two-thirds of locations. None the less, the vast majority of word processor operators remained on fairly low points on the 'Spine', as the local government pay scale in the UK is known.

Health and safety

Both in CRC and in Australia, the surveys turned up widespread reports of health problems associated with the use of VDUs, with 45 per cent of locations reporting problems in CRC, for instance. Interviews in CRC suggested that the survey may well have under-estimated the incidence of problems. NALGO's national survey also uncovered complaints paralleling those in CRC, concerning sore eyes, headaches, tiredness and fatigue, and back and neck aches in particular, yet in 39 per cent of locations it was reported that no action had been taken on these matters.

Official union policy placed considerable emphasis on this issue, which is one of the established, familiar and perhaps more 'comfortable' terrains for trade union activity. NALGO's own guidelines on IT examined the relevant problems in some detail, and several of the Australian unions interviewed had vigorously pursued the issue locally by circulating guidelines for representatives and members. None the less in CRC, the health and safety clause of the NTA was fairly vaguely worded and, as we noted earlier, at first the issue seemed to have been largely marginalized by the union and management (to the frustration of both management and union health and safety officers). In later stages of the OAP (after our own survey), it should be added that management were to place a great deal more official emphasis on attempts to improve health and safety standards, even to the extent of designing their own office furniture, after consultation with equipment users in the pilot scheme. The tables and chairs were then manufactured in a Blindcraft factory run under the aegis of the Social Work Department. Whether this reduced the incidence of backache and other muscle-related ailments is not known.

Satisfaction and interest

On balance, the evidence in CRC suggests that, initially at any rate, job satisfaction was increased by the introduction of IT (though see the discussion later concerning impact on different groups): 43 per cent of locations reported increased satisfaction overall, and just 10 per cent a deterioration. In the OAP, expressions of enhanced interest and satisfaction were almost universal, particularly among typists who had moved to become word processor operators. 'The work satisfaction is totally different; I love it,' was a typical comment.

None the less, there was frequent mention of some standardization of job content, and sometimes loss of task identification (for example, with the splitting of work on long documents). Apart from other factors discussed below, a combination of novelty and a number of features consistent with a 'Hawthorne effect' was noted as a likely major influence on attitudes. The women interviewed were on a special project, with a strong group identity and sense of isolation from other employees, and a receptive management style. It is hard to disentangle the effects of the technology itself in these circumstances, but research subsequent to our survey indicates that these positive factors were later outweighed by negative ones, especially as the project spread from the original location to other secretarial locations in the local authority.

One issue which was explored through the OAP interviews concerned the effect of IT on social contact. Pessimistic characterizations of the new office technology in the early 1980s had suggested that automation would reduce social interaction with managers and fellow workers. The reports at the time of our survey were universally to the contrary on this point; the new equipment was felt to allow much more scope for contact with a variety of people, both official and informal, and this contributed to the positive feelings which the operators had about the project. Again this would seem to have been a feature of the experimental and relatively unregulated nature of the initial pilot group, as personal interviews by the authors with staff in the later years of office automation expansion produced a very different picture. Apparently, operators by this stage were complaining of being isolated in pools with little opportunity to communicate with either their peers or with document authors. The quality of work performed had declined, and absence, turnover and overtime had soared. It was felt by our correspondent that the high standard of ergonomic design incorporated by management into the equipment and furniture (see p. 163) had been more than offset by the negative nature of the organization of work and job design.

In the Australian context, where IT was more widely and in many cases longer established, the climate of opinion was less sanguine from the start. A union representing primarily clerical and other routine non-manual workers opined that increased routine and declining job satisfaction were in practice more serious problems than threats to employment, and other unions were similarly pessimistic (though those representing managerial or technical staff reported less negative experience). Management were more positive in their assessment of the changes for their staff, but did not claim major advances on this score either.

Skill, responsibility and control

The lack of widespread regrading implies that management took the view that by and large the new labour processes involved no significant upgrading in skill for non-manual workers. In NALGO's national survey, on the other hand, only 21 per cent of locations reported a trend to deskilling or routinization of work. In Australia, most of the unions reported no significant general pattern, though one union did claim a general deskilling of lower-graded jobs, especially for women members. The survey evidence suggests that there was little support for the more pessimistic, labour subordination expectations of the effect of IT common in some predictions of the early 1980s, but little support for the more fervent optimism in other circles.

In the OAP interviews in CRC, however, it was clearly felt by all those interviewed that their responsibilities, range of work and the adaptability demanded of them had markedly increased. To some extent this was a feature of their unusual status – the assumption of training functions mentioned earlier, for instance, which was very much a feature of the experimental status of the project. The word processor operators also felt that the new systems gave them greater freedom to decide how to do their work, this being partly a consequence of having to explore the capacities of equipment with which management had little familiarity. Autonomy was thus high, but for reasons which, as already indicated, were always unlikely to endure. As one word processor operator put it: 'It gives you freedom because it's new.'

Consultation and negotiation

Given the favourable responses of OAP interviewees to their initial experience of the new equipment, it might be expected that the role of the union and of negotiation over such matters would be valued little. This was not the case. All of the operators interviewed saw the union's role as important, and although several said they knew little about it in principle they thought the NTA a necessary move. As one woman put it: 'No matter how much I enjoy using it, I'm in the union first and they introduced this second.'

There had, in fact, been a dispute over grading which had delayed the implementation of the project for some of those interviewed for several months. Not only was this felt by several respondents to have been inadequately resolved, but all were emphatic that there had been no consultation with users on the new systems before they were introduced:

No, nothing at all. From my grade downwards we weren't involved. It came as a shock actually . . . (Committee Clerk)

> We were more or less told . . . it was a sort of *fait accompli* . . .
> You know, it makes all the difference in the world if someone asks
> you for something rather than being told. (Secretary)

> No, we were just told that we were the dummies . . . (Secretary)

To repeat, to start with these respondents all enjoyed working with
the new equipment and enjoyed the challenge of acquiring new
computer-related skills: it was how work on the equipment came to
be organized as its use spread through the organization that seems
to have reversed these early positive feelings. In addition, the manner
of its introduction had not gone unnoticed, and helped to emphasize
the continuing potential conflicts of interest. In the OAP the manner
in which the project was set up, described earlier, clearly constrained
the scope for consultation, but the other evidence on the problems
of negotiation and consultation discussed earlier and in other
chapters in this volume suggest that the problem cannot be reduced
to such specific contingencies.

DIVISIONS OF LABOUR

The discussion thus far has proceeded largely in terms of generaliza-
tions concerning the experience of IT in local authority work. The
assumption of homogeneity in the consequences of IT for employees
across the labour force is obviously an untenable one, however. Our
research on CRC indicated that different types of equipment, and
different groups of workers using that equipment, displayed differing
patterns of experience. The research method employed, relying as it
did on departmental reports from union representatives, was not
ideally suited to a detailed exploration of these differences, but in an
earlier article (Ramsay *et al.* 1991) we explored these issues to the
extent the data permitted. The discussion here draws on the
findings reported there, supplemented by some information from the
Australian interviews.

First, local authority adminstration embraces an heterogeneous
range of functions. Certain tasks, such as word processing and some
clerical work, are found across the spectrum of functional divisions,
but others are distinctive. We found it helpful in CRC to distinguish
between three types of department for which the introduction of IT
could be expected to have different meanings:

1 '*Social*' departments, such as Social Work, Careers or Education,
  concentrated on providing face-to-face services to the public. They

had little prior experience of IT, and the unfamiliarity might cause some uncertainty, reluctance and perhaps negative reactions. It also created the likelihood of discrimination and division, depending on which employees were supplied with or learned to use the new equipment. The main impact of the new equipment could be expected to be an improvement in record-keeping and information recall.

2 *'Central support'* departments such as Finance, Manpower Services or the Chief Executive's office would be expected to have longer experience of work with mainframes. Local terminals or even distributed processing might be expected to the main change for these departments, potentially making achievement of work tasks more flexible and controllable through reduced dependence on communication with centralized data processing. Much of the data analysis involved would be fairly standardized, however.

3 *'Technical'* departments, such as Roads, Architects, or Surveyors, had still more familiarity with the use of mainframe, and to an increasing extent specialized stand-alone equipment. Their use of such facilities would typically be far more specialized, and seen as supportive of technical tasks, easing calculation or the preparing of drawings for instance. In KSG, for example, the union organizing 'professional' workers reported having great difficulty convincing members that there were any problems associated with the introduction of IT for functions such as cartography or other technical tasks. They were seen simply as sophisticated aids to their work, and ones enjoyable to use.

While the validity of these distinctions, and of the general expectations of reactions to IT which yielded them, were largely borne out by our informal observations and discussions in CRC (and in the Australian cases), they are not the only ones which call for consideration. The general recurrence of certain kinds of task associated with typing/word processing, clerical and general administrative work, also implies a need to look at divisions within departments between these staff and the 'professional' workers associated with the specific departmental functions.

In the event, a scan of the data from the CRC survey quickly confirmed that the clearest difference in reported experiences from local representatives was between 'technical/professional' locations and 'non-technical' ones, the latter including mainly clerical and administrative workers in 'central support' and 'social' locations. Because of the hold imposed by management on the introduction of word processors until the evaluation of the OAP was complete, the main reported innovations concerned mainframe terminals and, to a lesser extent, stand-alone microcomputers.

Local government workers' experience of terminals differed markedly between the technical and non-technical locations. The non-technical locations were far more likely to report an increased volume and especially an increased pace of work. It was also usual in non-technical locations for only a few regular operators to use the equipment, whilst in technical locations all staff would normally make use of the terminals. Job satisfaction was reported to have increased or (most commonly) not been affected in most technical locations with terminals, but for non-technical departments over half the responses indicated a decrease both in their job satisfaction and in their ability to pace and organize their work. In fact, non-technical workers were more likely to see some change, for better *or* for worse, than their technical counterparts, suggesting that IT was far more likely to have made a significant impact on their working lives.

The experience of micros reflected similar but less marked differences between the two groups. This is partly explained by the relative newness of micros even to most technical departments. Technical departments were still more likely to report increased job satisfaction, and to have a larger proportion of staff working with the equipment. For both groups, and particularly for non-technical staff, the volume of work was even more likely to have increased than with terminals, but the experienced pressure of work was none the less markedly less likely to have risen. The explanation of these differences between the effects of micros and terminals is considered further in our earlier discussion cited above, but their consequence seems to be that although micros performed somewhat different functions in the different types of location, they are as yet generally less subject to supervision and codification of work activity. This may have been more a consequence of their relative newness than something inherent in the particular technology.

The discussion of variations in experience with IT has thus far considered only task definitions. Yet it is well-established, in local government and other walks of work organization, that task divisions are associated with other divisions of labour, and most prominently with gender. As argued by Valentine (Chapter 7, this volume), gender role definitions are closely tied up with beliefs about respective abilities of males and females, and with the power relations which help to impose perceptions advantageous to males on women workers.

These definitions, moreover, have become closely entangled with conceptions of who can handle what type of information technology, often carrying forward and reinforcing task divisions already present (as between typing/word processing and more 'technical' functions involving data manipulation, for instance), however arbitrary and artificial these may seem from an objective standpoint. Thus IT may not recast internal stratification of the work-force along gender (or other) lines, but rather may even reinforce it through the self-fulfilling confirmation of divisions.

In the Australian authorities investigated, employment of women was at a far lower level than in Britain. Whereas over half of all local government employees are female in Britain, in Australia generally it was around one in five, and in WCC the figure was just 11 per cent. None the less in both countries the link between women and technology was pictured in similar ways by some of those interviewed – for example, that there was a strong sense of new equipment as 'toys for the boys' in many departments. This was most obvious, predictably, in technical areas of work where the division of labour was commonly between male professionals and female secretarial and clerical 'support'.

To a considerable extent, though, the division between technical and non-technical locations is also a distinction between predominantly male and predominantly female locations in CRC. When we seek to fine-tune this analysis by separating out locations we know to be chiefly male or female, the differences already observed sharpen further, thus emphasizing the independent significance of gender differences. In these locations, reduced control over and increases in work pace, lack of control over working method, and less freedom from supervision are all typical. Those whose work had already been most routine were most likely to report a further reduction on work satisfaction (contrary to the relative enthusiasm reported by those moving from typing pools to new word processing tasks in the special conditions of the OAP). Use of terminals was likely to be almost entirely by women in those locations where the equipment was associated with adverse consequences for operators.

In the male-dominated technical departments, on the other hand, where the new equipment was more favourably received, use was entirely by males. Control over use of the equipment, work pace, and reported increased satisfaction were all high. In short, male-gendered work was associated closely with the ability to exert control and so with more rewarding work experience, in stark contrast to the pattern for most female workers.

CONCLUSIONS: WORKPLACE DEMOCRACY AND IT IN LOCAL GOVERNMENT

Overall, the evidence suggests that the increase in pace and volume of work throughput typically associated with IT in the office, combined with the highly variable changes in experienced job control and responsibility reported here, can push job interest and satisfaction in either direction. The outcome is highly dependent on specific context and combination of changes, and perhaps on management's approach to the changes. A willingess to consult, at both employee and representative levels, and to negotiate meaningfully on the change process and associated rewards (given the marked collective awareness of many local government employees), together with the effectiveness of the union in that renegotiation, will play an important role in shaping employee responses.

However, we have found that job satisfaction and other positive or negative experiences of the changes associated with IT introduction are closely tied up with the pre-existing differential capacity of different groups of staff for exerting control over their work. Most important here were the technical/non-technical divisions, and these were found to be very much tied up with gender divisions in the workforce. The significance of occupational role and of gender for the democratizing or subordinating effects of IT is thus undeniable.

At the level of representation and the attempts at collective participation in the change process, the union record was not encouraging. The key gender issues were hardly addressed at all at the local level, and other aspects of work experience were little attended to in labour–management bargaining. Apart from delaying the use of some equipment in pursuit of regrading claims, with limited success, there is no evidence of a significant labour input to the implementation of IT programmes. This may cause little surprise, since the labour movement has developed no convincing alternative perspectives or policies which go beyond general exhortations for participation. To be of any use to local negotiators, there would need to be detailed guidelines on the alternative possibilities that might be sought through their efforts.

The failure of the unions should not be attributed to some imaginary powerful subtlety on the employers' side. Management strategy in local government was not particularly elaborate or sophisticated, and may well have been given greater *post hoc* coherence in our account above than it deserves. Indeed, a recent official report is highly critical of both strategic planning and of the absence of cost-effective utilization of IT by local authorities (Audit Commission 1989). In the event, in CRC the authority's decision to hold off investment until after the OAP was evaluated could also have given the union some space to reconsider their own policy.

Instead it seemed to surprise and disarm the union, even leading to some apparent loss of concern over the IT issue. The Australian cases afforded even less cause for celebration of union influence on management. It would appear to be extremely difficult for even quite sophisticated understandings of the IT question at national level to be translated into local strategy and motivation. From this follows an inability to take up key democratization issues with any real effect. Yet local government still has more potential for such an effort than most other sectors. It would seem there is a long way to go before democracy is a term of any relevance to the design, implementation and operation of information technologies.

NOTES

1 Figures for June 1989 from *Employment Gazette*.
2 The initial interviews were conducted by Harvie Ramsay during a visiting lecture and research programme funded jointly by Griffith University and a fellowship from the Australian Studies Centre. A collaborative project using parallel survey questions was then established and carried out by Chilla Bulbeck, Margaret Gardener and Ian Low at Griffith University. We gratefully acknowledge the information concerning the survey which our Australian colleagues have supplied to us, and would emphasize that the interpretations offered here are our own and are not necessarily shared by them.
3 Other examples of which we are aware include a two-year evaluation of a word-processing centre by Surrey CC (Smith 1982, though his glowing report of the outcome is contradicted by a Labour Research study 1983), and those reported by an Urwick/*Computing* survey of systems usage, which confirms this suggested pattern (*Computing*, 20 October 1983).
4 Technology Implementation Agreements (TIAs) are the equivalent of the British NTA.
5 Grateful acknowledgement is made to NALGO for supplying the results of their survey material and agreeing to allow us to make use of it.

REFERENCES

Audit Commission (1989) *IT Trends in Local Government*, Management Paper No. 7, London, HMSO.
Baldry, C. (1988) *Computers, Jobs and Skills*, New York, Plenum.
—— and Connolly, A. (1986) 'Drawing the line: computer aided design and organisation of the drawing office', *New Technology, Work and Employment* 1 (1).

Barras, R. and Swann, J. (1983) *The Adaptation and Impact of Information Technology in UK Local Government*, London, Technical Change Centre.

Butler, D. (1989) 'Secretarial skills and office technology', in E. Willis, (ed.) *Technology and the Labour Process*, London, Allen & Unwin.

Deery, S. and Plowman, D. (1991) *Australian Industrial Relations*, Sydney, McGraw-Hill.

Gardiner, J. (1981) 'The development of the British working class', in S. Aaronovitch and R. Smith (eds), *The Political Economy of British Capitalism*, London, McGraw-Hill.

Immel, A. (1985) 'The automated office: myth versus reality', in T. Forester (ed.), *The Information Technology Revolution*, Oxford, Blackwell.

Labour Research Department (1983) *IT Case Study – Surrey County Council*, London, Labour Research Department.

Lane, C. (1988) 'New technology and clerical work', in D. Gallie (ed.), *Employment in Britain*, Oxford, Blackwell.

Markey, R. (1987) 'Neo-corporatism and technological change in Australia', *New Technology, Work and Employment* 2 (2).

NALGO (1980) *New Technology – A Guide for NALGO Negotiators*, London, NALGO.

—— (1981) *The Future with New Technology – A NALGO View*, London, NALGO.

Nicholson, G., Ursell, G. and Blyton, P. (1981) *The Dynamics of White Collar Unionism*, London, Academic Press.

Ramsay, H., Baldry, C., Connolly, A. and Lockyer, C. (1991) 'Municipal microchips: the computerised labour process in the public service sector'. in C. Smith, D. Knights and H. Willmott (eds), *The White Collar Labour Process*, London, Macmillan.

Smith, R. (1982) 'Word processing installation', *Employment Gazette*, June.

Terry, M. (1982) 'Organising a fragmented workforce: shop stewards in local government', *British Journal of Industrial Relations* 20 (1).

Webster, J. (1986) *Office Automation*, Brighton, Wheatsheaf.

Williams, R. and Steward, F. (1985) 'New Technology Agreements: an assessment', *Industrial Relations Journal* 16 (3).

6 Technology and banking

The use of information technology

Peter Cressey

This chapter is based on longitudinal research conducted in the banking sector in the mid to late 1980s.[1] The research was particularly concerned with developments in staff participation consequent upon the introduction of new technology. In part this emphasis on banking was a deliberate attempt to situate technological innovation in a sector other than manufacturing. In banking the introduction of technology in the form of computerization was seen as a catalyst – a potentially transformative agent that would have profound influences upon the landscape of the industry.

The questions raised in the research centred on how it would reshape and redraw the staff–management relation, and whether and to what extent it would signal a transformation from what was generally seen as a paternalistic environment to one in which a technocratic ethos predominated. In particular we were interested in the effects of technological innovation in this service sector area of employment and claims made about its radical impact. Also, how did the question of union and worker influence in the process of change arise? Did such a setting provide opportunities for greater control by the staff involved? How were the interests of different groups combined, and with what effect? Was the introduction of information technology significantly different, that is to say more participative than had been found to be the case in the more researched manufacturing sector?

A somewhat surprising and, from a trade union perspective, a depressing picture emerged. Although there had been a wide-ranging and extensive introduction of new technology, there had been little general sustained involvement of the work-force or union in the method of its introduction. Indeed the process of innovation had been largely management's province, conducted at a senior level, planned and implemented without the branches or their staff having much to say regarding its use and impact. Whilst the trade unions had exerted pressure and expressed their anxieties about the changes envisaged, they had achieved little in the form of regulatory controls or influence in the overall design process. Additionally, the branch staff expressed little in the way of concern or anxiety over the pace and direction of technical change. Interviews with branch staff revealed that they tended to be at a loss to describe the industrial relations effects of new technology, or to indicate ways in which they could actively intervene in the process of its introduction. Our overall impression was, first, of a smooth transition to, and incorporation of, the new technology, and second, of a marginalized staff with little control but with few anxieties regarding the changes taking place.

How did this situation come about? This sector has been seen as a potential flashpoint because of its extensive technological restructuring. Dire forecasts and warnings have been issued by both union and independent observers[2] who foresaw decisive shifts in the nature of the industry, changes that would subvert the career structure and at the same time lead to an upsurge in union activity over the issue. This chapter aims to assess the limitations of the union's institutional approach to regulating technological change, and also to explore the work-force's responses and attitudes to the effects of new technology at the workplace. These two aspects together may go some way to explain why we find the profile of involvement that we do.

UNION REACTION TO NEW TECHNOLOGY

In common with many unions when faced with extensive techno-logical change, the banking unions attempted to enmesh the banks in collective agreements that regulated both the pace and impact of change. In the context of the British situation this could not be statutorily based or drawn within a national framework of rules as such mechanisms were lacking. Instead it meant seeking agreement at sectoral level or with individual banks.

Both the Banking, Insurance and Finance Union (BIFU) and the (now defunct) Clearing Bank Union (CBU) called for the establish-ment of agreements on technological change with each bank. They produced pamphlets and documents outlining their scenarios for the industry based upon the worst case consequences, and detailing the possible impact that these would have.[3] In tandem with some other unions and staff bodies in other sectors, and in line with TUC thinking on technical change, one of the main approaches adopted was to propose that comprehensive New Technology Agreements (NTAs) be drawn up and agreed. The main thrust of such agreements are twofold. First the inauguration of *procedures* for consultation and negotiation over technological change is sought, including provisions relating to:

- mutuality/prior agreement before introduction of change;
- agreement on a host of associated areas;
- full provision of information;
- use of joint working parties committees;
- guarantees on equal rights and non-discrimination;
- written agreement as basis of proceeding;
- job guarantees written in.

The second set of elements refer more to the *substantive* aspects of change. Here the effect on jobs, job content, rewards, health and safety and other areas can be scrutinized and made the subject of bargaining. This structure is similar to the TUC/CBI Concordat on New Technology drawn up in 1979 but subsequently dropped after the CBI was prevented by membership hostility from being able to sign the jointly agreed package.[4] Both BIFU and the former Clearing Bank Union drew up model NTAs based on these broad principles.

However, since the publication of these model agreements, hardly any successful developments in this direction have been apparent. The BIFU has had localized success in the Co-operative Bank where an agreement was signed, and in the TSB where an 'arrangement' is in force that allows for consultation on a regular basis over the implementation of all new technology. Besides these, a branch of Lloyds Bank in Jersey concluded an agreement over a specific piece of equipment, but this local level could not be seen as a precursor to a more generalized approach. This failure to install NTAs was mirrored by the CBU who could not persuade any of the London Clearers to enter such agreements. The unions, it seems, could clearly document the likely process of technical change and its effects but were excluded from the process of its regulation. They could not take the initial steps towards a jointly written agreement allowing consultation or negotiation procedures. In assessing the kind of participation possible the CBU was clear:

All three staff unions are critical of the facilities for genuine involvement in the decision-making process and for real debate about the worrying problems of job deskilling and job loss arising from technological innovation. All too frequently the information provided is about projects already being implemented in an atmosphere which is more that of a courtesy briefing than a consultation.[5]

Far from achieving joint agreement, joint decision-making or even consultation, there was a tendency for the management to decide unilaterally, and then notify when it saw fit. In the interim the banking unions have, in line with the majority of unions, positively welcomed the new technology and accepted the competitive and business forces impelling the banks along this route.[6]

The absence of agreements seems to match the absence of membership pressure for change. The unions, in keeping with their long-term aim of securing NTAs, base this on the premise that the changes threatened by new technology will eventually lead to mass activity. 'What will change this is the build up of frustration-as the career progression that they believed was theirs is not happening.'[7] The issue is the subject of an uneasy peace; in this context it is the unions who appear to be scaremongers, with the banks pointing to a different appreciation of new technology at the membership level. Put simply, at national level the banking unions appear to have achieved less than many other white-collar unions when it comes to arranging new technology agreements.[8]

Why is this? Why is that the unions have been apparently wrong-footed in their new technology policies. As always there is no one answer to this question, but there are a number of interlocking points that might contribute to an explanation.

NEW TECHNOLOGY AND ITS EFFECT IN BANKING

Many of the claims regarding the effects of introducng information technology to banking have pointed to radical impacts in three main areas – rapid and substantial technological change; important effects on the branch structure made possible by this new technology; and finally the employment effect involving both job losses and revolutionary changes in working conditions. It was against this broad background that the debate on the changes and trends within the industry was conducted. In that debate there was a general over-emphasis on the importance of technological factors themselves, and an underestimation of the organizational and social moderators that can adapt and absorb change. In the event, these latter constraints meant that the expected developments either failed to happen or did so much more slowly.

Incrementalism

The timetable for transformation was thus not as sudden as the union statements were implying. Instead it was marked by incrementalism, taking place over a much longer period with a more complex and staged process than they had expected. The broad plan of technological change can be seen both chronologically and in relation to the automation of various banking functions. If we follow this latter classification we can identify three phases of technological innovation: back office automation; front office automation; and out of office automation.

Back office automation

This has tackled the processing of transactions involved in cheque handling, direct debiting, standing orders, bill payment and the ancillary business generated by corporate and personal customers. The growth of paperwork and its circulation within the system has been a major target of information technology. This means a largely paperless system is introduced which relieves the bank branches of much monotonous issuing and checking of vouchers. In 1981 the Back Office Automated Clearing System (BACS) handled over 489 million separate items of business.

Front office automation

Many of the innovations in the back office are linked with developments in front office automation. If the former can be designated as involving predominantly the servicing, storing and retrieval of customer accounts, then a simple description of front office functions is the transmission of money and the direct handling of customer accounts. The key to innovation here has been the personalized plastic card which is secure and gives access to a range of automated machinery. The most visible innovation has been the Automatic Teller Machines (ATMs) which, through the use of the plastic card and personal identification number, allow customers 24-hour access to cash. The other innovation spun off from the use of plastic cards has been the introduction of teller terminals or interactive counter terminals. These allow for a range of transactions to be handled without paper being exchanged.

Out of office automation

These are essentially extensions of the front office technology in three main areas. First, ATMs are not now necessarily linked to banking sites but can be 'stand alone' machines in supermarkets, shops, High Street or other locations. Second, there is the development of EFTPOS (Electronic Fund Transfer at the Point of Sale). Rather than using cheques or credit cards for retail transactions, this allows for the direct debiting of customer accounts by retail outlets. Potentially any point of sale, be it retail or commercial, can be linked to the central computer system to directly transfer funds between accounts. This development has been experimental, but is now coming on-stream due to an agreement between the banks on its extended use. This also allows for the vendor to issue money up to a fixed amount via the use of the plastic card, hence potentially expanding the cash transmission outlets for the banks well beyond the branch and ATM network. The final development – home banking – has now gone beyond the experimental stage and has a potential for the further fragmentation of banking business since it involves a direct or telephone link to domestic or office micros allowing transactions to be conducted that are normally only available in the branch. All of this suggests a general trend towards the detachment of certain functions historically restricted to the branch and their wider dispersal throughout the economy, but with this being achieved gradually and without the feared rapid closure of branches originally seen as the inevitable effect of new delivery mechanisms.

Branch structure

The process begun by the automation of banking functions does not end with the installation of the hardware. The reorganization of the money transmission and other services did mean a rethink about the expensive branch structure, and whether there was a need for all branches to retain all of their historic functions.

Satellite Banking as a concept was first introduced following the Midland Banks' branch network reorganization. The Midland proposed a structure that could capitalize on the changes technology had brought by the grouping of bank branches into area and service branches. Essentially, satellite banking involves the establishment of a central branch with corporate, administrative and directive powers surrounded by a number of service branches which take responsibility for money transmission, play an extended role in the marketing of bank services, and yet cater for the normal everyday needs of customers.

As 70 per cent of bank staff are employed in the branch network, any threat to that structure is perceived by the union and staff as very important: 'its diminution implies job loss and career blockage as the number of management posts decline' (BIS 1982). Again the evidence so far is inconclusive. The Banking Information Services study showed a drop of 1,100 branches in the period 1970–84. Whilst figures for branch reduction are modest overall, in the same period employment increased by more than 35 per cent (Willman and Cowan 1984). Once again the predicted effects were much less dramatic than had been originally forecast, and the branch structure has remained essentially intact.

Employment effect

In numerous pamphlets the unions have expressed anxieties about the direction of technological change, its likely impact on employment, and the overall long-term organizational/structural consequences that such developments suggest. Whilst it may be that the employment effects of new technology have not yet been significant, the major unions in the industry, the BIFU and the erstwhile CBU, have highlighted the potential for staff reductions consequent upon all of these developments and their potential combined impact on career prospects in what threatens to become a fragmented money transmission and branch structure. The chief fears are therefore concentrated upon the bank's strategy for reorganiza- tion, the development of 'out of office' and fragmented money transmission systems with their knock-on effects in terms of branch viability, and on the rationale for an extensive branch structure in expensive High Street locations.

The stated fears regarding direct unemployment appear not to have been realized to date.[9] Rather we find evidence of the increased use of part-time staff and a slow down in recruitment. The more dramatic effects of new technology have been in the field of transac- tion growth, in part spurred on by the ease of use of some of the machines but primarily in their ability to service a growth in all transactions. Hence the result has been the use of new technology to keep productivity (as measured by transaction/worker) rising. Figures given by the London Clearing Bank Statistical Unit suggest a staff increase over the period 1972–84 of just over 30 per cent, whilst there has been an increase in transactions of approximately

125 per cent in the same time span. More recent figures on employment show a continuation of the expansion of employment, with an increase in the national employment figure of 35 per cent between 1980 and 1990.[10] Measures of productivity are difficult to construct and must be treated with some caution; however, if we use the measure of cheques cleared/employees then a significant increase is again detected as Table 6.1 shows.

Table 6.1 Changes in cheque-processing productivity, 1971–81

	Cheques processed	No. of employees	Cheque/employee
1971	1,032m	176,000	586,000
1981	2,042m	233,000	874,000
Increase	+ 98%	+33%	+49%

Overall then, at the national level we find two contending accounts of technological change in banking being constructed. The unions' account stresses restructuring, job loss and work reorganization of a radical kind, with long-term career structures being undermined. The senior figures in the banks, however, stress the evolutionary nature of technological development, its adaptiveness, and its essentially supportive nature in so far as it can ease the routine work of bank staff, reducing paper handling and lessening the boring elements of the working day. They underline their perspective by drawing attention to the increase in both the application of new technology and the increase in bank staff employment.

In the struggle to define the situation, it appears that the reality has tended to confirm the employers' interpretation rather than that of the unions. However, there are other actors whose interpretation is critical – namely, staff in the branches. The Glasgow University research sought their opinions through a survey of over 320 bank members. Half of the sample was drawn from BIFU members spread across all the clearing banks, while the other half was drawn randomly from the clerical staff of a single clearing bank.[11] We wanted to know whether the branch staff saw technology as threatening or benign, what effect they felt it was having on their skills and job content, and how satisfied they were with the introduction, regulation and monitoring of technological change.

NEW TECHNOLOGY – THE WORK-FORCE APPROACH

The foregoing section has indicated the union position on new technology, and in some respects its weakness. The piecemeal but sustained introduction of automation largely bypassed the union negotiating machinery so that the working practices, the conditions and recruitment of staff were largely determined by management. The responses to our questionaire showed that the work-force's own fears about technological restructuring did not surface as a key industrial relations issue. Technology was merely one factor amongst others contributing to longer-term changes in the industry, and one that was not perceived as primarily threatening by the staff interviewed.

Even amongst union members the union's NTA strategy was seen as somewhat out of touch, and there was no question of the membership taking any action in support of it. That said, staff *did* perceive the introduction of new technology differently, as a previous longitudinal study of a Scottish Bank also revealed (MacInnes 1989). This seems due, first, to the general paternalistic environment. As many as 80 per cent of staff accepted that 'it's management's job to manage', especially in the area of new technology. More particularly, as new technology was implemented in a period of business growth, and amid transaction rate increases of 6–7 per cent per annum, this meant that pressure on staff to process the increasing business was actually relieved by the introduction of new information technology. This pattern of views was reinforced by the survey of bank staffs. When asked if technology had helped or hindered them in their job the result was clear, as Table 6.2 indicates.

Table 6.2 What difference has new technology made to your job?

	Bank staffs (%)	BIFU (%)
Job more boring	7	14
Made job easier	77	62
Made some other jobs worse	23	37
Made some other jobs better	74	67

There was some willingness to admit that other people's jobs had been made worse by new technology, especially among union members, but this was still a minority amidst an overwhelmingly positive evaluation. Research on the effect on skills and work pressure by Child *et al.* supports this position. They interviewed staff in three branches and found that:

The use of newer on-line technology improved the quality of staff employment both as assessed by observation and as expressed by the employees. Processing inputs and outputs at an on-line terminal required the new skill of terminal operation but also constituted a more rounded task. . . . On the whole the new technology also permitted staff to have a greater control over the pace and timing of their work.

(Child *et al.* 1983, 174)

In neither of our groups did female respondents indicate that they had suffered disproportionately from new technology, contrary to observations in other settings (Ramsay *et al.*, Chapter 5, this volume; Valentine, Chapter 7, this volume). However, other findings cited below sharply qualify this observation. There was a tendency for the unionized group to express slightly greater dissatisfaction in line with the figures quoted above. This is reflected in their response to whether they welcomed new technology, as shown in Table 6.3.

Table 6.3 Do you welcome new technology?

	Yes unreservedly (%)	Yes with reservations (%)	Worry about it (%)	NA (%)
BIFU Male	30	65	4	1
Female	20	76	3	0
BS Male	27	72	1	0
Female	23	70	4	2
Overall*	81 (25%)	225 (70%)	11 (3%)	3 (1%)

Note: * Refers to actual number of survey returns. The figures in parentheses are percentages of the response rate (see note 11 at chapter end).

The main worries that were put forward centred around the change in job content, a worsening environment, the limitation of promotion, and job satisfaction. Yet, as Table 6.4 suggests, none of these are mentioned by more than 20 per cent of bank staffs or 28 per cent of union members. Table 6.4 shows some notable differences between male and female responses, with male staff fears centring on career worries, whilst female respondents exhibited higher adverse reactions regarding job content, job satisfaction, environment and hours of work. In order to distinguish between the innovations, we asked which had the greatest impact in the past, and which was thought likely to affect them in the future. The responses showed how ATMs are being discounted as a threat to them. Two-fifths of staff had been affected in the past, but only a quarter see any influence on their jobs in the future. On the other hand, EFTPOS is seen as a potential threat, with 59 per cent of staff rating it of growing importance in the future. When asked if they had any

Table 6.4 Is new technology having an adverse effect on your job?

	BS			BIFU		
	M (%)	All (%)	F (%)	M (%)	All (%)	F (%)
Yes, promotion	17	11	5	33	27	18
Job content	13	20	24	21	28	39
Job satisfaction	11	15	18	20	21	21
Job security	11	11	11	20	19	17
Work environment	13	15	16	22	27	35
Hours of work	8	14	18	12	17	24

particular concerns, 34 per cent replied in the affirmative and, unprompted, these were overwhelmingly couched in terms of job loss and lack of future employment security.

The trade unions do not appear to have markedly raised their profile in dealing with new technology. Most employees felt that they had dealt adequately with the issue, but no more (see Table 6.5). They saw the process of introduction as one where they or their representatives were largely excluded from decision-making (see Table 6.6). The preferred format for handling technological change, on the other hand, would require active consultation or greater influence for the great majority (see Table 6.7).

These responses demonstrate the fact that even among BIFU members the need to secure New Technology Agreements has not struck home, with a preference being stated for general negotitaion. The gap between the actual perceived and preferred methods for dealing with the introduction of technology does not stop bank staff from expressing satisfaction with the unions' handling of the process,

Table 6.5 How have staff bodies dealt with new technology?

	Very well (%)	Adequately (%)	Poorly (%)	Badly (%)	NA (%)
BS	28	61	7	1	3
BIFU	13	70	13	3	1

Table 6.6 Format for work-force involvement in new technology

	Fully involved (%)	Consulted before (%)	Consulted after (%)	Informed before (%)	Informed during (%)	Not involved (%)
BS	1	6	8	35	27	15
BIFU	2	4	5	34	25	24

Table 6.7 How should new technology be introduced?

	Use NTA (%)	Negotiate mgt/union (%)	Consult about introduction (%)	Mgt act unilaterally (%)	Other answer (%)
BS	7	41	38	10	4
BIFU	12	55	23	8	2

Table 6.8 Has management protected work-force interests?

	Yes (%)	No (%)	Don't know (%)
BS	63	31	6
BIFU	42	54	4

yet at the same time seeing the process as one firmly within managements' prerogative. Indeed, there remains a minority in both samples who see it as a legitimate management area. This is underlined to some degree by Table 6.8 which shows that a high proportion of our respondents felt that management in their actions had looked out for staff interests during the implementation of technological change.

In sum, the respondents tended to display a relaxed and trusting approach to the banks' use of new technology. It did not appear as a threat, nor was its impact perceived to be as negative as many previous researchers, observers and experts predicted. The expectations of staff, their experience of conventional technology and their prior job content, combined with the benign perceived effect of the new technology in easing work load, reducing routine paper handling and opening up other areas of skill, led to positive evaluations of new technology overall. As Rajan has pointed out in relation to the finance sector in general:

> It is arguable whether new technology has 'deskilled' the clerical work. It has reduced demand for certain job-specific skills and promoted extreme job specialisation amongst keyboard operators. But clerical work in these industries was never skilled in the accepted sense that it involved significant discretion and autonomy. . . . Under the emerging work practices, there is an increasing emphasis on diagnostic skills needed for a number of separate functions now performed by clerical staff. Job enlargement is one outcome.

(Rajan 1984: 127)

One can see clearly how the subjective appreciation of the introduction of new technology by staff in the banks is incongruent with that put across by the unions in their literature and demands. This highlights the gulf between the unions' attempts to tightly regulate the innovation process and the more relaxed reality experienced by the workers who – lacking the sense of threat and perception of menace from technology – did not press for the inauguration of the participation formats that they clearly favoured.

OTHER INTERVENING FACTORS

A great deal of the explanation regarding the negative involvement of staff can be attributed to the evidence presented above. However, there are a number of other contextual features that supplement that explanation. One of these relates to the actual way technological innovation occurs in the banks. In discussions with branch staff, computer development people and senior management representatives, one can detect an exclusion of branch staff from the process of change, and identify how the circle of discussions about planning and implementation is circumscribed. To illustrate this, when asked if the branches had the opportunity to amend, detail or propose changes to new technology – if there was space for a role in the design and specification of the function of the technology – the reply was again almost wholly in the negative. This was put down to a number of factors.

First, the computer services section or electronic data processing divisions were physically separate and distinct units, apart from the retail body of the banks. Their staff had different qualifications, training and career structures. This meant that the opportunity for extensive involvement about the form and functions of the technology was, in the main, denied. Technical development of both hardware and software was highly centralized, and 'gifted' to the branches ready-made; it came in the form of a black box, as techniques to be learned, or as new disciplines to be mastered.

A further obstacle to participation developed out of the divisions between the computer literate and the computer illiterate, or between the centre and the periphery. Whilst this categorization overdraws the distinction somewhat, one of the reasons given for not putting bank managers 'on-line' was the lack of knowledge that would allow safe access to the centrally stored data. This had resulted in the systems developing a top-down orientation, rather than being an interactive end-user-oriented system. Accordingly, little concern was expressed about the technical problem-solving or participative abilities of branch staff. On the contrary, in the eyes of management this division of labour downgrades any serious role for whole layers of staff in the different phases of innovation.

Another factor to be considered is that the nature of technological innovation was not wholly within the control of the banks themselves. The number of suppliers to the industry was itself limited, with large multinationals such as IBM, NCB, Honeywell-Bull, etc. dominating the field. The banks' computer staffs admitted to a high degree of supplier direction in the design and specification of the actual technology, with often minimal input from them on the hardware side. Where some measure of discussion and involvement did occur, it was again at a level above the branch via specialist committees with the presence of a token branch banker to aid the planning unit. The range or potential for participation is thus circumscribed, and it remains difficult for branch personnel to gain any meaningful access to decision-making.

To speak of the division between the branch and the centre in terms of technological planning and development raises the question of other forms of 'division' between staffs that obstruct full participation in the innovation process. The 'gender' issue in banks is one such division that separates men's and women's experience of promotion, work task, and job satisfaction. In terms of new technology we saw from the survey that women as a group foresaw a worsening in their job content, work environment and job satisfaction as a result of its introduction. The other major feature to note was the increase in part-time workers as a way of dealing with transaction peaks during the day; in virtually all cases these part-timers were women.

The effects of new technology will continue to bear predominantly upon women, but within the banks it is this group that has the lowest expectations about careers and personal progress. The opening up of two-tier recruitment, part-time posts and reduced facility branches tied to lessened customer services has meant a greater use of women in ways that have re-emphasized the sexual discrimination of career opportunities rather than improving them. So, whilst the combined changes brought about by new technology are undermining internal labour markets within banks, they do not pose a similar challenge to all staff. For the male banker the threat is seen as marginal, hence the ideology of career progression can proceed whilst the reality of its breakdown is borne by others. Part of the problem of low participation may be the way in which the costs of technology have been adapted within the banks to bear on these who are least vocal, committed or involved in the regulatory process.

Connected with the gender issue is the banks' tradition of industrial relations based on paternalism, another element that contributes to staff acquiescence. Paternalism stems in part from male domination of the hierarchy, but is also expressive of a kind of relationship, a tenor or industrial relations based on a series of expectations about staff loyalty, staff deference to the bank, and to the right of management to manage. This is a two-sided relationship. The management expect their staff to be committed and loyal to the organization, while the grading system establishes a pattern of deference, subservience and respect that is accepted, provided all who are within it feel it will deliver to them similar status and deference in the future. Certain of the methods of promotion are based in the branch structure, leading to a tiered dependency relationship. Also the grades emphasize a diffuse rather than sharp division between management and staff. Indeed management are a strong force in the union, and this also effaces the clear distinction of them and us. The strength of the managerial prerogative and its legitimation depends on that code of 'gentlemanly behaviour' being followed, with the tenor of the industrial relations also placing obligations on management to provide a career structure, security, promotion chances, adequate remuneration, and a series of ancillary perks not found in other settings. Such paternalism is bolstered by the hierarchical division of labour and the sense of knowing one's place precisely within the organizational structure.

Changed technology and skills, and the need for different relationships of accommodation were thought to be breaking this down. Cowan describes the banks as traditionally fitting Tom Burns's description of a mechanistic organization:

> this type of structure has served them very well in the past. The question is whether it will serve them well in the future in a rapidly changing economic and technological environment. It would be wise to assume not and human resourcing managers should be considering how their organisation becomes more organic.
>
> (Cowan 1983: 22)

The mechanistic structure is suited to organizations faced with stabilized regularity, whereas the new competitive, technocratic and changing structures could demand an 'organic' approach to management and staff policies. There are some misconceptions in this picture: as we have seen, the organization of banks did not change radically at any stage having absorbed a great deal of change over a sustained period. In this sense paternalism and its practice within banks is a tangible asset in such circumstances. Staff trust in, and reliance upon, management acting in their interests has been noted in the survey results. Such a flexibility for management to act would be highly valued in such periods of change and innovation. This, together with the gathering evidence that the new technologies have few harmful effects on employees, has allowed great latitude to manage the social aspect. What we found was a general overemphasis of the technological influence, and an underemphasis of the organizational and social moderators that can adapt and absorb change. We found that the timetable for such a transformation was much longer and more complex than we anticipated, and that the work-force's own sense of anxiety about technological restructuring did not surface as a key industrial relations issue. Technology was one factor among others contributing to longer-term changes in the industry, but one that did not emerge as primarily threatening to the staff interviewed.

A final factor to be added to the explanation of the null-participation hypothesis in banking refers to the structure of the industry and its representation. The banking sector has strong similarities to the retail trade with its very high division of staff across numerous outlets. On average a branch size of twelve would be considered quite large. This situation may encourage personal contact but does not constitute an adequate basis for an industrial situation to develop, nor for a strong system of branch representation. Banks are centralized in their industrial relations. The seconded representatives (career bankers who take two years or so to represent the unions inside the banks) are given office space, secretarial provision and their wages from the banks. These representatives are national bank-wide figures who have contact with 'branches' but are no substitute for branch representation. The attempts at installing jointly accredited officed representatives have only achieved limited success, and the regional basis of many union branches effectively disenfranchises a number of the bank staff from influencing union policy, and even in some cases from voicing grievances.

These representational problems and the diffuseness of decision-making over new technology provide additional explanations regarding the low level of workplace/worker involvement in the innovation processes. This last point is by no means specific to banks. As Cressey and Williams (1990) have pointed out, the structure of workplace representation is problematic in a number of industries, being effectively inoperative at the enterprise or extra-enterprise sites where decisions are taken. Also, the diffuseness and abstract character of the decision-chain, representing a 'process' rather than an event, is not exclusive to banks. Rather, it is illustrative of many problems facing trade unions in their attempts to gain some purchase on change and its impact.

CONCLUSION

There has been an important shift in the 'technological problematic' facing the senior management of banks. This is premised on the deregulation of the industry and its growing market orientation, the changing role of new technology, and so the need to decisively revamp the human relations strategies they employ. These are the areas of concern that are now exercising the managers of all of the large British banks, and it seems the European ones as well. Researchers have found very similar processes at work in the French and Dutch banking system, with an impetus to modernize stemming from the twin pressures of internal deregulation and the threat of an open financial market post-1992 (see Bernoux *et al*. 1990). This latter pressure could prove catastrophic to certain banks if they fail to modernize and commercialize in time: 'Europe with 20% more branches and only 50% of the deposits per capita [compared with the USA] is grossly overbanked and will be the scene of a bloody battle between the banking giants, a banking industry "shake-out"' (Foreman 1989).

There are claims being made in some countries that the banking sector could turn out to be the 'steel industry of tomorrow', with wholesale and extensive restructuring required unless it improves its ability to sell new products and services and reach new customers. This indicates strongly that the banks' focus on the role of new technology is being reassessed, with new technology seen increasingly as a facilitator of market and product expansion, as an element in the struggle for competitive advantage. Research that solely centres upon the impact of new technology on a series of staff-based measures – redundancy, work-group practice, work satisfaction, deskilling, and so on, may obscure the wider role of transformation that new technology is making possible. The drive now on in most parts of the banking sector to adopt a new commerciality, founded on new technology based products, is coming up against the social, organizational and cultural aspects of these enterprises – that 'cultural baggage' that enterprises have inherited and cannot quickly jettison.

Examples of assets which may then become obstacles include staff expectations about their careers, jobs and environment; the stable if paternalistic pattern of industrial relations, training and its distribution; and the old hierarchies and patterns of deference. The banks appear to be having difficulties in making the transition to being market-driven organizations without an opening up of the branch structure and the inauguration of a new and more participative staff culture.

So, although the studies have found little in terms of participation, there is a need to widen out the discussion a little in order to speculate. Rather than look for a direct impact on staff attitudes or industrial relations procedures, we need to assess what information technology is doing in the medium to long term and its consequences for work-force involvement and participation. Seen in these terms, the innovations appear to be breaking down, albeit slowly, those hierarchical structures and strong internal labour markets that have existed within the industry.

These points give us some understanding of why the gulf exists between the stated union position of rigid controls over new technology and the divergent views of their members. However, this does not mean that the members' views are necessarily correct. Changes in the composition of the labour force that are now proceeding slowly may rupture due to the gathering market pressures, and may indeed challenge the male career structure. Once that is threatened by change, the need for extensive joint regulation and participation may be expressed more forcibly.

NOTES

1 This chapter draws upon evidence based in part upon research conducted during the period 1984–6 and financed by the ESRC. This research was primarily concerned with the development of industrial relations in the Banking sector between 1973–83. In addition to the author, the team also included Professor J. Eldridge and J. MacInnes.

2 Various reports have indicated that, given the maturity of technology, a harsher and more competitive environment and the need for branch reorganization spells the end of the 'honeymoon period' of innovation. Increases in business volume and staff employment are coming to an end. The PACTEL Report (1984) estimated a 5 per cent reduction in bank branches and a 10 per cent employment drop in Banking across Europe by 1990. Shaw and Coulbeck (1983) indicated a 12 per cent fall in employment from 1983–90, whilst Kirchner's 1984 study of British and European retail banking suggested; 'a medium-sized fall in employment is probable by 1990'. See also *Banking Information Services*, Lombard Street, London, 1982, page 5.

3 Union technology publications include *Jobs for the Girls? The Impact of Automation on Women's Jobs in the Finance Industry*, BIFU, Wimbledon, 1984. *Microtechnology: A programme for Action*, BIFU, Wimbledon, 1983.
4 For a detailed description of the Concordat see I. Benson and J. Lloyd, *New Technology and Industrial Change*, Kogan Page, London, 1983.
5 Interview conducted with John Cousins, then General Secretary of CBU, 1986.
6 W. Daniel has published a book detailing the WIRS response to a range of questions specifically related to new technology. See *Workplace Industrial Relations and Technical Change*, Frances Pinter, London, 1986.
7 Interview with Lief Mills, 1986.
8 P. Willman, *New Technology and Industrial Relations; A Review of the Literature*, Dept. of Employment Discussion Paper No. 56, London, 1983. For a review of the characteristics of white-collar new technology agreements see Williams and Steward, 'New technology agreements: an assessment', *Industrial Relations Journal* 16 (3), 1985.
9 See P. Cressey, *Industrial Relations in British Clearing Banks*, CRIDP Report, Glasgow, 1985. A. Rajan, *New Technology and Employment in the Financial Service Sector*, Gower, Aldershot, 1984; and P. Willman and A. Cowan, 'New technology in banking: the impact of auto-tellers on staff number', in M. Warner (ed.), *Microprocessors, Manpower and Society*, Gower, Aldershot, 1984. Recent evidence collected in 1990 is beginning to tell a slightly different story. The adverse market situation and the growth in bank and finance sector competition is now drawing banks into large-scale job cuts, including for the first time compulsory redundancies. See *Industrial Relations and Innovation in Services: The British Banking Sector*, a report to the French Ministry of Labour by P. Cressey and P. Scott, IRIS, Paris, 1991.
10 ibid. (note 9 applies in its entirety).
11 Two samples each of 500 were randomly drawn from the current BIFU membership list and the participating bank. The response rate was 32 per cent, about average for a mail-shot questionnaire.

REFERENCES

Banking Information Services (1982) Lombard Street, London.
Benson, I. and Lloyd, J. (1983) *New Technology and Industrial Change*, London, Kogan Page.
Bernoux, P., Eldridge, J., Cressey, P. and MacInnes, J. (1990) *New Technology, Organisation and Culture in a Scottish and French Bank* ESRC/CNRS Report, Bath/Glasgow, May.
BIFU (1983) *Microtechnology: A Programme for Action*, Wimbledon, BIFU.
—— (1984) *Jobs for the Girls? The Impact of Automation on Womens' Jobs in the Finance Industry*, Wimbledon, BIFU.
Child, J., Loveridge, B., Harvey, J. and Spencer, A. (1984) 'Micro Electronics and the Quality of Employment in Services', in P. Marstand (ed.), *New Technology and the Future of Work and Services*, London, Frances Pinter.

Cowan, L. C. (1983) *Personnel Management and Banking*, Institute of Bankers pamphlet, London.

Cressey, P. (1985) *Industrial Relations in British Clearing Banks*, CRIDP Report, Glasgow.

—— and Williams, R. (1990) *Participation in Change: New Technology and the Role of Employee Involvement*, Dublin, European Foundation.

—— and Scott, P. (1991) *Industrial Relations and Innovation in Services: The British Banking Sector*, Report to the French Ministry of Labour, Paris, IRIS.

Foreman, C. (1989) *Wall Street Journal*, April.

Daniel, W. W. (1986) *Workplace Industrial Relations and Technical Change*, London, Frances Pinter.

Kirchner, E. (1984) *The Social Implications of Introducing New Technology in the Banking Sector*, Brussels, EC DGV.

MacInnes, J. (1988) 'Participation in Scotbank', in R. Hyman and W. Streeck (eds), *New Technology and Industrial Relations: International Experience*, Oxford, Blackwell.

Rajan, A. (1984) *New Technology and Employment in the Financial Service Sector*, Aldershot, Gower.

Shaw, E. and Coulbeck, N. (1983) *UK Retail Banking Prospects in the Competitive 1980s*, London, Stanisland Hall.

Williams, R. and Steward, F. (1985) 'New technology agreements: an assessment', *Industrial Relations Journal* 16 (3).

Willman, P. (1983) *New Technology and Industrial Relations; A Review of the Literature*, Dept of Employment Discussion Paper No. 56, London.

—— and Cowan, A. (1984) 'New technology in banking: the impact of auto-tellers on staff number', in M. Warner (ed.), *Microprocessors, Manpower and Society*, Aldershot, Gower.

7 Gender, technology, and democracy at work

Lynn Valentine

The introduction of information technology, it is widely argued, may well have significant consequences for those who work with it. But those consequences are not innate in the technology itself, which affords a range of choices of application, including alternative options for work organization. Management may impose the changes, or may willingly or unwillingly negotiate them with its employees or their representatives. The ensuing arrangements may enskill those working with IT, deskill them, or recompose work in a more complex fashion not easily labelled in these ways. Optimistic discussions of the potentially liberating and skill-enhancing nature of IT are qualified by the gloomy predictions of labour process theory, stressing the capacity of computerization to routinize and control most work where it does not eliminate it altogether.

The analysis of management policy has been predominantly shaped by one of two approaches. Feldberg and Glenn (1981) identifiy these as the 'consensual research model' and the 'critical research model'. The former stresses harmony between employees and management, assured by the mutual benefits for workers and management arising from IT. The latter, on the other hand, views IT as a means for management to increase control over the workplace by centralizing knowledge in their own hands and directing more employees more closely. Thus Franco di Benedetti, when managing director of Olivetti, argued that IT was 'basically a technology of coordination and control of . . . the white collar workers taylorian organisation does not cover' (quoted in Huws 1982: 26).

A third possibility is that management neglects or is unable to apply any clear policy on work organization related to the introduction of IT. Thus Storey, in his study of computerization in the insurance industry, comments on the 'apparent lack of constraint', in which an expected management assault on employee control had not materialized, creating what he calls a 'phoney war'. Crompton and Jones (1984), however, have suggested that there is a long-run tendency towards task routinization and the centralization of control arising from computerization, even where this is not pursued in a direct and clear-cut manner.

Findings relating to these different approaches seem to offer conflicting conclusions. Optimistic, consensual expectations appear confirmed by some studies, while others affirm a process of increasing management control, reducing skill levels, and work intensification. In support of Storey, change is often far less radical than either of these views predicts. Yet each of these interpretations seems flawed not only by its partiality, but by its tendency to aggregate and generalize. This is linked with a particular weakness in the conceptualization of choice and determination with which we began.

While technology may afford choices, and in this sense IT equipment may be relatively neutral in its effects, it is neither designed nor applied in a vacuum. Rather, the way it is fashioned, and the way it is subsequently operated, will reflect the prevailing climate into which it is introduced. Determinations and constraints may thus be built into the *social* structures within which IT is set. Management ideologies, market circumstances, and dominant available understandings of what the new technology does and in what manner, are amongst the factors which shape managerial policy and practice, however much they appear to have (and feel themselves to have) a choice.

This chapter is particularly concerned with one area of social constraints – the influence of relations and perceptions on the question of gender. It seeks to ask how far this factor is determinate in its effects, and in what ways it influences the implementation and impact of IT on women at work. This returns us to the other related point: that to talk of effects of IT in general terms fails to consider that effects may be differential. To some extent this is recognized by Feldberg and Glenn (1981) when they argue that a critical approach requires attention to the fact that particular groups of workers may suffer job loss or degradation. That this will tend to be true in particular for those already with least control prior to the introduction of IT has been argued elsewhere in this volume (see Chapter 1), and that power relations tend particularly to disfavour women is now almost universally accepted.

The discussion will continue with a brief review of the dimensions of gender inequality as it relates to contemporary technological change. The extent to which this is an immutable state of affairs, locked in place and reproduced by power and ideological perception based in the wider society, or else subject to change and possible improvement over time, will also be examined. To test the possibilities for change, it is argued that we must look not only at routine clerical work, where powerlessness is most compounded, but at professional and technical occupations with a significant female presence. The main body of the chapter examines the case of gender and computerization of librarianship to contribute to this inquiry.

INFORMATION TECHNOLOGY AND WOMEN'S PAID WORK

A pessimistic feminist analysis would conclude that women's experience at work has been and will continue to be shaped primarily by patriarchal gender relations. Patriarchy can be broadly defined as 'a system of interrelated social structures through which men exploit women' (Walby 1986). Its prime focus has been variously located in the domestic sphere of motherhood and housework (Eisenstein 1979, Delphy 1984), or in the workplace and the capitalist labour process itself (Hartmann 1979). Either way, gendered power is seen as a system of closure through which male advantage and female disadvantage is reproduced and even extended through control over computerization and related changes in work organization (Game and Pringle 1983, Cockburn 1985).

A more optimistic and less deterministic analysis would accept the existence of inequality and disadvantage for women, including that defined by supposed technical expertise. A number of factors may operate to weaken this, including the economic pressures on employers to maximize talent utilization, and to obtain skilled labour in the context of such challenges as the so-called 'demographic time-bomb', or the ground made by the counter-ideology and powerful reasoning of feminism itself. The openings for change may be particularly evident in professions where both sexes are present, but women are in the majority and have seen past (if isolated) examples of significant advance. Here, in occupations such as teaching or various areas of medicine, the denial that women can exercise technical and management skills may become ever-harder to maintain. The disadvantages of domestic commitments and career breaks are not thereby removed, of course, so marked inequalities are likely to endure, thus weakening the optimists' argument.

A review of evidence on the dynamic of work organization and technological change as it relates to gender lends considerable force to a pessimistic reading of experience to date. Broadly, three mutually reinforcing aspects of female disadvantage emerge: childhood and adult socialization, non-work responsibilities and burdens, and handicaps in the workplace itself. Even if the first, and perhaps the second, of these are weakened, the third may remain in place: in other words, even if women cease to perceive themselves as unsuited for certain work roles, other constraints on their advance may continue to thrive. Since our own focus is the workplace, the remainder of this discussion will concentrate there.

Workplace disadvantage itself has a number of interconnected dimensions. One is the sex-typing of work tasks, which entails that most women work in occupations that are seen as 'feminized'. This has been described as 'the ten deadly 'c's: catering, cleaning, cashiering, clerking, counter-minding, clothes-washing, clothes-making, coiffure, child minding, and care of the sick' (Reid and Wormald 1982). Women are thereby concentrated in the lower-paid, lower-status, more routine jobs. These are also the tasks with least control vested in them, most likely to be subjected to management control, and so, too, the women performing them are usually subordinate to a male.

These jobs are also those most likely to be subjected to insecurity (for example via the use of part-time or temporary labour routinization – Crewe 1991), and to be deskilled and routinized by the application of computerized information systems. Clerical or typing non-manual work is particularly subject to the new technologies (Baldry 1988), which some believe are being deskilled in a long-term process (beginning long before current innovations) of office rationalization (Crompton and Jones 1984). There are problems in measuring this process, created by the relativistic notions of 'skill' itself. Skill may be identified by technical complexity or by the exercise of discretion (Rolfe 1990), but it may also be read onto tasks through the power of a group of workers to get themselves defined as skilled, a capacity more likely to be available to men in practice (Cockburn 1985). Thus the ability to resist deskilling in the first two senses is reinforced by the virtuous circle of status and control wielded over official perception. There is, conversely, a vicious circle for the less powerful groups.

This is echoed further in the problems of regrading and training. Particularly (but not at all exceptionally) where new technology is introduced, there will be conflict over demands for training to use it, and for regrading to recognize newly acquired skills. But if job changes cannot be defined as requiring greater skill, and/or if employees are left to obtain the knowledge to operate the new equipment themselves, the pressures of change will not receive concomitant rewards. Again, there is plentiful evidence that these are key issues, and that women are disadvantaged sharply in these spheres also (Liff 1990). Crompton and Jones (1984) argue that in mixed-sex office settings, men actually 'need' women who are disadvantaged in obtaining the credentials (including formal quali-fications through night-school) required for promotion; it is this which makes their own life-chances better.

When we turn to the processes of representation and participation, once again the disadvantages of women workers tend to be reinforced rather than alleviated. The problems of women in gaining an equal voice with male members in trade unions is thoroughly documented (Cockburn 1983, Boston 1980, Pollert 1981, Wajcman 1983), so that even were the unions effective in gaining influence over changes (which several contributions in this volume alone show they are not) this might well not benefit them as greatly as men. Notwithstanding this, there are some signs that unions are trying to respond to these shortcomings, and that women are exerting increasing if still limited influence over the setting of priorities (Ellis 1988, Kelly and Heery 1988). None the less, it has been argued that the tone and content of typical labour movement demands for 'industrial democracy' have remained fixated largely on the needs of skilled male workers, neglecting the democratic expression of women's needs (Phillips 1983).

As for management attempts to encourage participation, these may well be more popular with women than men, but largely perhaps because they offer at least some channel of influence when the union blocks them out, as in Pollert's study (1981) of female tobacco workers. Attempts to draw women into user-involvement in the implementation of computerized information systems have failed for the most part to afford genuine influence, and appear at times more as a means for gaining the acceptance and co-operation of employees in the process of change (Liff 1990, Beirne and Ramsay 1988).

The effect of IT on this system of disadvantage has been suggested already at various points in the discussion. While IT might be thought to reduce the need for job segregation in many areas, in practice it more often replicates and even reinforces it. Control over the knowledge and discretionary use of computerized systems tends to be cornered by those with existing work control. The ideology of 'technical' skills also sets it firmly in the male camp; equipment which women use (for example, for word processing) is not thought of as technology in use. Moreover, 'Every woman knows that when she is operating a machine – any machine – if it breaks down and she asks a man to help her she is likely to be blamed, criticised and patronised by the man' (Rowe 1986). The problems of training access, and of obtaining the acknowledgement that new skills have been learned, is thus made all the more difficult for women.

The experience of IT is thus likely to be far less positive for women than men, especially men in technical or professional jobs (see Ramsay *et al.*, Chapter 5, this volume). Yet studies of employee attitudes to IT suggest that even amongst women it is generally well-received. Liff's (1990) study of women office workers in the West Midlands found that almost three-fifths thought the skill level of their jobs higher after the introduction of IT, while two-fifths thought the interest level higher. Two-fifths also thought the stress level higher, though. A more general study of attitudes to new technology conducted as part of the British Social Attitudes survey in 1987 (Witherspoon 1988) found that 75 per cent of the 'salariat' (professional and managerial, predominantly male) class said new technology had affected their work for the better, as did 67 per cent of the (predominantly female) routine non-manual group. Indeed, attitudes to new technology remain generally positive, though such responses should be interpreted with caution (see Liff 1990, and Chapter 1 of this volume).

None the less, there appear to be grounds for examining whether the gender issue overwhelms other factors relating to new technology in all contexts of female work. Rolfe (1990) has reported that professional workers had a markedly more positive experience of IT introduction than clerical workers, though the possible gender dimensions of this difference are not explored. As indicated earlier, this chapter will now examine the position of women in the librarianship profession, and their experience and reaction to IT relative to males in the same profession, as a means of exploring the more general themes raised in this section.

LIBRARIES AND WOMEN'S EMPLOYMENT

Prior to the information technology 'revolution', librarianship had its roots in the humanities and social sciences, with library work being characterized by 'traditional' methods of working – on cataloguing and classifying text acquisitions, for instance. Most library employment is within the public sector, and involves the accumulation by individuals of extensive skills and knowledge beyond the obvious levels of literacy required. The professional status of the work has long been promoted through the existence of a professional body, the Library Association (LA), which awards the Associate and full Fellowship membership status which exerts an important influence on career progression, and the establishment of training courses (with the first University-level school opening in 1918).

As with many administrative and clerical types of work, librarianship was initially a male preserve. When three female library assistants were appointed in 1871 in the Manchester Free Public Libraries (Baker 1880), this was the first 'breakthrough' appearance of women outside of a few employed in private subscription libraries. Gradually, though, their numbers increased, and a role was recognized for them in the profession. Their role was a 'helpful' or supportive one to males (though the work content of the sexes differed for the most part), and also they were seen as 'decorative' and so more popular for attendance on readers (Burrington 1987, Baker 1880). Finally, their pay was typically about two-thirds of that of male librarians, affording a further attraction to those who held the purse-strings.

Although initial advances in the proportion of library employment occupied by women were slow in the UK (far more so than in the USA, for instance), 25 per cent of library workers were female by the 1920s, this figure rising to around 60 per cent by the 1940s, then stabilizing until the mid-1960s, after which it increased to its present level of around 75 per cent (Burrington 1987). In a familiar pattern, however, men continued to dominate senior positions, a feature which some (male) commentators regarded as the only factor rescuing the profession from being downgraded by feminization. In 1987, female chief librarians were only 11 per cent of all chief librarians in English public libraries, 27 per cent of those in Scottish public libraries, 3 per cent of those in Polytechnic libraries, and 23 per cent of those in Universities (Ritchie 1987).

This was reinforced by the ban on married women, which operated in some places until the early 1960s, forcing many female librarians to 'resign' if they chose not to remain single (Liddle 1941, Fransella 1973). Subsequent labour shortages in the 1960s, now being reproduced in the 'demographic crisis' of the 1990s, have led to desperate efforts to attract married women back to the profession, but a period away is still likely to leave its mark on career progress.

The general level of pay in library work has traditionally been poor by professional standards, but even within the existing pay scales, Siebert and Young (1978) found strong evidence of discrimination, with married men consistently receiving the highest reward and married women the poorest even after allowing for seniority differences (and all the inequalities we have seen those imply). Far greater inequalities between rewards for men and women, though, arise from the prevalence of women in part-time and lower grade work, these two factors overlapping heavily. In a recent study in a University Library, Luck (1991) found that 94 per cent of women employees were employed on the lowest grades, as library 'assistants', while the few males occupied the senior posts. Three-quartes of women worked part-time, and occupied all but one part-time post in the library.

While the part-time women on the assistant grades were defined as less skilled, Luck found that they had comparable educational qualifications to full-timers. Moreover, they reported that the work they were actually allocated required them to use skills and knowledge officially needed only for higher grade work, which went unrewarded under the existing system. Nor were the part-time women an unstable work-force, with four-fifths having over four years' service in their present job. Work was seen as an important feature of their lives by most, though their present work patterns were constrained in most cases by domestic responsibilities. Luck's study thus confirms the disadvantage and inequality discussed earlier for women at work in general, though socialization appears to play a lesser role than domestic constraints or structures of unequal employment chances and recognition of skills at work.

Representation provides one possible counter to this situation. But there are few signs of it having a major impact on improving women's position, and it may even reinforce inequality. Thus the LA took until 1987 to issue any statement at all on the question of equal pay. The Association itself has had only two female presidents (in 1966 and 1988), and its council remains male-dominated despite the prevalence of women in the profession as a whole (only 31 per cent of its membership being female in 1988). In response to this a Women in Libraries group was established in 1980, remaining separate from the LA to maintain independence (but thereby losing an important channel for articulating its case). In University libraries, AUT and NALGO have gradually recognized and publicized aspects of women's position, but not with any great apparent impact to date, as Luck's (1991) survey seems to confirm.

INFORMATION TECHNOLOGY AND LIBRARY WORK

The arrival of IT has impacted on and been shaped within this situation. The traditional skills derived from the humanities and arts are still of relevance to the profession, but new skills are having to be learned as a direct result of innovations affecting the structure of the work. By its very nature, librarianship is a profession that is central to the emergent information society, and the nature of librarianship is changing to meet this role.

Information technology is increasingly likely to occupy a central role in the work of librarians. Whereas microelectronics 'is often thought to herald the death of the professions' (Newton 1981), in some respects it could be the making of librarianship. The possibilities IT holds for libraries have hardly begun to be realized, but several major innovations have already taken place. Most large library systems are using some form of computerized catalogue production (for example, confiche) with cataloguing (OPACS) and network access. These systems have changed the ways in which libraries handle most of their basic internal routines and processes, as well as offering them the ability to link with other libraries in a more effective manner than in the past (Dowlin 1984).

While these developments are to a large extent dependent on the library's own resources, it is significant that most librarians will have to be trained to deal with them as they are realized. This raises particular issues for women's employment, as we have seen in other contexts. Domestic and other social pressures may well make it harder for women to find the time and energy to undertake additional training courses. Moreover, those women taking career breaks might be expected to find re-entry and subsequent progression still harder in a time of technological change, when their earlier skills are being superseded; technology may thus act as a further disadvantaging barrier, reinforcing socialization and life-cycle pressures as well as surviving discriminatory practices.

The surveys

In order to examine some of the general features of gendered work expectations in libraries, and to explore the specific changes in these areas associated with the introduction of IT, it is necessary to rely largely on the results of the fieldwork carried out by the author from this point in the analysis.

The research reported here was carried out in 1989 among practising librarians and among students on undergraduate and postgraduate librarianship courses. In all, sixty-nine questionnaires were collected from those studying to be librarians (a response rate of 56 per cent), examining their career aspirations (and, where relevant, their past experience of employment in the profession). This will be referred to below as the Student Survey.

A further sixty-two questionnaires (a response rate of 52 per cent) were returned by practising librarians (male and female) in Scotland. These provide the basis of some of the career information discussed here, but also the findings on work organization and the impact of IT which are the central concern of the chapter. Questionnaires were distributed to various types of libraries, and returns were distributed representatively across the different departments and functions in each. This element of the research will be referred to below as the Librarian Survey.

TRAINING, CAREERS AND IT

Training and retraining are seen as vital in opening up information technology opportunities in all areas of employment, but the fact that libraries have undergone such rapid information technology changes in the past decade makes it doubly important. Most library schools now offer high standards of information technology training, but for many practising librarians any technological training has come about almost by accident. For example, most of the practising librarians in the Librarian Survey had experienced on-the-job training. Some had attended external or internal courses supplementing this, but the majority (60 per cent) had experienced on-the-job training and nothing more. Where formal training had been given (for example in on-line accessing), this usually involved only an introduction over one or two days (and one woman reported that she had missed even this as she was on maternity leave at the time, with no further provision being made).

The rating given to overall training (not just in information technology, since the library survey question was of a wider scope than this) is summarized in Table 7.1. This reveals a fairly moderate assessment overall, with females more likely than males to make both a definite positive or negative evaluation. None the less, differences in the view of training between the two sexes are not great.

Formal access to training did not differ as between males and females although, as we have seen from the example above, females may miss out on training 'informally' as a consequence of domestic commitments. Of those who suggested improvements to training, most just wanted 'more', although of those who elaborated their response 34 per cent thought that training specifically in information technology aspects of the job could be improved.

Table 7.1 Evaluation of training provision (Librarian Survey)

	Rating	
	Males (%)	Females (%)
Good	7.5	19
Adequate	50	39
Rather inadequate	12	22
Very poor	7.5	17
No answer	23	3

If we consider career patterns and aspirations more widely, it is useful to look first at the Student Survey, and to subdivide the results further as between undergraduate and postgraduate respondents. Amongst undergraduates, reasons for undertaking the course primarily involved 'interest' or 'self-development', rather than a more focused or instrumental aim. Male/female differences were small and suggested no particular pattern. Self-development was far less important for postgraduates, and while interest still figured prominently, career matters now came to the fore (promotion chances, obtaining licentiateship, career change). While male respondents were markedly more likely than females to emphasize self-development and obtaining licentiateship, the overall pattern is still not suggestive of a consistent and coherent gender difference in reasons for studying.

Most of the students were quite ambitious in their aspirations of the level they hoped to reach in library work, though postgraduates (more of whom had perhaps tempering experience of work in the service already) seemed a little less so. Again, and for both undergraduates and postgraduates, there were no significant differences between men and women on this issue. Membership of professional bodies was almost universal, and reported attendance at meetings showed similar patterns from each sex. Contrary to findings in many professions, then, career aspirations are strikingly similar across the gender divide.

If we look at the Librarian Survey, this demonstrates that more than three-quarters of both men and women are members of the Library Association. As with the students, reported attendance rates (which may be taken as a reasonable indicator of professional commitment and involvement) were fairly similar between the two sexes, though males were a little more likely to attend 'regularly' or 'sometimes' (54 per cent as against 44 per cent of female respondents).

None the less the positions achieved on the occupational ladder give a strong echo of the position in other professions, or those reported earlier from Luck. Over 80 per cent of males, but only 36 per cent of females, were at departmental/service head level or higher. Women were much more likely, consequently, to be at assistant librarian or trainee status levels. Of the women replying to the questionnaire, 22 per cent reported specific experience of discrimination, between them mentioning promotion, training, work allocation, and access to new technology support systems. As one general comment by a female senior librarian put it, most disadvantage is less specific:

> The assumption seems to be that in a low status and lowly paid profession like librarianship it is only fitting that any men in it should rise to the top. Women are permitted to assist them provided they behave as temporary men. Men managers display photographs of their families on their desks; women with desks do not. Such a display would work against their 'working' persona.

It appears, then, that it is external rather than internal constraints which predominate in disadvantaging female librarians (see also Ritchie 1987). They experience disadvantage despite attitudes and behaviour which seems to be indistinguishable from that of their male colleagues in key respects.

THE EXPERIENCE OF NEW TECHNOLOGY

Newton (1981) suggests that 'new technology in libraries at present has a tendency to be used to economise, at the expense of jobs. . . . Women are not necessarily freed to enjoy more interesting work as this work isn't available.' In order to confirm or correct this statement it is helpful to see how technology has affected the working conditions of those taking part in the Librarian Survey, male and female.

A total of 23 per cent of males and 28 per cent of females in the Librarian Survey reported that they had not experienced any technological change at work. The changes experienced by the remainder can be broken down into different areas, as indicated in Table 7.2 where it can be seen that a wide range of applications of IT have affected a large proportion of staff, both male and female. The fact that males use desktop publishing and word processing to a greater extent even than females indicates a difference between the library and an ordinary office, where these would be expected to be the

Table 7.2 Impact of technology on librarians

	Males (%)	Females (%)	All (%)
Word processing	50	35	41
Use of PRESTEL, CEEFAX, ORACLE	15	8	13
Database management	40	33	43
On-line retrieval from external databases	35	58	61
On-line retrieval from in-house databases	55	28	46
Electronic interlibrary loan system	–	14	11
Electronic mail system	30	11	22
Automated data entry	50	25	41
Electronic/desktop publishing	50	11	21
Other	25	14	21

preserves of mainly female secretarial workers. While there are other differences in the gender pattern of use of IT, there is no very obvious pattern beyond those attaching to seniority (with its gender base, of course) in the use of equipment.

However, the important questions, as we have argued earlier, concern not what technologies exist *per se*, but the context in which they are put to use. As Crompton and Jones (1984) put it, 'The benefits of microtechnology could well be invaluable if used in the proper manner.' But how far has the 'proper manner' been adopted in libraries? Alternatively, have patterns emerged along the lines found for much clerical work where IT has been used to a significant extent as a controlling and discriminatory device?

Those male and female librarians who had experienced technological change in their present workplace (77 per cent of men, 72 per cent of women) were asked to indicate in what direction and how far selected aspects of their job had changed. The results are shown in Table 7.3. First, the overall reported effects of IT as experienced by these practising librarians are of interest. The most stable of the factors (those that have not changed to any great degree) are, in descending order: sociability of job; job security; relations with management; and promotion prospects. The first and third of these indicate that IT has not affected everyday interaction, a feature of other forms of professional and administrative work (see, for example, Ramsay *et al.*, Chapter 5, this volume). In other respects, too, the findings echo those in comparable work elsewhere. Thus on balance an increase in the pace of work is reported (by 65 per cent), and 42 per cent also reported increased stress. The range of work performed is reported to have increased, rather than jobs becoming more repetitive for the majority (63 per cent), though this may be

Table 7.3 The effects of IT on aspects of work

	Increased greatly (%)	Increased a little (%)	Unchanged (%)	Decreased a little (%)	Decreased greatly (%)
Job security	–	8	70	20	2
Promotion prospects	4	17	61	11	7
Work supervision	2	24	48	24	2
Pace of work	17	48	28	7	–
Responsibility	11	46	30	9	4
Amount of stress	14	28	54	2	2
Job interest	28	32	22	7	11
Decisions on work method	11	17	50	20	2
Range of activities performed	24	39	26	11	–
Sociability of job	2	15	74	7	2
Relations with management	4	20	61	8	7

seen as a possible source of pressure also. The same two-edged interpretation may be given to the increase in reported responsibility (especially without concomitant promotion) by 57 per cent.

On the other hand, reported job interest has also risen for three-fifths of the librarians replying, indicating as in other studies the positive side of changes arising from the introduction of IT. However, the ability to make decisions on their own job has not apparently increased in line with other changes for these respondents, with only 28 per cent reporting an increase on this dimension and 22 per cent reporting a reduction. Given the reported increase in responsibility noted above, this is a disappointing (not to say potentially disturbing) finding.

None the less, these results do not substantiate the more pessimistic views of IT, which suggest that it will undermine autonomy and job control. They reflect the fact that technology remains for the most part a supportive aid to the provision of existing facilities, rather than displacing or transforming the nature of the professional librarian's labour process. Of course, these are early days to be making a long-term judgement on such issues, since much of the equipment is still settling in and further systems developments are certain.

GENDER DIFFERENCES IN THE EXPERIENCE OF IT

Let us now analyse these results further, to investigate the effects of IT on patterns of inequality between male and female librarians. In Table 7.4, 'M' stands for male respondents, and 'F' for females. An analysis of Table 7.4 reveals a number of sharp differences between men and women, markedly changing some of the impressions given by the combined results. More than a third of females experienced a decline in job security as a result of information technology, for instance. A significant minority (31 per cent) also perceived a worsening of promotion prospects, in contrast to males, who all saw these extrinsic aspects of their jobs as unchanged or improved. These findings are consistent with the observations on actual (though not formal) access to training and use of equipment reported earlier. The figures for this area seem to correlate with a gendered revision of the reskilling/deskilling thesis, whereby some jobs are upgraded (particularly for males) while others remain static or become deskilled. They also imply that the 'protection' that professional work at first sight gives through the supportive rather than displacing or routinizing application of IT is heavily compromised for women, partly through their concentration in the lower grades of the occupation.

None the less, on a number of aspects of work content and workplace relations, fairly similar results are reported by males and females. These include pace of work, responsibility, amount of stress, range of activities performed, sociability of the job, and relations with management (though stress and pace are reported to have increased by rather more women than men). These results taken by themselves might be seen to suggest that the effect of new technology on the experience of work was roughly the same for both males and females. Apart from the differences noted already, though, other divergences contradict this picture.

Most notable are the aspects of work experience with IT relating most closely to the theme of this collection: those related to control, and so to democracy at work. For instance, 31 per cent of females but no males indicated that job interest had decreased (and 19 per cent that it had decreased 'greatly'), reviving the deskilling issue. This is reinforced in the area of decisions on work methods, where 30 per cent of females indicated that autonomy on decision-making had

Table 7.4 Work changes experienced (by gender)

	Increased greatly (%)	Increased a little (%)	Unchanged (%)	Decreased a little (%)	Decreased greatly (%)
Job security	–	M 15	M 80	–	M 5
	–	F 4	F 61	F 35	–
Promotion prospects	M 5	M 20	M 75	–	–
	F 4	F 15	F 50	F 19	F 12
Pace of work	M 15	M 45	M 35	M 5	–
	F 19	F 50	F 23	F 8	–
Responsibility	M 5	M 50	M 40	M 5	–
	F 15	F 42	F 23	F 12	F 8
Amount of stress	M 10	M 25	M 60	M 5	–
	F 15	F 31	F 50	–	F 4
Job interest	M 30	M 45	M 25	–	–
	F 27	F 23	F 19	F 12	F 19
Decisions on work method	M 10	M 25	M 55	M 10	–
	F 12	F 12	F 46	F 26	F 4
Range of activities performed	M 25	M 35	M 30	M 10	–
	F 23	F 42	F 23	F 12	–
Sociability of job	–	M 20	M 70	M 5	M 5
	F 4	F 12	F 77	F 7	–
Relations with management	M 5	M 20	M 65	M 10	–
	F 4	F 19	F 57	F 8	F 12

decreased as a result of information technology, though only 10 per cent of males thought this.

These results show the danger of generalized conclusions about the impact of IT on work control which do not consider the differential impact on various sub-groups, in which gender divisions are likely to play the most important part. When added together, the findings reported here point to the conclusion that information technology has led to a degree of degradation in work for a large minority of female librarians. These findings are consistent with the view that the strategy of control practised by management in connection with the introduction of information technology can be seen as gender-differentiated in important respects.

CONCLUSIONS

From a selective reading of the evidence of the two surveys reported in this Chapter, it might seem reasonable to conclude that access to using the new technology, and the consequences of this for job content, is in significant respects comparable for both males and females engaged in library work. On this evidence, taken with that we have presented showing the relative willingness of female librarians to seek promotion, the prospects for changes associated with the introduction of IT to promote rather than obstruct the advance of women towards greater equality in the occupation appear to be at least fair.

However, in other respects the findings are less supportive of the optimistic thesis. Work control is felt to have decreased for a significant proportion of female librarians as a result of information technology, in contrast to their male counterparts, though they are somewhat more likely to report increased work pace and stress. Promotion prospects are also seen as being unaffected or reduced, again for women rather than men. Female librarians also perceive more of a threat to their jobs via information technology. Although jobs have in general not been deskilled, others (particularly those occupied by males, it seems) have been reskilled, leading to a potential disparity with (some) females bearing the brunt of this widening gap.

It may well be that the nature and context of female access to equipment, whilst often as great as that of males in frequency terms, entails a rather different and less empowering relationship to the machine (for comparison see Ramsay *et al.* Chapter 5, this volume). Of course, this is probably in part at least due to females being in lower status and so generally less influential occupational roles. But this merely takes us further back in the chain of causation, to the evidence on the links between job status and control on the one hand, and the process which ties 'feminization' and low status work together on the other. The evidence both from the surveys reported here, and from other work on women in libraries reviewed earlier, suggests that women are consistently disadvantaged in library work, partly through their external commitments and thus restriction to part-time jobs which remain low status, but also through persistent inequality of treatment. This may not be as severe as in non-professional occupations, or in more singularly male-dominated professions, but it remains significant.

In practice, these various factors have become almost impossible to disentangle for many predominantly female occupations. In short, for females working in libraries, as for those in many other types of work, information technology has acted as yet another discriminatory barrier to their ability to exercise control over their working lives.

The balance of the evidence is that technology has not reduced but has tended to reinforce those inequalities which exist in the profession.

REFERENCES

Baker, A. (1880) *Transactions and Proceedings of the Second Annual Meeting of the Library Assocation of the UK*, London.

Baldry, C. (1988) *Computers, Jobs and Skills*, New York, Plenum.

Beirne, M. and Ramsay, H. (1988) 'Computer redesign and "labour process" theory', in D. Knights and H. Willmott (eds), *New Technology and the Labour Process*, London, Macmillan.

Boston, S. (1980) *Women Workers and Trade Unions*, London, Lawrence & Wishart.

Burrington, G. (1987) *Equal Opportunities in Librarianship: Gender and Career Aspirations*, London, Library Association.

Cockburn, C. (1983) *Brothers: Male Dominance and Technological Change*, London, Pluto.

—— (1985) *Machinery of Dominance: Women, Men and Technical-knowhow*, London, Pluto.

Crewe, L. (1991) 'New technologies, employment shifts and gender divisions within the textile industry', *New Technology, Work and Employment* 6 (1).

Crompton, R. and Jones, G. (1984) *White Collar Proletariat*, London, Macmillan.

Delphy, C. (1984) *Close to Home*, London, Hutchinson.

Dewey, M. (1986) 'Women in libraries: how they are handicapped', *Library Notes*, October.

Dowlin, K. (1984) *The Electronic Library*, London, Neal Schuman.

Eisenstein, Z. (1979) *Capitalist Patriarchy and the Case for Socialist Feminism*, New York, Monthly Review Press.

Ellis, V. (1988) 'Current trade union attempts to remove occupational segregation in the employment of women', in S. Walby, *Gender Segregation at Work*, Milton Keynes, Open University Press.

Feldberg, R. and Glenn, E. (1981) 'Technology and work degradation; effects of automation on women clerical workers', in J. Rothschild (ed.), *Machina Ex Dea*, London, Pergamon.

Fransella, M. (1973) 'Marriage and the profession', *New Library World* 74.

Game, A, and Pringle, R. (1983) *Gender at Work*, Sydney, Allen & Unwin.

Hartmann, H. (1979) 'The unhappy marriage of Marxism and feminism', in L. Sargent (ed.), *Women and Revolution*, London, Pluto.

Huws, U. (1982) *Your Job in the Eighties – A Women's Guide to the New Technology*, London, Pluto.

Kelly, J. and Heery, E. (1988) 'Do female representatives make a difference?', *Work, Employment and Society* 3 (4).

Liddle, H. (1941) 'Resigned on marriage', *Assistant Librarian* 34.

Liff, S. (1990) 'Clerical workers and information technology: gender relations and occupational change', *New Technology, Work and Employment* 5 (1).

Luck, M. (1991) 'Gender and library work: the limitations of dual labour market theory', in N. Redclift and M. Sinclair (eds), *Working Women*, London, Routledge.

Newton, M. (1981) 'Libraries, automation and women', *Librarians for Social Change* 9 (1).

Phillips, A. (1983) *Hidden Hands: Women and Economic Policies*, London, Pluto.

Pollert, A. (1981) *Girls, Wives, Factory Lives*, London, Macmillan.

Reid, I. and Wormald, E. (1982) *Sex Differences in Britain*, London, Grant McIntyre.

Ritchie, S. (1987) 'Women in libraries: ten years on', *Information and Library Manager* 7 (2).

Rolfe, H. (1990) 'In the name of progress? Skills and attitudes towards technological change', *New Technology, Work and Employment* 5 (2).

Rowe, C. (1986) *People and Chips – The Human Implications of Information Technology*, London, Paradigm.

Siebert, W. S. and Young, J. (1978) *Sex Differentials in Professional Earnings: The Case of Librarians*, SSRC Report, London.

Wajcman, J. (1983) *Women in Control*, Milton Keynes, Open University Press.

Walby, S. (1986) *Patriarchy at Work*, Cambridge, Polity.

Witherspoon, S. (1988) 'New technology: workers' views, the public's views', *British Social Attitudes* 87.

8 Trade union involvement and influence over technological decisions

Stephen Deery

INTRODUCTION

It is now widely recognized that the effects of information technology are not preordained. They depend on more than the technical capabilities of computers and microelectronics. Organizations have room for choice in the way in which work is organized and jobs are structured around technology. Although the employment consequences will depend primarily on the goals and values of management, there are clear opportunities for union mediation. The choices that are made about the use of technology and the reorganization of the labour process can be affected by the intervention of workers and their representatives in the decision-making processes of the organization.

During the 1970s trade unions in general sought to establish procedural rights to participate in decisions about technological change. In some countries these were achieved by way of collective bargaining, and took the form of data or new technology agreements, while in others parliamentary processes were used to impose mandatory requirements on employers to consult and share information about the proposed changes. Notwithstanding the wide variations in these participative rights, there has been little evidence to indicate that managerial prerogatives were seriously infringed. Indeed, for most trade unions effective participation in technological decisions has remained an elusive goal.

Yet there have been exceptions. Some successful agreements have been negotiated which have safeguarded jobs, protected skill levels and generally guaranteed a flow of benefits to their members (Deery 1982, Gustavsen 1985, Batstone *et al.* 1987). No doubt, the assignment of legal rights to employees and their collective representatives to be notified and consulted about technological changes has strengthened the opportunities for union influence over the substantive effects of change. But as a number of research studies have shown, the presence of statutory rights has done little to guarantee effective participation in the introduction of new technology (Cressey 1987, Tallard 1988, Levie and Moore 1984). Surprisingly, little attention has been directed towards providing an explanation of the types of factors that may assist or retard possibilities of trade union involvement and influence in the planning of technological change.

The main difficulty for unions would seem to lie in their inability to gain entry to the process of management decision-making at a sufficiently early stage to participate in the questions affecting the design and application of new technology. Invariably their role has been confined to *ex post facto* bargaining about pay and related issues once the technological systems have been implemented. In those particular situations where trade unions have actually managed to secure a participative role, they have faced additional problems. A lack of resources, combined with insufficient expertise to assess the technology, evaluate its consequences and design alternative strategies for its use, has seriously handicapped their ability to contest management decisions.

The purpose of this chapter is, first, to identify the circumstances under which trade unions may best be able to secure access to the decision-making process and, second, to outline the factors that will affect their ability to participate effectively in that process. Before examining these issues it is necessary to discuss briefly the process of technological decision-making and the possible forms of union participation.

PARTICIPATION AND TECHNOLOGICAL DECISION-MAKING

The kinds of decisions that are made in any organization will be highly dependent on those who participate in their formulation. Normally technological decisions will be made by groups consisting of senior executives, technical data processing staff, designers and managers. These groups will tend to have a strong influence over the design and choice of new production systems and ultimately their organizational effects. Computer professionals in particular can have an extremely wide sphere of influence over the selection and design of technological systems (Wainwright and Francis 1984). Their possession of specialist information and understanding of the technological options can often give them considerable organizational power. As a consequence they can be in a position to affect not only the results of decisions, but also the issues which are raised for decision. This may mean that issues which are not a data processing priority, or matters of which computing specialists are unaware, are ignored.

In the absence of a participatory process through which employee interests are represented, design decisions can centre purely on questions of technical performance and be informed by a rather imperfect understanding of the needs and requirements of those using the equipment. It is obvious, however, that participation in itself will not endow an interest group with power to influence a technological decision one way or another. That influence will depend very much on the form of participation, the types of issues that are brought within the participatory framework, the organizational level at which participation takes place and the timing or stage at which the party is involved in the decision-making process. Participation may take the shape of consultation or joint decision-making, it may involve discussions with individuals about job-related issues or with their representatives about investment planning. It may occur at the workplace or the corporate level of an organization and it can take place at the time of technological planning or at the stage of its implementation.

A particularly important question for trade unions is the decision-making phase at which participation takes place. The choices that determine the effects of technological change on skills, work organization, and other industrial relations outcomes will tend to be made at the earlier stages of the decision-making process. Often the decisions will take place at the upper levels of an enterprise, and may even form part of wider business strategies and investment policies. Certainly, by the time of implementation at the plant or office level many of the alternative working arrangements that could have been chosen to accompany the introduction of technological change will have been closed off. This is not to overlook, however, the considerable discretionary opportunities that may still exist at the implementation stage (see Clark *et al.* 1988).

CIRCUMSTANCES AFFECTING UNION INVOLVEMENT IN TECHNOLOGICAL DECISIONS

In this section we will examine the circumstances which shape the opportunities for union involvement in the process of technological decision-making. It is suggested that those opportunities will depend principally on four variables: first, management's dependency on labour to achieve its technological objectives; second, pre-existing management styles and attitudes to participation; third, the scale and type of technological innovation; and last, the ability of organized labour to force management to consult and discuss those changes in the absence of any voluntary disposition on management's behalf to do so. These variables will not only shape the opportunities for participation but affect the subject matter and timing of involvement. They will not, however, determine the extent to which trade unions can influence the organizational effects of technological change. It is one thing to secure access to the forums in which technological decisions are being made, but it is quite another to translate these participative opportunities into an actual ability to shape the way in which new technology will affect the nature and performance of jobs. This requires amongst other things an organizational capacity to encourage and support the representation of members in those areas where technological decisions are planned and implemented, and clear and well-articulated strategies to influence technological choices. Before examining this issue we will first look at the circumstances which are likely to affect union access to the process of technological decision-making.

Technological objectives and dependency on labour

Organizations have a variety of reasons for introducing new technology. They may make such investments to enhance the quality of the goods and services sold, or they may seek to achieve savings in manpower, raw materials, inventory or space costs. Alternatively, their motives might lie in obtaining better information for production scheduling and control or increased speed or quality of text processing. The decision to invest may be made for strategic purposes in circumstances where the technology is applied to maintain or improve the commercial position of the organization, or it may be the subject of more *ad hoc*, short-term and issued-based appraisals (Hirschheim 1982). Child has observed that:

> Managers will normally have several goals in mind when introducing new technology into companies' operations. The emphasis between these is likely to vary according to the priorities and purposes of their organisation and the context in which it operates.
>
> (Child 1984: 213)

There is increasing evidence to indicate that competitive considerations are being incorporated into the planning of new technology

(Parsons 1983, Pyburn 1983, Galliers 1987, Earl 1987). Greater attention is being focused on technological applications which support activities and processes critical to the continued survival or growth of the firm. In these circumstances the business strategies that organizations adopt in response to different market pressures will have a bearing on their objectives for technology. They will also influence the opportunities that exist for employee participation in the process of change.

Those companies whose activities are located within mature price-competitive markets and who concentrate largely on the sale of fairly standardized products – textiles, chemicals and staple canned foods, for example – are likely to assess the benefits of new technology in terms of its effect on their cost structure. Process innovations will be used for the purpose of achieving improvements in material usage, the simplification of the production process and the lowering of labour input. The tendency will also be to strengthen managerial controls over the work process (Kochan and Tamir 1986: 205–6). Where new technology is utilized in cases of large, undifferentiated production runs the organizational outcome tends to be characterized by higher and more rigid segmentation of work with a greater concentration of programming-related functions in specialized departments or positions (Sorge *et al.* 1983). In these circumstances management is unlikely to show a disposition towards engaging employees or their representatives in the planning or implementation of technological change, except where they may be forced to by the threat of industrial disruption or a reluctance by the work-force to accept the changes. Neither the application of employee insight nor the use of skilled worker knowledge is particularly important to successful process innovation. Similarly, where office technology is used to reduce costs by standardizing the collection or processing of information, thereby making the work task more routine and predictable, there will be little technical or operational necessity to involve employees in the process of change.

Other organizations may pursue quite different competitive strategies and have alternative technological objectives. These competitive strategies may, for example, be built around the concept of differentiation with an emphasis on high product or service quality. Here greater attention will be given to design requirements, product performance and technical sophistication (Porter 1985). In line with these demands, process changes will tend to focus on enhancing product quality features and providing support for greater quality control, more flexible scheduling and faster response to orders.

The supply of specialized goods through shorter and more varied production runs will tend to lead to a concentration on exploiting the adaptability inherent in computer-controlled production systems. As a number of research studies have shown, this is often associated with greater shop-floor responsibility for process integrity and results, and with the identification and solving of problems at the place of work (Katz and Sabel 1985, Adler 1988). This restricts, as Sorge and Streeck have observed, 'the usefulness of constraining standards and central plans . . . [and] gives rise to a need for developing and involving human competence' (1988: 25–6). More flexible production systems require more adaptable and broadly skilled operators. The knowledge of those involved in production is important for the effective use of technology. Employee insight and problem-solving skills are highly valued (Willman 1986b: 77–8). Where technological changes enlarge the discretionary element in work roles it may be accompanied, as Fox has suggested, by a management attempt to create high trust relations:

> It becomes apparent that high-discretion roles call for a set of high-trust rules, relations and modes of conduct on top management's part that are quite different from those deemed appropriate to low-discretion roles. If they are not observed the full potentialities of high-discretion work will not be realised.

(Fox 1974: 114)

Management may therefore show a greater propensity to pursue a participative approach to change in circumstances where the successful introduction and operation of the new technologies relies less directly on the skills and expertise of computer specialists and senior managers and more centrally on the problem-solving capacity of lower-level personnel and their willingness to use their knowledge. It is probable that this situation will be more common in those organizations where competition tends to be on product performance rather than cost, and where new process technology is applied to achieve economies of scope rather than scale (Goldbar and Jelinek 1983). Here the process capabilities of the technology cannot be fully realized through the use of a 'command and control' form of management more suited to the execution of a standard, stable set of procedures (Adler 1988). In association with this, the prospects of a participative approach will be enhanced in those organizational settings where the work-force posseses high skill levels (Sorge and Streeck 1988).

A number of observations, however, should be made about the

form of participation, its content and timing. Typically it will involve informal discussions with individual workers (users) over job-related issues (see Cressey 1987: 44–5). The stage at which employees are involved will be determined by management in line with technical requirements – most probably towards the early or middle phase of the implementation stage. In itself this form of participation does little to disturb the rights of management. The parties, agenda and timing are of their choosing and the participative mechanism is more likely to be that of consultation rather than negotiation. None the less, opportunities are created for some degree of employee influence over the process of change. Where user knowledge and motivation are important elements in the successful design and operation of the new technology an avenue is formed for employees and their representatives to shape the skill and employment outcomes. Whether that opportunity will be realized, and union influence brought to bear on the decisions affecting technological change, will depend on a number of factors that are discussed later in the chapter.

Pre-existing management styles and attitudes to participation

Whether organizations carry out technological change by participative means or by managerial fiat will depend on more than their technological objectives. Prevailing industrial relations practices and traditions will have an important bearing on the manner in which technological change is introduced. Both Di Martino and Cressey (1985) and Price (1988) found a strong relationship between pre-existing styles of management and the methods used to accompany technology innovation. Where co-operative industrial relations prevailed the approach tended to be marked by consultation and participation. Where a pattern of distrust and antagonism existed between the parties, this too was reflected in the handling of technological change.

Management attitudes, values and ideologies can act as crucial influences over the choice of industrial relations practices. Attitudes which reflect a 'factor-input' or commodity conception of labour and place a high degree of emphasis on managerial discretion may be so ingrained as to preclude the development of a participative style more suited to the requirements of certain types of technological change. Wainwright and Francis (1984), for example, provide evidence of such a case involving the unsuccessful implementation of a word processing system in the offices of a major insurance broker. Despite the complexity and variability of the work performed, and the consequent need for operator involvement in the design process, a highly centralized and non-participatory approach was adopted, largely because of the authoritarian values of the technical systems manager and other senior staff in the company.

Many organizations may find it very difficult to break from historical patterns of antagonistic behaviour in spite of the particular need for collaborative relations. It is conceivable that in numerous organizational settings, relations between management and unions are paralysed by past events and a lack of mutual trust. Their interpretation of economic and technological changes may be significantly based on previous experiences and the manner in which these changes have been historically managed, rather than on contemporary assessments of their present requirements.

This is not to suggest that industrial relations practices or management styles are immutable or incapable of being changed in order to match the competitive and technological needs of the business. According to Purcell (1987: 545) firms may pursue a variety of management styles differentiated between broad occupational groups and their perceived value to the firm, and these may be modified in line with pressures exerted in the product market and by technological change. However, the adaptation of managerial practices to new environmental pressures can be difficult. Even in those situations where senior management may actively encourage a change towards 'high trust' rules and relations more consistent with a particular competitive strategy and the use of technology, they may be thwarted by a lack of commitment from lower levels of management. In any large organization there will be multiple constituencies and coalitions that will evaluate the merits of any proposed change more in terms of their immediate self-interest than in terms of the goals of the total organization. Different responses to change can be expected across and within various layers of the managerial hierarchy, depending on whether an individual or group sees its power or prestige being augmented or eroded. Wainwright and Francis (1984: 108–12) provide such an example of a computer director whose initial attempts to involve secretarial staff in work systems design were obstructed by a number of middle managers who were opposed to a decentralized and broadly based participative approach to change. The involvement of subordinates was perceived as a threat to their sphere of authority. In many cases middle managers themselves may feel that they have insufficient opportunity to participate in or influence important decisions in their organization. In a study of British attitudes towards employee participation, Heller *et al.* observed that:

The average middle manager cannot usually do more than give an opinion even on routine decisions like [the] assignment of tasks. . . . He does not usually feel his opinions are taken into account, and he certainly does not get involved in joint decision-making.

(Heller *et al.* 1979: 50)

Understandably, this may act to constrain their desire for participative decision-making by subordinates. In Canada, Long found evidence to indicate that the amount of responsibility managers were willing to grant to employees was directly related to the amount of influence that they believed they had in performing their own jobs (Long and Warner 1987: 73). In a different setting, Edwards (1987: 496) also found a congruence between factory managers' approach to industrial relations and the way in which they were themselves controlled from above. This might suggest that those managers who are less circumscribed in carrying out their activities will be more comfortable about extending some decision-making activities to those below them.

Nevertheless, the influence which is extended to employees is likely to be kept within very strict limits and directed towards the achievement of quite specific management objectives. Cressey *et al.* (1981) concluded from their research that most middle managers saw participation as 'complementary' to their right to manage and make decisions, and not a challenge to that power. Those managers wished to retain the initiative in the decision-making process, as well as complete discretion over the subject matter, timing and handling of any participation. This appears to be similar to the approach taken by senior site managers in the manufacturing establishments surveyed by Edwards (1987). Although factory managers attached considerable importance to employee involvement and participation, this did not extend to the provision of opportunities for the sharing of decision-making. Overwhelmingly it was seen in terms of 'telling workers what the needs of the business were [and] persuading them to accept . . . the new technologies and new working practices that went with them' (Edwards 1987: 488).

If these studies can be used as any guide, participation in the process of technological change will tend to be limited to employees rather than union representatives, and to involvement in specific task-related matters rather than questions of investment plans and corporate policy. Management may also offer direct user involvement to avoid trade union or shop steward intervention. Should trade unions be admitted to the decision-making process it is likely to be at a stage where the major technological design questions have been completed. The Union participation will not usually be extended voluntarily to issues such as work methods, job design and the speed of work, let alone to matters such as personnel decisions, choices of technological hardware or software or investment policies. Thus, Wilson *et al.*'s (1982) study of the process of organizational decision-making in a wide range of British companies found almost no serious involvement of unions in 'strategic' management decisions. Their work highlighted the prerogative of management to control the agenda of decision-making and to decide which issues were open to participation and which were not. Invariably, bi-lateral decision-making was not seen as appropriate or necessary. In fact, possible union involvement actually led management to speed up decision-making.

The type of innovations introduced

The possibilities for trade union participation in technological decisions will also depend on the type and extent of the innovations. Where, for example, the new technology involves major changes in the production process, such as the use of electronic point of sale systems in retailing operations, the introduction of photo-composition in the newspaper industry, or the application of robotics or automated warehousing in manufacturing, the technical obstacles to union involvement may be quite formidable. Invariably, invest-ment decisions of this sort will be made at the highest level of the organization. Senior management will be supported by specialized project teams, which themselves carry out systems work with equip-ment suppliers, thereby removing the design process even further from its level of eventual application (Child and Tarbuck 1985: 22–5). The remoteness of the new technology decision process will not normally facilitate wide discussion and participation. Moreover, the investment decision could be of a strategic kind designed to create or maintain a competitive advantage and not one that the organization would want widely disseminated. Unions may also find it difficult to gain access to the decision-making process because of the highly technical and scientific knowledge that may be required to understand these types of technological change. The skills and experiences of their members working in the organization may not be of sufficient assistance to challenge the domination of technical experts.

In contrast to these major types of technological innovation there are other changes which may be small scale and simply involve incremental improvements in process efficiency. These may take the form of additional word processing facilities, the introduction of semi-automated metal presses or the installation of computer numerically controlled machine tools. Such changes may not require substantial alterations in the form or character of work. They are the types of innovation which are introduced on a more or less regular basis and are usually part of a planned process linked to annual investment budgets. Importantly, the key decisions here are often the responsibility of managers who are much closer to the production process than to the boardroom.

For trade unions, this distinction is significant for two reasons. First, managers at this level in the organization are more likely to concern themselves about the industrial relations issues involved in implementation than are senior managers (Child 1985). They may be much more more conscious of the contribution of good industrial relations to company performance (Edwards 1987). Second, the levels at which the investment decisions are made are lower in the managerial hierarchy and more within the reach of trade unions. Furthermore, the incremental rather than radical nature of the technological innovations will assist unions in another way. Participation in decisions relating to job design questions, for example, can be supported by shop-floor knowledge and experience. Demands that machine tool operators should be trained to do their own programming and data entry are assisted by a practical understanding of the existing organization and planning system.

Union power

The final factor that will determine the extent to which unions can gain access to decisions over technological change and new systems of work organization is their actual power to force management to consult and bargain with them. That power will depend on the presence of a number of interrelated factors, the most important of which include membership density, the strategic importance of individuals and work groups in the production process, and their readiness to act collectively to protect perceived interests. Union members must not only have the capacity to inflict damage on an employer, they must also possess the willingness to realize that potential through industrial action. That requires, as Hyman and Fryer (1977) have suggested, some degree of conflict-consciousness and solidarity. Workers who see no major conflict of interest with their employer are less likely to organize effectively. Alternatively, those who perceive a need for mutual protection against the vagaries of market forces, technological changes or managerial power may form a more developed understanding of the divergence between their own interests and those of the employer. Group solidarity and support for the use of collective as opposed to individualistic means of interest pursuit are also important determinants of union power. In some organizations the level of unionization may be seen as an indicator of perceived interest differences and of the likelihood of workers acting collectively (Batstone and Gourlay 1986: 21).

In his study of the introduction of technology in Britain, Daniel (1987) found an association between the incidence of consultation and the level of unionization. For both manual and non-manual workers there was a tendency for all channels of consultation to be used more frequently the higher the proportion of union members at the workplace. Daniel (1987: 121) also reported more common use of consultation and negotiation where technological change was more unpopular and reactions more hostile to its introduction. Reactions to new technology may be affected by the character of the work-force and their job expectations. Where employees lack a permanent or substantial attachment to work, and tend to express dissatisfaction with workplace problems through resignations rather than collective action, it may prove difficult for unions to mobilize the work-force around the issue of technological change. Based on Australian case study data, Deery (1987) has suggested that the perception of new technology as a threat to job security or career progression is one of the necessary preconditions for the use of industrial action to force management to negotiate its introduction.

It is important to understand, however, that new technology is quite different from those items that normally form the subject matter of collective bargaining and naturally give rise to the possibility of industrial disruption. The complexity and differential impact of technological change makes it hard to identify its precise effects on job content and job security. The introduction of new technology will not simply produce a single uniform consequence. More probably it will involve a number of more or less simultaneous changes which may affect more than one aspect of a job and, perhaps more importantly, alter jobs in dissimilar ways. Consequently, it is unlikely that all those affected by technological change will view the outcome in the same light (Roskies *et al.* 1988). There will be differences in the perception and interpretation of the changes with some individuals defining themselves as 'winners' while others will see themselves as 'losers'. Whereas some may see their jobs being deskilled or their job security threatened, others may well find that the new technology has widened their responsibilities, enhanced their pay or improved their promotion opportunities.

In circumstances where a union's membership appraises the consequences differently it may prove difficult to develop a common and united position on new technology. Those who perceive the changes as having positive benefits for them may simply be unwilling to take action in support of those whose employment security or job content is adversely affected. This problem may be particularly acute for a union where the potential 'losers' occupy a position of marginal influence in the production process and cannot, themselves, exercise sufficient power to cause management to adopt a more bipartite approach to change. Management practices may also act to undermine collective responses to technological change. Discussions with workers on an individual basis about the possible effects of change on them can neutralize opposition and reduce the possibilities of a union bargaining collectively on behalf of its members.

In the preceding section we have identified four variables which would appear to play an important part in shaping the opportunities for union involvement in the process of technological decision-making. It has been suggested that those opportunities will be enhanced where management is reliant upon the skills and knowledge of shop-floor or office workers to achieve their technological objectives; where management's approach to trade unions is co-operative and underpinned by collaborative industrial relations

Table 8.1 Circumstances affecting union participation

Variable	Favourable conditions	Unfavourable conditions
Technological objectives	Quality/performance enhancement and problem-solving skills integral to success	Cost reduction with little technical or operational dependence on workers
Management style	Collaborative and open approach adopted throughout organization	Conflictual and closed with different and competing managerial interests
Type of innovations	Incremental changes with moderate workplace implications	Radical changes initiated at the top with major organizational implications
Union power	Members strategically placed, highly unionized and facing common and recognized technological threat	Members marginally located, weakly unionized and faced with uncertain or variable effects from technology

procedures; where technological changes are incremental; and finally where trade union members have the capacity and willingness to force management to bargain over the process of change. This information is summarized in Table 8.1.

FACTORS AFFECTING UNION INFLUENCE OVER TECHNOLOGICAL DECISIONS

Securing access to the decision-making process does not in itself guarantee influence over the technological choices or their workplace outcomes. The ability to exploit the participative opportunities that may exist will be affected by factors of organizational expertise and organizational structure. For a union to be able to shape the direction of technological change it must first possess the ability to assess and evaluate its possible effects and, in the event of disagreement, be able to devise strategies to contest and challenge management's decisions. Second, it must develop an appropriate organizational structure at the levels at which technological decisions are made and implemented.

Organizational expertise

For most unions the process of negotiating such matters as investment planning, systems selection and job design is quite new. Their traditional work has been in the areas of wages, working hours, pensions and leave entitlements. These have been relatively straightforward matters on which union members have formulated clear mandates for their representatives. Invariably, they have been easily made subject to some form of quantification or expression in monetary terms. Furthermore, these matters have been comfortably processed through the established means of collective bargaining or conciliation and arbitration. By and large, union officials have developed considerable expertise in dealing with them. A body of principles and established criteria has developed over time to assist and guide the parties in the settlement of their disputes.

The issues raised by computerization are very much more complex and often quite different from those that unions normally confront. Unlike those matters most immediately relevant to the wage-effort bargain, negotiations will involve *ex ante* considerations of decisions whose consequences are problematic and uncertain. A union's role cannot simply be confined to *ex post* distributional bargaining. The purpose of intervening in the decision-making process is to help shape aspects of the work environment as they affect task performance, labour usage and rewards and benefits. This is far from easy. At the corporate level, for example, the practices and methods of strategic planning are unfamiliar to most unions. Technological changes may frequently be embedded in wider changes that are made in response to market or financial pressures. The rationalization of branch outlets in banking, the upgrading of product quality in areas of manufacturing and the diversification and expansion in the range of customer services in telecommunications have all involved considerable investments in new technology. These types of developments can take years to be finalized, they can involve various experts and layers of management in their planning and implementation, and may embrace a whole range of financial and technical variables that affect both the process and outcome of change.

This raises two obstacles to effective trade union intervention. First, the changes are most unlikely to fit into a pattern which is susceptible to regular periodic negotiations. Second, the effects of the new technology may be hard to separate or disentangle from those changes induced by other factors. The union's position will be further weakened where the choice of technology and questions of equipment and process design are made by senior managers or project teams. Their knowledge and technical expertise will contrast sharply with that of union representatives, and limit the ability of labour to challenge corporate plans and initiatives. The influence and exclusivity of the centralized decision-makers will make it difficult for unions to inject social considerations into the design stage before new technology is introduced. Furthermore, they will not be assisted by senior management's apparent neglect of labour considerations in technological planning (Batstone *et al.* 1987: 213). Research based on information supplied by a large group of European managers indicated that personnel managers exerted practically no influence whatsoever over technological decisions (Hegarty and Hoffman 1987). Similar findings have been reported by Millward and Stevens (1986) and Martin (1988). In contrast, those in finance, marketing, production managememt and research and development have played a much more significant role. The absence of an established function for personnel managers in the early stages of the decision-making process gives support to the view that the problems associated with the introduction of computer technology are seen predominantly in technical rather than human terms (Daniel 1987: 107–111).

The evidence from a number of studies suggests that these obstacles are not insurmountable and that the degree of overall influence exerted by unions will be affected by five interrelated factors. These include the depth and strength of a union's organizational arrangements within the enterprise (Batstone *et al.* 1987), the technical knowledge and experience of its membership (Deery 1987, Clark *et al.* 1988), the resources that it is able to apply to the task of developing alternative technological options (Gustavsen 1985, Dodgson and Martin 1987), the ability to develop detailed strategies to guide and assist its membership in the actual process of change (Levie and Moore 1984) and finally, the capacity to threaten and possibly use sanctions to induce management to make concessions on union proposals (Batstone and Gourlay 1986).

In most cases, effective representation in technological decisions can only be achieved through a process of continuous bargaining both at the level at which decisions are made, and with those managers responsible for planning and implementation. A reliance on external union officials is clearly impractical in these situations. A sound representative structure at the workplace integrated with and supported by branch and national levels of the union is a necessary foundation for this type of bargaining. The negotiating process must also draw upon and mobilize the existing competencies and skills that lie within the membership, their detailed knowledge of the existing work organization and production of new technology.

Indeed, one of the most successful examples of trade union intervention in Australia involved the development by unionists of alternative solutions for the design of work and the use of computer equipment in the telecommunications industry. This arose in response to the modernization of the telephone exchange network in the late 1970s and management's initiatives to create a highly centralized maintenance arrangement to service the new technology. This would have involved a substantial reduction in the numbers of skilled staff required for its operation. Drawing upon the extensive technical knowledge of its members, the Australian Telecommunications Employees Association devised an alternative maintenance system which not only retained existing skill levels but widened prospective career opportunities. Following a lengthy dispute, management were forced to introduce both systems on an 18-month trial basis and have them evaluated by a team of independent experts. The evaluation reports judged the union model to be as efficient in the technical service it provided to customers and superior on other criteria related to job satisfaction, the retention of technical expertise and career opportunities. The final organizational arrangements which accompanied the new computerized telephone exchanges embodied most of the principles developed by the union (Deery 1987). Similar alternative technological plans have been initiated in Scandinavia (Bansler 1989). Although it is too early to judge the particular accomplishments of these plans, it is clear that employee skills can be utilized to develop alternative technological solutions and ways of organizing work.

Those skills and abilities, however, may not be sufficient in themselves to affect decisions on the application of new equipment and work organizations. Workplace representatives require not only professional support and guidance, but a 'strategic orientation' combining both long-term general objectives with short-term detailed substantive demands related to particular projects (Williams and Steward 1985). Effective intervention in management decision-making calls for specialized technical–scientific knowledge to understand the implications for the reorganization of work and to formulate independent options for manning levels, skill requirements and the layout of work. For employee representatives to make a real input into the process of change they need access to technical, computing, and engineering personnel within the organization, and to external resources and professional support from unions or research bodies (Levie and Moore 1984).

In Britain and Australia in particular there has been a clear weakness in terms of union support for research initiatives to examine alternatives to existing patterns of computer-based developments. The quality of training programmes to inform and educate the membership on both policy and practical issues has also been judged sorely deficient (Willman 1986a, 1986b; Dodgson and Martin 1987). The effectiveness of trade union negotiations over technological change will depend, to a large extent, on the views of the members who will be affected by these changes (MacInnes 1988); yet in many companies the formation of opinion on new technology is left almost entirely to the employer. It is not uncommon for larger firms to use quite sophisticated forms of communication to attempt to convince employees of the benefits of technological change to the organization. Without alternative information about the proposed changes, union members are left with only a vague and general understanding of the possible negative features of the technology on which to base their responses. Scandinavian experience has shown that a key factor affecting the ability of unions to influence the direction of technological change has been the provision of educational support programmes for their membership at the local level (Gustavsen 1985). Union access to research and development information independent of employers has also been important in this regard. Often these education programmes have been assisted by legislation which has required substantial subsidies by employers and government (Eiger 1986).

The threat and possible use of industrial action to support union alternatives, however, is also crucial if change is to be jointly regulated. The studies by Batstone and Gourlay (1986) found that management was more ready to agree to union proposals when these were backed up by a readiness to use sanctions. This reinforces the importance of a union's organizational strength within the establishment and the relationship between the membership, lay shop representatives and external officials. It also brings us to the question of organizational structure.

Organizational structure

The structure of unions and the concentration of their resources will tend to be influenced by the level at which collective bargaining is typically conducted. Where negotiations are normally focused at an industry or national level, union organizations will inevitably become more centralized. In contrast, where bargaining is located closer to the level of the individual establishment, the union organization is likely to be associated with stronger representative arrangements at the workplace.

These structures may not, however, be entirely suitable for union intervention in matters of technological change. The considerable flexibility offered by computer technology in terms of the range of possible alternatives for work organization in one and the same technical system, for example, makes negotiations at the industry level quite inappropriate. Questions of job content, involving such elements as variety, challenge, discretion and the like contain an important subjective dimension. Compared with issues such as wages, hours and leave conditions, they are difficult to standardize and formalize across companies or throughout an industry.

There are two critical points in the process of technological decision-making where trade unions need to be represented: at the company level where the key investment decisions are made and questions of equipment selection and design are resolved, and at the establishment or workplace level where those decisions are implemented. An effective organizational structure, therefore, is one which enables both the negotiation of broader strategic issues at the company level and more detailed and specific issues at a localized level. In the multi-establishment organizations surveyed by Daniel (1987) a clear dichotomy was found between the location of decisions to introduce technology – which showed a strong tendency to be centralized – and decisions about how to implement the changes, which were more likely to be made at the individual establishment. Perhaps even more interesting is the finding that those techno-logical decisions that had a negative effect on earnings or manning levels were far more prone to be taken at the centre (Daniel 1987: 90, 96).

A union structure that can support negotiations at those junctures where the planning and selection decisions are made is clearly critical for successful intervention. But unions can also achieve important concessions by negotiation during the implementation of the techno-logy at the workplace. Indeed Batstone and Gourlay's research indicated that employers were more ready to make significant conces-sions to union proposals where bargaining was conducted widely at all organizational levels and a comprehensive range of issues was subjected to the negotiation process (Batstone and Gourlay 1986: 206–9). Often the limited attention paid to the labour aspects of new technology by central decision planners can provide considerable scope for local variations in matters such as staffing levels and the content and design of jobs. Inevitable delays and unforeseen difficulties in installing and debugging the new equipment, combined with a possible 'looseness' between corporate management decisions to introduce new technology and the approach taken to imple-mentation, can also widen the opportunities for union influence over the eventual outcomes of change (Clark *et al.* 1988: 211). This might relate to the selection of employees for skills training, arrangements covering manning levels and the extent to which companies can enforce an intensification of work effort. Inevitably, the accom-modations that are made will be between managers, engineers and shop-floor workers, and the bargaining method used will be informal and unofficial (Wilkinson 1983: 98).

The issue of the organizational structure of the union movement as a whole is also relevant to the question of exercising control over the effects of technological change. Conflicting interests created by multi-unionism can often make it difficult to reach a co-ordinated or uniform approach to technological change within a company. Clearly, the members of different unions will not be affected equally by the introduction of new technology. Martin (1981) showed, for example, how the use of computerized photocomposition in the British newspaper industry was able to undermine the skills and employment opportunities of compositors at the same time as it increased career opportunities for other occupational groups such as journalists and those who were proficient in electronics. Understandably, this can lead to division and conflict between various unions and their members as they seek to defend jobs and their territory against each other. It may also enable employers to mobilize the support of certain occupational groups and their unions who see opportunities to profit from the discomfiture of others. Even the trade-union-based UTOPIA project in Sweden, which sought to create advanced computer-based skills for printing workers, fell hostage to inter-union rivalries. In one of the first attempts to introduce the new production system at the Swedish newspaper, *Aftonbladet*, the project had to be abandoned following opposition from the journalists' union who saw it as a threat to their members' jobs (Bansler 1989).

Table 8.2 Factors affecting union influence

Variable	Favourable conditions	Unfavourable conditions
Organizational expertise	United and cohesive organization	Inadequate internal co-ordination and communications
	Technically knowledge-able and skilled membership	Work-groups unable to design organizational alternatives
	Internal and external assistance	Lack of research resources
	Strategic policy orientation	Short-term and tactical policy orientation
	Ability to obstruct change and force consideration of own proposals	Difficulty in use of sanctions where disagreements arise
Organizational structure	Robust at key levels where management decisions made and implemented	Gaps in intra-union organization at company or workplace level
	Single union or co-ordinated approach by multiple unions	Competitive multi-union structure

In order to formulate and enforce a common policy on technological change, inter-occupational differences must be capable of being resolved. Obviously, this is more difficult where most of those occupational groupings are represented by different unions. In those countries where labour movements have largely been successful in implementing the principle of 'one plant one union' – as is the case in West Germany – conflicts about contradictory interests between occupational groups will not be absent but they can be dealt with in a single representative structure (Hingel 1983). A summary of the main factors that will affect the ability of trade unions to shape the process and outcome of technological change is given in Table 8.2.

CONCLUSION

A union's ability to convert its participative opportunities into actual influence over technological decisions will lie largely within the organization itself. The willingness and ability of union members to negotiate the planning and implementation of change is crucial for successful intervention. Unions must be able to mobilize their rank and file around a clear set of objectives, and develop their awareness of the potential to influence technological decisions. Obviously, this will be easier where union members possess a detailed knowledge of the production process and are able to make informed judgements about the proposed innovations, and to possibly formulate alternative plans for the actual performance of work. Major organizational changes may be required to support an extension of activities in these areas. Membership involvement in the system of internal union government and in the process of policy formation may be necessary to obtain an understanding and commitment to workplace participation in technological change decisions. Union education and research, and facilities for the servicing of employee representatives, are also critically important. The opacity of the language of computer technology can act as a significant deterrent to lay participation in the decision-making process. Consequently, access to technical expertise within the company as well as external assistance is vital if technological options are to be developed. Trade union members ultimately must be equipped with both a capacity to assess management's proposals for technological change and the ability to provide alternative solutions where they are seen as necessary to protect jobs and skill levels. To date, however, there is little evidence that trade unions are willing to commit the organizational resources necessary to achieve this level of workplace competence.

REFERENCES

Adler, P. (1988) 'Managing flexible automation', *California Management Review*, Spring.
Bansler, J. (1989) 'Trade unions and alternative technology in Scandinavia', *New Technology, Work and Employment* 4 (2).

Batstone, E. and Gourlay, S. (1986) *Unions, Unemployment and Innovation*, Oxford, Blackwell.

——, ——, Levie, H. and Moore, R. (1987) *New Technology and the Process of Labour Regulation*, Oxford, Clarendon.

Child, J. (1984) 'New technology and development in management organisation', *Omega* 12 (3).

——, (1985) 'Managerial strategies, new technology and the labour process', in D. Knights, H. Willmot and D. Collinson (eds), *Job Redesign*, Aldershot, Gower.

—— and Tarbuck, M. (1985) 'The introduction of new technologies: managerial initiative and union response in British banks', *Industrial Relations Journal* 16 (3).

Clark, J., McLoughlin, I., Rose, H. and King, R. (1988) *The Process of Technological Change*, Cambridge, Cambridge University Press.

Cressey, P. (1987) *Participation Review*, Luxembourg, European Foundation for the Improvement of Living and Working Conditions.

——, Eldridge, J., MacInnes, J. and Norris, G. (1981) *Industrial Democracy and Participation: A Scottish Survey*, Research Paper No. 28, Department of Employment.

Daniel, W. (1987) *Workplace Industrial Relations and Technical Change*, London, Frances Pinter.

Deery, S. (1982) 'Trade unions, technological change and redundancy protection in Australia', *The Journal of Industrial Relations* 24 (2).

—— (1987) 'Trade union involvement in the process of technological change', Unpublished Ph.D. thesis, Latrobe University.

Di Martino, V. and Cressey, P. (1985) *Introducing New Technology: A Participative Approach*, Discussion Paper 14, Centre for Research in Industrial Democracy and Participation, University of Glasgow.

Dodgson, M. and Martin, R. (1987) 'Trade union policies on new technology: facing the challenge of the 1980s', *New Technology, Work and Employment* 2 (1).

Earl, M. J. (1987) 'Information systems strategy formulation', in R. Boland and R. Hirschheim (eds), *Critical Issues in Information Systems Research*, Chichester, Wiley.

Edwards, P. K. (1987) 'Factory managers; their role in personnel management and their place in the company', *Journal of Management Studies* 24 (5).

Eiger, N. (1986) 'Education for workplace democracy in Sweden and West Germany', in R. N. Stern and S. McCarthy (eds), *The Organizational Practice of Democracy*, New York, John Wiley & Sons.

Fox, A. (1974) *Beyond Contract: Work, Power and Trust Relations*, London, Faber.

Galliers, R. D. (1987) 'Information systems planning in the United Kingdom and Australia – a comparison of current practice', in P. I. Zorkoczy (ed.), *Oxford Surveys in Information Technology* (Vol. 4), Oxford, Oxford University Press.

Goldbar, J. and Jelinek, M. (1983) 'Plan for economies of scope', *Harvard Business Review*, November–December.

Gustavsen, B. (1985) 'Technology and collective agreements: some recent Scandinavian developments', *Industrial Relations Journal* 16 (3).

Hegarty, W. H. and Hoffman, R. C. (1987) 'Who influences strategic decisions?', *Long Range Planning* 20 (2).

Heller, F., Wilders, M., Abell, P. and Warner, M. (1979) *What do the British want from Participation and Industrial Democracy?*, A Report to the Anglo-German Foundation, Mimeo.

Hingel, A. (1983) 'The challenge of new technology for European unions – a comparative approach', in V. Briefs, C. Ciborra and L. Schneider (eds), *Systems Design For, With, and By the Users*, Amsterdam, North Holland.

Hirschheim, R. A. (1982) *Information Management Planning in Organisations – Part One: A Framework for Analysis*, LSE Working Paper.

Hyman, R. and Fryer, R. (1977) 'Trade unions: sociology and political economy', in T. Clarke and L. Clements (eds), *Trade Unions Under Capitalism*, Glasgow, Fontana.

Katz, H. and Sabel, C. (1985) 'Industrial relations and industrial adjustment in the car industry', *Industrial Relations* 24 (3).

Kochan, T. and Tamir, B. (1986) 'Collective bargaining and new technology: some preliminary propositions', International Industrial Relations Association, 7th World Congress, Hamburg, September.

Levie, H. and Moore, R. (1984) *Workers and New Technology; Disclosure and the Use of Company Information*, Oxford, Ruskin College.

Long, R. and Warner, M. (1987) 'Organizations, participation and recession', *Relations Industrielles* 42 (1).

MacInnes, J. (1988) 'New technology in Scotbank: gender, class and work', in R. Hyman and W. Streeck (eds), *New Technology and Industrial Relations*, Oxford, Blackwell.

Martin, R. (1981) *New Technology and Industrial Relations in Fleet Street*, Oxford, Clarendon Press.

—— (1988) 'The management of industrial relations and new technology', in P. Marginson, P. K. Edwards, R. Martin, J. Purcell and K. Sisson (eds), *Beyond the Workplace*, Oxford, Blackwell.

Millward, N. and Stevens, M. (1986) *British Workplace Industrial Relations 1980–1984: The DE/ESRC/PSI/ACAS Surveys*, Aldershot, Gower.

Parsons, G. L. (1983) 'Information technology: a new competitive weapon', *Sloan Management Review*, Fall.

Porter, M. (1985) *Competitive Advantage*, New York, The Free Press.

Price, R. (1988) 'Information, consultation and the control of new technology', in R. Hyman and W. Streeck (eds), *New Technology and Industrial Relations*, Oxford, Blackwell.

Purcell, J. (1987) 'Mapping management styles in employee relations', *Journal of Management Studies* 24 (5).

Pyburn, P. J. (1983) 'Linking the MIS plan with corporate strategy: an explanatory study', *MIS Quarterly*, June.

Roskies, E., Liker, J. and Roitman, D. (1988) 'Winners and losers: employee perceptions of their company's technological transformation', *Journal of Organizational Behaviour*, 9.

Sorge, A., Hartmann, G., Warner, M. and Nicholas, I. (1983) *Microelectronics and Manpower in Manufacturing*, Aldershot, Gower.

—— and Streeck, W. (1988) 'Industrial relations and technical change: the case for an extended perspective', in R. Hyman and W. Streeck (eds), *New Technology and Industrial Relations*, Oxford, Blackwell.

Tallard, M. (1988) 'Bargaining over new technology: a comparison of France and West Germany', in R. Hyman and W. Streeck (eds), *New Technology and Industrial Relations*, Oxford, Blackwell.

Wainwright, J. and Francis, A. (1984) *Office Automation, Organisation and the Nature of Work*, Aldershot, Gower.

Wilkinson, B. (1983) *The Shopfloor Politics of New Technology*, London, Heinemann.

Williams, R. and Steward, F. (1985) 'New Technology Agreements: an assessment', *Industrial Relations Journal* 16 (3).

Willman, P. (1986a) *New Technology and Industrial Relations: A Review of the Literature*, London, Department of Employment.

—— (1986b) *Technological Change, Collective Bargaining and Industrial Efficiency*, Oxford, Clarendon Press.

Wilson, D., Butler, R., Cray, D., Hickson, D. and Mallory, G. (1982) 'The limits of trade union power in organisational decision making', *British Journal of Industrial Relations* 20 (3).

9 Trade unions and new technology
European experience and strategic questions

Peter Cressey

The introduction of new technology has recently come to represent something of a catalyst for trade union activities, providing unions with an opportunity to reassess and redraw their policies on a much wider front. This potential for redefinition stems from the impact that new technologies are having on employment levels, the structuring of work and skills (including long-term occupational changes) and the prospects for different and possibly more stringent forms of organizational control. The response by the national union movements across Europe to these challenges has not been uniform; nor is there any single agreed strategy for handling them. Rather, unions have dealt with technological innovation at a number of different levels, without clear indications as to its direction, often with minimal expertise and quite often with the highly ambiguous notion that technology is both a long-term positive force and yet an immediate threat to their organization and the capacity for effective action.

There is a very real question mark here against trade union capabilities for handling the transformative issues that technology places on the agenda. In effect the issue of technology becomes a litmus test for the character of unionism itself. Will a future dominated by the new technology mean the demise of the old reactive and instrumental approach and the installation of a collaborative trade unionism? The question itself should be recast in terms that allow an empirical assessment. For instance, is the experience of new technology leading to a new set of 'participative' arrangements? Or is technology refocusing attention on unions' ability to act as a proactive force? How far are the trade unions structurally constrained in their responses to new technology? What are their limitations as reactive institutions within an unequal labour contract? How can trade unions best defend their interests, expand their areas of experience, and develop their strategies in positive directions? To what extent do unions have the organizational capacities to shadow management in ever more complex and multinational enterprises?

This chapter sets out to answer some of these questions and to examine how trade unions have become involved in technological change, what participation they have achieved and what strategies they have adopted. It also looks briefly at the regulatory provisions established in different European countries for dealing with such innovation. Evidence is presented from research in a number of European countries, based on case studies of new technology and changes in work organization.[1] The findings of these studies provide a background against which to judge the coherence of trade union strategies in situations of change, especially, but not exclusively, at the level of the enterprise and below.

The chapter is organized in two main parts. First, it examines the trade union reaction to new technology and the ability of the unions to implement effective strategies inside enterprises. It goes on to look at the overall context in which European trade unions presently operate and the kinds of participative relationships they currently accept. The second part will examine the different possible levels of union and work-force activity, identifying the key determinants of strategies and asking how unions can achieve some measure of positive control over the process of technological development.

THE TRADE UNION REACTION TO NEW TECHNOLOGY

Faced with a situation of diversity and experimentation across Europe and within each national context, it has been difficult for unions to offer broad coherent strategies at these levels. Although trade unions have easily enough identified fears with regard to several key features of the introduction of new technology, their attention has unsurprisingly centred upon threatened job loss. Whilst the trend towards a wholesale 'collapse of work' (Jenkins and Sherman 1979) has clearly been overstated, new technology is affecting employment unevenly, with manufacturing industry being the hardest hit. Estimates of the size of this impact vary widely. Ciborra (1984) predicts a 35–70 per cent reduction in 'direct labour' consequent upon the introduction of 'production related technologies' – that is, those with a direct effect upon the manufacture of goods. This category would include innovations such as robotics, flexible manufacturing systems, numerically controlled machine tools, etc. He also expects a 15–30 per cent employment reduction to follow the introduction of 'organisational related technologies' in such areas as the development of management information systems and office automation. These figures refer to the 'direct' impact of innovations and not to their implications for overall enterprise employment. They also mask a number of compensatory factors that could absorb labour, both at the site of the introduction and in the production of the hardware and software being introduced. Yet, such counteracting, positive effects on employment typically take place over a longer time-scale and do not guarantee work for those displaced. Thus there is unanimity from the European level down to the work-group that the primary objectives of unions in this area must include securing job guarantees.

Other worrying aspects of innovation for unions relate to work-force recomposition, through skill squeeze as well as job loss. As the printing cases from the European Foundation studies illustrate, whole strata of occupations can face the danger of being wiped out. Less dramatic, but more general, are the changing needs, skills and responsibilities brought about by the innovations. In many instances entire job grades, and with them areas of high union density, are under presure, leading to long-term and decisive changes in the character of the work-force and thereby in the composition, size and influence of the unions themselves. Yet other anxieties centre around worsening conditions, with evidence of increased stress, noise and general concern over the changing nature of work demands – bringing an increase in mental fatigue greater psychological disorders, and so on. There are also a host of fears surrounding issues of a contractual nature, such as pay and conditions, shift working, task flexibility and diluted employment contracts. These particular effects vary across the innovations but an abundance of evidence exists on intensified manning, greater use of shifts, bonuses and performance ratings, as well as the often expressed pressure for all round flexibility. The question of increased managerial control has been raised in terms of enhanced surveillance and performance indices, control in the planning and direction of work, and the dismantling of established methods of regulating production within enterprises. A corollary of this is that work-force self-regulation is reduced as technology makes possible new forms of management control over work pace, output and methods of production. This may weaken key 'hot spots' in production processes, for instance marginalizing maintenance workers or bypassing industrial relations practices that retain worker inputs into the work process.

The fact that the trade unions have fears does not necessarily mean a negative appreciation of new technology by union members. Indeed evidence from the case studies and other surveys by the European Foundation (see Di Martino 1987) and from the British Workplace Industrial Relations Survey (Daniel 1987) points to a decisive break with the old Luddite imagery surrounding technical change, showing instead a strong welcome for technological innovation from the work-force and its lay representatives.

Nor is the evidence on many of the effects feared by unions straightforward, since their contestation of each of the above effects generates uncertainties in strategic approaches. This is exemplified in recent publications that paint a very different picture of new technology as an agent in the restructuring of old mass production processes. It is suggested in these accounts that management can combine technological innovation with more flexible forms of production which are often 'Post-Taylorist' in their application. Multiskilled, flexible and integrated work-groups are a central feature of the resulting labour processes. These themes are developed in numerous sources, notably in the work by the Technical Change Centre in the UK, whose report *Towards the Flexible Craftsman* (Cross 1985) suggests the emergence of the multiskilled/multirole engineering craftsman who combines the functions of operator and maintenance worker. Such flexibility is, nevertheless, seen as a challenge to existing union structures and forms of work-group representation, threatening a loss of occupational identity and of the collective and unifying set of interests that underwrite it. Thus Atkinson (1984) sees new technology as one element pushing towards greater segmentation of the work-force. His model of the 'flexible firm' identifies various levels of 'core' and 'peripheral' workers who offer different kinds of flexibility. It also shows the varied ways in which the labour market within a firm can be adapted to change, be it technological or otherwise.

However, the nature and extent of the new flexibility, and the acceptance of what they argue is a new form of managerial ideology, is challenged by recent critics (Pollert 1988, MacInnes 1988). They argue *inter alia* that the notion of a 'core' work-force has to be handled carefully, given the multifarious ways in which different companies respond to different situations. The demand for management direction of flexibility may well undermine participation and influence for employees. On the other hand, sustained influence in or over some decisions taken by management may be offered to key groups in the labour process. That said, these may or may not correspond to those new 'core' groups identified by Atkinson and

Cross. It would be difficult, though perhaps not impossible, for some forms of involvement to be extended to subcontract fee-paid or temporary staffs. Certainly there are other forms of managerial dependency on employee skill and discretion than those presumed in the core-periphery model which may require such a policy.

Overall, there has tended to be an unhelpful simplification and generalization of the positions of the main actors. This has been misleadingly focused on such points as the trade union aim for security through regulation, requiring a protection of their employment, skill and material position. On the other hand, the fundamental aim in management's technology strategy has become identified as flexibility, where new technology is presumed to reorder the labour process in ways that undermine trade union control and allow management strategic use of participative methods among the new core 'work-force'. Neither of these characteristics is valid or adequate as a means to understand actual strategies and responses.

TRADE UNIONS AND PARTICIPATION

It is evident that any detailed assessment of work-force responses and strategies must recognize the variation that results from the diverse changes wrought by innovation, and by the different forms of agreement constructed to deal with these. The European Foundation's work (Cressey 1985, Depoali *et al.* 1988, Cressey and Williams 1990) draws upon a programme of cross-national case studies of technological innovation, and highlights those where worker-participation formats are being used. These different national case studies draw our attention to the range and scope of such provision. Table 9.1 displays, in the form of a continuum, the possible range of regulatory mechanisms in use.

Table 9.1 The possible range of regulatory mechanisms in use

No involvement	Information provision	Consultation	Negotiation	Joint decision-making
● Management planned and executed schemes	● Briefing sessions ● Information agreements ● Group forums	● Advisory /technology /steering committees ● Project groups	● Productivity /planning /technology agreements ● Protective clauses in general agreements	● Veto powers ● *Status quo* clauses ● Joint-decision bodies

These existing practices shown in Table 9.1 can be formally classified under the general headings of joint decision-making, negotiation, consultation, and information based on the degree of labour influence within the enterprise. In some particular instances it may be that information disclosure had a significance beyond that of bargaining, but for most practical purposes this continuum of influence did hold good, thus making it more than a mere heuristic device. The Foundation studies found that the stronger formats were thin on the ground. Where participation was installed it tended to be of a weak character. Information provision accounted for the bulk of the cases, together with some use of *ad hoc* joint consultation methods. Management and manual sections of the unions gave much less priority than white-collar sections to the creation of New Technology Agreements (NTAs) or the establishment of joint decision-making bodies to oversee change.

REGULATION DURING DIFFERENT PHASES OF CHANGE

Describing the major forms of involvement found in the case study companies tells us little about the actual depth of influence that the parties had during the constituent stages of the innovation process. For this we have to distinguish the different phases of decision-making and see how, if at all, the work-force became involved at each stage. To explore this, the process of introducing new technology was broken down into planning, selection and implementation phases, and these were considered for each of the forms of participation on offer in five European countries. Figure 9.1 gives a composite picture of the format of participation (for which see Table 9.1) and its timing, in two sets of studies looking at employee involvement in change.[2]

Looking at the earliest stage in the process, namely the Planning Phase, the graph shows how this process is marked by relatively high incidence of 'no involvement'. The respondents suggested certain reasons why this configuration and style of regulation might occur. Management respondents stressed that planning, by its very nature, is a specialist task that does not allow for extended involvement. Further, they argued that planning has to take place at higher levels within the company, possibly many months or years prior to any effect upon the work-force. They also emphasized that the period of planning is one marked by uncertainties which extensive consultation may exacerbate rather than aid.

Union and work-force respondents tended to agree with the

Figure 9.1 Employee involvement in change
(a) Work organization research – type of participation evident in the different phases of the change process

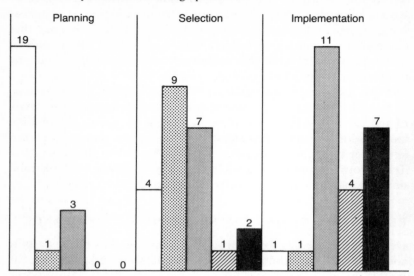

(b) New technology research – type of participation evident in the different phases of the change process

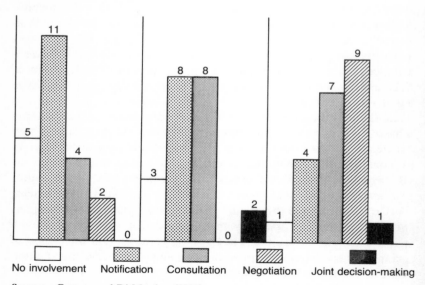

Source: Cressey and Di Martino (1991).

assessment that the planning phase requires specialist input and involves functional experts. Largely because of this, planning was considered an area of managerial initiative. Yet planning may also involve objectives which are themselves contentious. For instance, decisions with implications for job loss, job flexibility and skill reductions are taken at this stage, and this potential for conflicting rather than shared interests constitutes one possible obstacle to enhanced participation.

In the Selection phase, a clear movement towards more notification and consultation may be observed. Consultation tends to be of a local nature and based on specific problems, however. There were few signs of any structured influence at all in this phase, especially in those national contexts where the work-force had few designated rights to draw upon. In certain cases, none the less, substantial evidence of high involvement did emerge, especially where the introduction of word processors and certain of the computer numerically controlled (CNC) machine tools was involved. In the Selection phase, however, involvement was often a purely formal affair due to the fact that the prior planning stage had largely determined the overall requirements for innovation, the type of machinery, and concomitant organizational structure. Very often the Selection process occurred within very narrow technical boundaries. Many work-force respondents in identifying this fact expressed a sense of powerlessness, a feeling that once the process of change was underway there was little they could do to influence the innovation in any fundamental sense.

The Implementation phase was characterized by the extensive use of bargaining and consultation. Once more a marked shift occurs in the form of involvement and regulation. This is the phase in which the shape and impact of new technology becomes fully visible to the work-force in a concrete rather than a paper sense. Here, too, the work-force and their representatives begin for the first time to put forward alternative demands regarding job security guarantees, *status quo* arrangements or mutuality provisions, and to make full use of the bargaining option. It was a feature of the case studies that where job protection arrangements were agreed in advance, a markedly different trajectory of involvement occurred. By contrast, in situations where non-involvement extended to the details of implementing the new technology, the whole question of new technology itself tended to become a conflict-centred issue. In this context, the association between offers of job guarantees and good market position shows through, while innovations made in response to market or cost pressures or a declining economic position severely limit the room for manoeuvre by management.

This overall pattern of participation can be supplemented by looking at the actors involved in the process of change. The Foundation studies show that the process draws in many different actors from both management and work-force. There is no indication that any one group of enterprise, company or plant management takes charge of the whole process – rather, such groups have varying responsibility for particular elements of the process within a complex web of decision-making. For the work-force the main involvement tends to be loaded towards union action at company level, and the increased use of direct work-group involvement in certain settings. Although evidence of a growth in this more individualized involvement is clear, its practice is difficult to specify in terms of any one model. The involvement of management and other parties varied significantly through the innovation process. What emerges is a complementary pattern to that of the phases of involvement, emphasizing the increased potential for wider experimentation as one enters the implementation phase.

The conclusions that may be drawn from this picture suggest that there is little real involvement in technological change outside of the implementation phase. The planning phase in particular appears to lie within management's prerogative: they may *choose* to inform the work-force, but little else is on offer. Where one does find involvement it tends to take the form of information disclosure, *ad hoc* advisory groups or some form of consultation, with the implementation stage being the primary period where joint discussions/decision-making might occur. Overall, the process of technological change was dominated by management who retained initiative and control throughout both the decision-making and realization processes. Work-force influence was mainly felt through negotiating channels, and tended to be restricted to the job-related issues thrown up in the implementation phase. Procedural aspects that related to control-oriented facets of change were addressed in few cases.

European evidence was unequivocal in its depiction of participation as limited and partial. With a few notable exceptions, the power to define, plan, initiate and secure objectives resided with managers – primarily those at central board level. Most studies were characterized by a lack of trade union or work-force alternatives to a managerial conception of things, and the absence of early work-force involvement. In effect, there was a 'gap' in work-force influence, and because of this a 'power imbalance' centred upon the exclusion of the work-force from the planning phase and minimal inclusion of trade unions in all but the implementation phase. Fundamentally, policy decisions were taken at enterprise level, whilst operational/ implementation decisions were the subject of plant discussions. Due to the pattern of work-force representation it was rare for work-force inputs into decision-making to touch any but these later transactions (see Cressey *et al.* 1981).

All these studies tend to confirm that the involvement of trade unions has primarily occurred at the 'micro' level, at company level and below, rather than through wider-ranging agreements at European, national or even sectoral levels. Locating enterprise activities in the broader national context, however, does not change the position greatly. With the exception of Denmark, and to some extent Germany, trade unions have not secured general protective legislation in the event of technological changes. In the Federal Republic of Germany there are some clauses to this effect, but these are the exceptions, and, as the European Trade Union Institute (ETUI) has observed, tend to be of a defensive nature (Evans 1982). The same applies to the Italian situation where unions have also secured the right to monitor workplaces and the right to relevant information on technological changes, together with compensation payments in the event of restructuring. Deficiencies were also identified in the support and training facilities available for employee representatives, including access to consultants for advice. More-over, as indicated earlier, the trade union forms of representation and organization were seen as mismatched when compared to those of company management structures. Trade unions did not have effective representation at levels where key decisions were routinely taken, and the existence of *comites des enterprises* as in the French case, does not guarantee the ability to be involved to any significant degree in the decision-making process.[3] The Danish LO had achieved most in this regard, thanks mainly to a national agreement that specified the creation of co-operation committees in each enterprise.[4]

In general, work-force/trade union strategies face a context that appears predominantly hostile, filled with problems regarding the legitimacy of their participation and lacking a general framework within which even rudimentary forms of regulation could be agreed. In the absence of such a framework, a plethora of voluntarist agreements have appeared at various levels as unions react to particular innovations in widely differing social, economic and political contexts.

A WORK-FORCE STRATEGY?

The formulation of an effective 'strategy' to deal with the prevailing situation faces some problems. If any one of the necessary components of such a response is missing then the strategy can be assessed as weak and doomed to be ineffective. A prioritized set of objectives must be constructed, yet this requires an infeasible level of knowledge about the changes that will take place and of their future impacts. The central problem that arises is that such strategic thinking may be possible for management, for with management resides initiatory or proactive powers in relation to new technology. They control the day-to-day operations of the enterprise, plant or unit, and enjoy decisive voice and representation in the network of decision-making sites within the organization. Hence management has power that allows 'strategic' planning, the strategic use of information, acceleration or delaying of decisions, the widespread promotion of new ideas, and so forth.

Can the same be said of trade unions? The unions, for their part, can indeed take part in exercises to define priorities, gain knowledge of the likely nature and impact of innovation, and they can attempt to assess options and resources. The real distinction between the coherence of a union strategy and that of management lies in the ability to take initiatory or positive control over the process of innovation. At best unions do so on the invitation of management, this being dependent on the 'style' that enterprise managements adopt. They can attempt to extend control through existing institutions, be they work councils, consultation committees or bargaining arrangements. However, this form of implementation of union strategies does seem to be qualitatively different at the level of the enterprise from that exercised by managements. This may explain why the trade unions persistently seek to extend the possible range of initiatory action beyond the organizational setting to national political levels in order to redress the balance.

In terms of the broad union movement in Europe, there are no general models that designate correct trade union approaches. Differences are evident on both inter- and intra-systems levels. The differences are starkly posed between the co-operative/legalistic models of Germany and Denmark and the antagonistic/voluntaristic ones in the UK, Italy and Ireland. However, it has also been noted, when looking at the specifics of new technology, that such national systems' differences appear markedly less significant than different approaches *within* countries (see Cressey 1988c). For instance, cases of information provision over job loss exist alongside formal institutions and/or formal negotiations in all of the countries investigated. No one approach to involvement was dominant under either of the two broad models, nor could one identify clear and distinct national patterns from the available cases.

That said, there was a widespread tendency for trade unions supported by national guidelines to seek formal agreements through collective bargaining, although this was not the primary method of regulating the introduction of technological change. Within companies, the unions found themselves in an ambiguous position, attempting to secure *status quo* clauses of formal agreements of a protective nature against a background of weakened positions. Due to restructuring or recession where managements were offering at best consultative or other less formal means for involvement, possibilities existed for joint interests to be realized only within restricted frames of reference. These considerations pulled trade unions in two directions. The first might be called the *oppositional* position, where trade unions sought to operate through collective bargaining strategies. Here they adopted formal positions of isolation from management, and were clear in their lines of opposition to changes as they affected members' interests. The alternative option was for trade unions to operate through *integrative* strategies. These took on many guises from tripartism down to works councils and consultation schemes, and were especially apparent where joint forums of union and/or work-force representatives met to oversee, monitor or decide on the introduction of innovations. This approach based its appeal on the search for, and possibility of, consensus and partnership. The premise was that power imbalances could be redressed through social partnership, through the accrediting of equal rights of representation and by sustained discussion to secure formal and informal agreements. In situations of this sort, trade union interests were recognized as were the interests of the company or institution.

This uncertainty in approach was found in many of the case studies, and compromised the clarity of trade union standpoints. Often both positions were held, with the conflict-mode reserved for certain aspects, primarily substantive ones, whilst an integrative approach was adopted on other matters. The latter tended to centre on the procedures or forums for reaching agreement, and the prior recognition of the legitimacy of union intervention was the premise upon which joint groupings of unions and management could be constructed.

NEW TECHNOLOGY AGREEMENTS

The major trade union approach has been the negotiation of specific New Technology Agreements (NTAs). When faced with the implications of change brought about by the increased use of robotics, automation and informational technology, the first response by trade unions was to attempt to control their impact and introduction by tightly defined agreements. The research shows, however, that NTAs do not seem to deliver the benefits that were expected of them, being limited in both number and impact. NTAs have been heavily concentrated in the white-collar sector, and have covered only limited numbers of the work-force.[5] Agreements studied in the UK were aimed predominantly at establishing basic *procedural* controls over the introduction and use of new technology. This was contrasted with NTAs in the manual sector that regulated the *substantive* effects of such new technology on pay, hours, conditions and so forth. The Ruskin study (see Levie 1985, Levie and Moore 1985) also noted the rather limited success of NTAs in terms of affecting either the decision-making or the existing structure of consultation. In addition, the European Foundation Study showed how NTAs suffered from their own specificity and how, in a period of corporate change represented by innovation, attempting to reach fixed agreements was fraught with difficulty.

In the European Foundation's case studies, a number of points were raised that illuminated these problems. For instance, there were no standard or potential model agreements that could cover different sectors or innovations, and the formal agreements that were made needed heavy supplementation and qualification according to the special conditions found in different companies. Often the provisions were open to variable interpretation, leading to interpretive struggles. Moreover, the issues covered tended to focus upon technological rather than socio-organizational issues, or dealt with these latter issues late in the innovation cycle, so offering little real chance of influence. This recognition of the limitations of NTAs suggest that traditional collective bargaining still has a key role to play in regulating innovation; in particular, the normal annual round of negotiations does not restrict union or work-force representatives in the same manner. Indeed the role of technological change could be integrated into agreements that are open, rather than specific to technology. These could take account of interlocking issues and, more importantly, could respond to the particular exigencies of the enterprise, plant or work-group. The German situation shows that even with a thorough and comprehensive national set of agreements and unique co-determination arrangements within companies, there is still a need for local company bargaining since it remains impossible to specify in advance the exact consequences of change or to legally define the responsibilities of the parties. The case studies show that agreements that attempted such tight specification frequently led to difficulties of interpretation. In those circumstances, work councils were often able to make company agreements and information arrangements that were 'more suited' to their domestic scene.

This does not mean to say that ongoing collective bargaining is without its problems. For instance, bargaining in the research sites was often restricted to a set of issues that dealt almost purely with the *effects* of change. Even though the studies dealt with national bargaining systems that operated at quite different levels, enterprise bargaining took place at a point in the organization where only operational issues rather than initial decisions could be affected. The more important policy and investment issues that determined the initiation of new technology programmes were usually made at enterprise headquarters. Additionally, in large multi-plant or multi-divisional companies the chain of decision-making surrounding new technology in all its aspects could be very complex. In contrast, the trade union organization tended to be strong at particular levels, at the plant or in national/industry bargaining groups. This meant that the influence exerted through bargaining was restricted, and only infrequently extended throughout the enterprise to cover key areas of decision-making. Many of the cases demonstrate the problem that such restricted bargaining entails. Frequently, high-level groupings were formed in order to start discussion on the policy and strategic issues that innovation involved. However, few cases revealed that bargaining did achieve influence in areas of investment or future financial planning. Indeed in the Italian, UK and Danish studies the point is forcibly made that current forms of involvement, including collective bargaining, simply do not have any effect in this area.

Given this broad context, which unions themselves judge to be hostile, no one approach seemed adequate to safeguard the multiple valid interests in innovation of the work-force and trade unions. Most unions have acknowledged this in their recognition of the limitations of new technology agreements as the all-embracing response:

> Central technology agreements can be useful. But it is more difficult to come to terms with the non-quantitative but potentially more significant questions of systems design, work organisation

and job quality. The development of local participation in the systems design process and influence over work organisation, says the ETUI, has therefore become an important factor for attempts to extend joint regulation of the introduction of new technology.

(Safarti and Cove 1986: 8)

In concrete terms, unions, and to a lesser extent work-force representatives, do have important choices regarding a participation strategy and the best method of regulating new technology. Should they seek to influence change prior to and independent of the specific processes of change happening with enterprises? Is it preferable that the main forms of control should exist at the level of the actual sites during the innovation process and whilst the specific effects are being felt? Alternatively, should they seek influence after the event, essentially dealing with the impacts of change? Looking at the European scene abstractly, one can discern various control strategies.

INFLUENCE PRIOR TO SPECIFIC CHANGE

In this model, power to influence change in relation to new techno-logy would exist in previously determined frameworks of rules, rights and responsibilities. These could be explicit in the form of legal provisions, tripartite agreements, national guidelines or sectoral models of activity. There would be a high element of consensus underlying such agreements, and agreed penalties for non-compliance. Such provision would then set the context and shape the agenda for involvement in new technology. The examples usually quoted to illustrate this approach are taken from the Scandinavian countries of Sweden and Denmark, but West Germany and Austria also have relevant frameworks of rights and duties in their Mitbestimmung and Betriebstrat arrangements.[6]

At national level the role of legislation remains important, especially in those countries with a tradition of institutional forms of participation. The legal situation does set the context for local and industrial bargaining, and the case studies showed that where items of conflict had been taken out of the parties' joint remit then participation could proceed on a qualitatively different plane. In Sweden, Denmark, the Netherlands and Germany one finds legal intervention directed to securing greater worker participation in enterprise decision-making. In other cases the powers of the work councils have been explicitly extended to include participation on technological matters, such as in the case of the 1982 'Auroux' laws in France where the *comite des enterprise* is informed and consulted in advance on all important projects concerning the introduction of new technologies which may have consequences for employment, qualifications, remuneration, training or working conditions of personnel.[7]

This approach essentially attempts to set the agenda prior to any specific change happening. It is largely fixed in place by wider traditions, such as the social engagement of trade unions, and whether their approach encourages active involvement with the state. Not surprisingly, this tends to be found in those countries that emphasise social partnership, whether in the form of a social contract or encased within neo-corporatist arrangements. These traditions may support some voluntaristic means of serving their members' interests, but a clear separation of the economic and political role of trade unions tends to be less important.

The major defining feature of this approach is the form of social mobilization the trade unions choose to employ, whether acting through existing institutional and party channels or through co-operative or bargaining relations based at national level. This implies that some union movements have greater opportunities to promote influence on the context of technological change, and to become involved at a higher level of activity where they can help frame the more general form that regulation will take.

INFLUENCE DURING THE PROCESS OF CHANGE

The process of technological change takes place almost entirely at the plant level, and correspondingly the main centres of control over the process are vested there. The evidence produced in the previous section suggested that this is one key area for trade union activity where they have to secure both substantive and procedural controls over the process as a whole. The British TUC has admitted that whilst its ten-point programme mixes substantive and procedural aims 'the thrust of its policy is procedural',[8] the emphasis indicating the importance of attempts to write-in controls over the process prior to the impacts being settled.

The ETUI (Asplund 1981) similarly contrasts these 'control' elements against more substantive ones and lists seven objectives for unions to secure:

- Joint commitment of parties to change and the satisfactory management of that change.

- Prior provision of adequate, intelligible and reliable information.
- Joint bodies with effective powers of decision-making.
- The appointment and training of trade union representatives responsible for handling new technology matters.
- Provision of outside expertise independent from management.
- Monitoring procedures on data/performance.
- *Status quo* clauses or veto powers for trade unions.

There is some evidence of model agreements being signed with such provisions. However, wide-ranging clauses of this sort tend not to have been secured in practice. Some of these items may be included in New Technology Agreements, but less are seen in general collective agreements. Without such procedural controls to establish the mutual responsibilities of the parties, there is a tendency to find weaker consultative forums being accepted.

None the less, the case study evidence of the Foundation revealed a number of very important company arrangements for extended participation during the change process. The Consolidated Report of the Foundation's first phase of new technology research detailed five such 'strategic cases' (see Cressey 1985: 59–64) that took the issue of participation further, in contrast to their normal domestic provisions. A number of these important cases were based upon a mixture of high-level consultation over the early phases of change, with a recognition and an accordance of bargaining rights to groups of workers involved in the changes. In this context, new forms of regulation have emerged. These are of an 'extended' type, with an enlargement of workers' participation in such issues as investment and organizational restructuring due to technological change.

The experience of the 'Saturn project' at General Motors is also illustrative. The agreement signed in 1985 between the General Motor Corporation and the United Automobile Workers represents an advanced experiment of 'new co-operation' in an industrial context where formalized participation in connection with techno-logical innovation had never previously played a major role. This was based on a systematic search for consensus, with the full involvement of the union and the workers at the various levels of the decision-making process. Altogether an extended participatory approach (even 'integrationist' in some aspects) is involved, marked by innovative features which go far beyond 'concession bargaining'.

In such instances a kind of participation has been attempted that captures new ground, being not merely reactive to management initiatives but striving for a measure of joint influence. These need not be enterprise-wide, as a project funded by ESPRIT covering three European countries on Human Centred Technology has shown.[9] The overall aim of this project was to investigate the potentialties of programmng and operating computer-integrated manufacturing on human-centred principles. The German group have chosen to develop a computer-sided information system, the Danish group a new means of computer aided design, whilst the British consortium are developing computer-integrated manufacturing by means of constructing and operating a prototype integrated turning cell. The 'human-centred approach' is based on the premise that computer-integrated manufacturing systems will be more efficient, more economical, more robust and more flexible if designed with and for the people who will be operating them. They see this as more productive and efficient than a comparable unmanned system. In concept, the thrust is anti-Taylorist, with emphasis on the use of technology to give more dignity and fulfilment, whilst at the same time offering more productivity and less unnecessary subdivision of tasks. The project aimed for a robustness of design which retains and enhances operator skills, maximizes operator choice and intervention in the work process, gives holistic knowledge, and optimizes ergonomic factors.

Significantly, the most intractable problems with this ambitious experimentation have not been in the area of software design or devising the 'open architecture' of such systems. Rather they have involved difficulties with the human factor. For instance, senior management have proved obstructive in many cases, with attempts made to block ideas emanating from the project. Similarly, there has been difficulty with the work-force in getting people to participate openly, especially in the early stage that tends to be largely 'abstract' in character. Moreover, engineering staff seem to have had great difficulty in understanding the reversal of criteria or the front loading of 'social' issues. Meanwhile, the trade unionists have been suspicious of the inversion of hierarchy that participation in design represents, and of the new responsibilities that accompany any acceptance of decentralized cell working.

INFLUENCE AFTER THE PROCESS

This, the most common model, is reactive and defensive. It tends to be found wherever voluntaristic bargaining attempts control over limited and clearly defined areas. It eschews elements of prior control and prior responsibilty, seeking instead the piecemeal amelioration of the specific effects of change. It is represented by the countless examples of restricted agreements centred upon job security/no redundancy claims, redeployment/retraining provisions, guarantees on work pace, and so on.

Whilst apparently limited, this approach does have the virtue of clarity in its single-minded defence of issues close to members' interests. The empirical evidence suggests that whilst serious attempts to extend the control of unions and work-forces by means of procedural controls are common, these are in the main being thwarted and channelled instead into consultative forums. Looking at Britain, Price indicated a serious lack of strategic thinking and awareness about the possibilities that involvement might offer:

> Overwhelmingly, British union involvement takes place after the initial planning stages have been carried out by management. Thus while it may not be totally inaccurate to speak of genuine areas of joint implementation of new technology, this must be understood to imply implementation within the acceptable limits for management.
>
> (Price 1988: 260–1)

The lack of influence detailed in the previous sections indicates that this problem is not limited to the UK. Nor is it a fact that those nations which possess institutional participation at top company level have necessarily achieved satisfactory procedures across the board. Whilst the British case is exacerbated by a distinct lack of an enabling framework that could support wider trade union strategies, this form of reactive bargaining was also popular in the other countries studied.

These considerations pull trade union and work-force strategies in differing directions, or as ARPES termed it, towards one perspective based on 'realism', the other on 'possibilism':

> The trade union movement is in fact undecided on the whole issue of participation, torn between two types of position: the 'traditional' one which sets clear boundaries around trade union activity, ruling out the possibility of taking a positive hand in managerial prerogatives regarding company decisions, and another position based on 'possible action', which sees an ongoing check on management activities as a chance to perform the union's role of protecting the workforce more effectively.
>
> (Depoali *et al.* 1988: 100)

These and other authors have pointed out the quandary that faces unions and work-force when confronting technological change. On the one hand they value the investment for the longer-term security it promises. They see positive elements in supporting work-force demands for improvements in environmental and substantive conditions, for new methods of co-operation, and for a better quality of working life. On the other hand, however, they cannot control the changes that technology brings by traditional union-means alone. New skills, new ways of regulating working time and work discipline, new divisions within the work-force, are all perceived as threats. So too is the unions' lack of ability to contest the long-term planning of management.

PROACTIVITY

The crucial question facing trade unions is whether they can enhance their control at each point in the process, and especially during the decision-making process. The emphasis on a 'proactive' role then becomes more urgent – for instance, in developing inputs into the design process; in the creation of a commitment and the organizational ability to pose alternatives to management plans; and in the assertion of those alternatives at an early and strategically important point. It appears that whilst the current practice is somewhat deficient, there is still the potential to develop openings for trade union action and to have trade union criteria adopted. This is in part a corollary of management's dependency on the work-force during technological change (Jones and Rose 1985).

The exploration of management uncertainty is the very ground upon which such openings for work-force and trade union involvement exist. However, just as management exhibit uncertainty about their response, so the trade unions are also uncertain, tending to vacillate in their belief in, and commitment to, the possibility of producing coherent new technology strategies. There are a number of structural, financial and strategic problems that can be fairly easily identified. These difficulties in the way of coherent trade union strategies are all related to the initial premise of the power imbalance existing in organizations. Trade unions do have severe resource, educational and structural problems. These are exacerbated by the lack of a framework in which they are assigned rights to regulate technical change.

Furthermore, the ideological *status quo* is one which places legitimacy for decision-making with management, and reinforces managerial styles of decision-making of an hierarchical kind. In relation to new technology, the failure to pose alternatives is buttressed by what David Noble (1979) has called the ideology of 'technicism' or 'scientism' that contributes to work-force exclusion and the designation of technology as a legitimate area of management control. Technological ignorance was 'expected', rather than actually discovered, by our research.

In this context, and amidst recession as well, it is little wonder that unions were suspicious of wholeheartedly embracing 'participative' involvement. Instead, in the absence of effective rights and formats, they opted for defensiveness and some distance from joint responsibility. For trade unions, direct involvement is a risk. Hence it is usually work-groups and lay union members who form the bulk of those willing to be involved. Yet, while matters are left to voluntary developments, the situation will remain a difficult one for trade unions. A decisive push would be required to move new technology decision-making into a consensual framework. Nor would this be painless, with the dismantling of some management shibboleths regarding their right to control, but also in relation to trade union thinking on their whole approach to social partnership.

The recession of the 1970s has also increased union uncertainty and averted their gaze somewhat from these longer-term and less pressing issues of change. Streeck, however, considers that it is precisely the issues such as technical change and the long-term nature of its restructuring of the environment that demand urgent action by unions. Despite their problems, he maintains that a posture of defensive resistance to change is insufficient and dangerous for the union movement. Identifying the opportunity for union action in the current period as being caused by the extent of management uncertainty, he goes on to say that:

> The single most important inducement from trade unions would be a credible commitment to contribute their share to the complex social and institutional pre-conditions of manufacturing beyond mass-production in a re-integrated system of industrial governance.
>
> (Streeck 1987: 303)

For such a commitment to be realized, unions would have to accept a number of crucial reorientations, including recognition of the need to restore efficiency and competitiveness through the modification of existing industrial relations; the development of a plausible conception of their own potential role in a decentralized and participation-oriented system; a change in their attitude towards wage differentials and measures such as share ownership; and, finally, the development of the organizational resources necessary for intervention in areas of managerial prerogatives such as design, investment and technology. To Streeck, this represents the development of a 'productivist' strategy based upon a new kind of 'conflictual cooperation', and he indicates that there will be differences in the possible ease of application of these changes from one country to the next.

On these questions, the degree of adaptation that has so far occurred is predictably variable. There has been some change towards an acceptance of the need for efficiency, and also for trade union 'openness' to technology, especially in Sweden and some other Northern European countries where the question of organizational resources has been tackled. However, the major problem of union uncertainty regarding participation and involvement has not been tackled. The fear remains that positive steps on this front will mark them as 'co-managers' of a capitalist enterprise. Sorge and Streeck (1988) maintain that whilst there is a current unevenness in the range of issues that concern management and unions, it is only through the extension of co-determination that the imbalance in industrial relations can be overcome. Product strategy, investment and planning, work design and the social context of technology, should all be targets for shared decision-making.

But what form should such proactivity take? The context within which trade unions can forge effective strategies in this vein varies enormously. Even with a firm commitment, they have to cope with national and internal diversity, plus the operation of managerial strategies that seek to neutralize or deflect their control. Because the concept of proactivity is of necessity associated with some reorientation of trade union activity that fits with the wider changes in industrial relations and manufacturing policy, it appears much more complicated to put into practice. None the less, much of the rhetoric surrounding new technology was found to emphasize the human resource element, suggesting that technology itself is simply a potential, and that its full realization requires a considered and compatible human resource strategy. The possibility of worker inputs into the design process confronts this rhetoric with very pertinent questions about the role, style and content of work-force participation and the potential for the full realization of human resources in the context of innovation. Specifically, participation experiments question the existing balance of organizational power and decision-making and the repression of certain forms of knowledge and interaction as normally greater importance is attached to abstract, technicist knowledge than to practical and tacit knowledge.

Yet most of the available research on participative design signals a highly limited role for the work-force. The emphasis is on the application of systems concepts in a way that renders a high degree of work-force involvement passive or unnecessary. The very different concepts of efficiency or rationality, and of organizational aims that management and trade unions adopt are highlighted by the Lucas Aerospace experiment which sought to provide workers with a major input into the design, choice and manufacture of new products. One of the changes signalled by the research at Lucas was the need for a new character of participation during innovation, one that went beyond the collective regulation of terms (essentially the negotiation of the peripheral impacts of technology), beyond a consultative format, or even one based on small group problem-solving.

Fundamentally, the Lucas shop stewards' proposals challenged deep-rooted organizational attitudes and behaviour normally associated with Taylorism. These prescribe a functional format premised on an ever-growing split between conception and execution. Hence in these views systems design is thoroughly separated from shop-floor operations and lodged elsewhere, perhaps in layout departments or management services. Planning, design, and research and development activities become a 'black box' as far as the work-force is concerned. Involvement, if it exists at all, is relegated to the margins of the implementation phase. The notion of proactivity in design questions whether this separation is necessary, and if one can operate 'efficiently' on the basis of a growing integration of tasks on the basis of an organizational reintegration of conception and execution. Indeed, proactivity changes the issue for investigation towards determining what form the reintegration of conception and execution should take. Human-centred technologies have been centrally concerned with this very issue, designing into work processes new 'unities' of conception and execution, opening up for re-examination work systems, job specifications and concepts of efficiency.

However, the problem which remains here is the abstraction of the process of design and planning from its wider context, and so the difficulties of achieving participation by users in this process. The ESPRIT programme of research exposed a form of 'participation by proxy'. Engineers, software designers, and technicians with a sympathy and understanding of 'human-centred criteria' were acting on behalf of the work-force, framing the format of participation in the systems innovation and subsequent operations in production. In terms of proactivity this would appear to be little different qualitatively from many other forms of organizational planning. However, the issues raised in this context are vital to the integrated use of the technical and human resources of the enterprise. We must, therefore, ask whether there are qualitatively new ways in which they may be integrated, if new forms of collaboration should be devised now, and how these might be visualized. Such conjectures, whilst isolated in themselves, do take on 'iconic' status, representing possible futures and highlighting possibly critical problems.

That said, a central question raised by experience of the current experiments is how far the union strategy can achieve a 'design with' as opposed to a 'design for' format of participation. Accepting this entails that controversial challenges to the existing role structures of technician, manager, accountant and operator must follow. More detailed investigation seems merited on the practical issues and constraints involved. There would appear to be four broad areas where design and participation might interact. The matrix in Table 9.2 tries to match the external environment with the internal constraints upon design choices, with each situation offering differing opportunities for (and restrictions on) active participation in design processes. Such an identification of the organizational opportunities in the process of design allows for a much finer tuning of the use of human resources and for user-participation in all of the boxes, with the possible exception of '2' where the pressures for decision-making emanate from outside the enterprise.

This brief look at the notion of proactivity as it relates to involvement in the design process indicates some of the real problems that trade unions face, and will continue to face, when confronting the challenge of strategy on innovation. These difficulties are not insuperable, as some of the Scandinavian examples in particular have shown. However, the resources, the time and the commitment needed to support the Arbeitslivcentrum, the projects on work redesign and improvement in the quality of working life, are beyond the grasp of most other trade union movements. In fact resource problems may be the tip of the iceberg, as many union movements even fail to recognize that some of the issues are resolvable at all. Too many refuse to recognize their potential capacity, either in the form of an intelligence/research function or as agents pressing for a different approach in the workplace.

Moreover, even if advances were made in this respect, we cannot simply read-off what the appropriate role or response to innovation

Table 9.2 Possibilities and constraints

| Form of decisions | Design variables: | |
	Intrinsic 1	Extrinsic 2
Taking	Technology assessment studies of costs/control of design process	Product market/ labour market pressures on design
Making	Allocation and negotiation of design roles	Institutuional aspects of industrial regulation

should be for different actors. The forces at play can result in contradictory positions being advanced, for instance from management, where needs for tighter control in a period of uncertainty are expressed alongside needs for greater decentralization and co-operation through shared decision-making. Similarly, divisions within the work-force are apparent especially between those using new technology – and so having a measure of job security – and groups downstream of the innovation who see in the technology a threat to their livelihood. The aims of the parties do diverge and conflict at many points, and because of this they seek different things from the process of regulation. Participation, then, has to accommodate and resolve these conflicting and different interests, and inasmuch as it does so is judged successful by the parties.

On the basis of my own findings it appears that the more rigid and formal the form of participation, the less it can accommodate the particular interests of the parties. Hence in the introduction of new technology, there does seem to be a move towards participative forums of an informal and highly differentiated character. This tendency towards informality and *ad hoc* participation, the lack of simple strategic aims, and the difficulties of gaining proactive positions inside enterprises will conspire to sustain the power imbalance inside European enterprises well into the 1990s. The promise of 'Social Europe' and the 'new' forms of Social Dialogue will be severely tested in this regard, and as yet seem to pose no real answers to the detailed questions listed in recent research.

NOTES

1 The results of the research in twenty-one cases have been published by the European Foundation for the improvement of Living and Working Conditions, Dublin, in a Consolidated Report called *The Role of the*

Parties Concerned in the Introduction of New Technology (Cressey 1985). Another twenty-three case studies were also used in the *Participation Review*, Cressey *et al.* (1988), published by the same institute. Use was also made of the twenty case studies in *The Control of Frontiers: Workers and New Technology, the Disclosure and Use of Company Information*, compiled by a group headed by Hugo Levie at Ruskin College, Oxford, 1985.

2 See Cressey and Di Martino (1991a). These studies refer to the twenty-one cases and the twenty-three referred to in Note 1. For an account of the latter see Della Rocca (1985).

3 For an account of the operation of these committees see Borsiex and Linhart (1986), and Marsden (1978).

4 However, even here the claim of decisive influence for trade unions during the innovation process has been contested. See Lorentzen (1988).

5 See Williams and Moseley (1982) who made a close and detailed study of the benefits and drawbacks of such agreements; also Williams (1985).

6 For an account of the German system see Fricke (1986) and also Furstenburg (1983). On the Austrian model, the ETUI (1985) Information Booklet No. 12, *The Trade Union Movement in Austria: the OGB*, is a good introduction.

7 Cressey and Di Martino (1991b) describe the main features of the Auroux reforms as they affect the introduction of new technology.

8 For the full text see the TUC/CBI Concordat on New Technology published by the TUC 1980, also quoted in Benson and Lloyd (1983).

9 For information on the Esprit project see Cooley and Crampton (1986). See also Corbett (1985) and Clegg and Corbett (1987), on the wider aspects of worker involvement in Human Centred Technology experiments.

REFERENCES

Altmann, N. and Dull, K. (1988) *Participation in Technological Change – Company Strategies and Participation*, Dublin, European Foundation for the Improvement of Living and Working Conditions.

ARPES (Analisi Ricerche Piani Economica e Sociale) (1985) *Company Strategies: Partial Report Role of the Parties Concerned in the Introduction of New Technology* (Phase Two), Dublin, European Foundation for the Improvement of Living and Working Conditions.

—— (1987) *Participation in Technological Change*, Consolidated and Summary Report, Dublin, European Foundation for the Improvement of Living and Working Conditions.

Asplund, C. (1981) *Redesigning Jobs: Western European Experiences*, Brussels, ETUI.

Atkinson, J. (1984) 'Manpower strategies for flexible organisations', *Personnel Management*, August.

Benson, I. and Lloyd, J. (1983) *New Technology and Industrial Change*, London, Kogan Page.

Borsiex, A. and Linhart, D. (1986) *Participation in France: The Emergence of a Consensus*, CRIDP Discussion Paper No. 15, Glasgow.

Ciborra, C. (1984) *New Technologies and Design Options*, Working Paper,

The Role of the Parties in the Introduction of New Technology, Mimeo, Dublin, European Foundation for the Improvement of Living and Working Conditions.

—— (1988) *Participation in Technological Change – A Design Perspective*, Dublin, European Foundation for the Improvment of Living and Working Conditions.

Clark, G. L. (1986) 'Restructuring the US economy: the NLRB, the Saturn Project and economic justice', Paper to 'Future of Labor Movement' Conference, Minnesota.

Clegg, S. and Corbett, M. (1987) 'Research and development into "Humanising" advanced manufacturing technology', in T. Wall, C. Clegg and N. Kemp (eds), London, John Wiley.

Cooley, M. and Crampton, S. (1986) 'Criteria for human centred systems', Paper to CIM Europe Conference, Bremen, May.

Corbett, M. (1985) 'Prospective work design of a human-centred CNC lathe', *Behaviour and Information Technology* 4 (3).

Cressey, P. (1985) *The Role of the Parties Concerned by the Introduction of New Technology*, Consolidated Report, Dublin, European Foundation for the Improvement of Living and Working Conditions.

—— (1988a) *Participation in Technological Change – Work Strategies and Participation*, Dublin, European Foundation for the Improvement of Living and Working Conditions.

—— (1988b) 'Participation and new technology: recent trends in Europe', Conference Paper to Congress on Technological Innovation and Participation, CNEL, Rome.

—— (1988c) Review of the European Foundation's research on new technology', in F. Butera and J. Thurman (eds), *Automation and Work Design*, Amsterdam, North Holland.

——, Eldridge, J. MacInnes, J. and Norris, G. (1981) *Industrial Democracy and Participation: A Scottish Survey*, Department of Employment Research Paper No. 28.

——, Bolle De Bal, M., Treu, T., Di Martino, V. and Traynor, K. (1988) *Participation Review*, Consolidated Report, Dublin, European Foundation for the Improvement of Living and Working Conditions.

—— and Williams, R. (1990) *Participation and New Technology*, Information Booklet, Dublin, European Foundation for the Improvement of Living and Working Conditions.

—— and Di Martino V. (1991a) *Workers' Participation in Technological Change*, forthcoming, ILLS Geneva.

——, —— (1991b) *Agreement and Innovation, The International Dimension of New Technology*, Cambridge, Prentice-Hall.

Cross, M. (1985) *Towards the Flexible Craftsman*, London, Technical Change Centre.

Daniel, W. W. (1987) *Workplace Industrial Relations and Technological Change*, London, Frances Pinter.

Della Rocca, G. (1985) *The Role of the Parties Concerned in the Design and Letting Up of New Forms of Work Organisation*, Dublin, European Foundation for the Improvement of Living and Working Conditions.

Depoali, P., Pantoni, A. and Miani, G. (1988) *Participation in Technological Change – Consolidated Report*, Dublin, European Foundation for the Improvement of Living and Working Conditions.

Di Martino, V. (1987) 'Social dialogue and new technologies in Europe', Paper presented to Second European Regional Congress of Industrial Relations, Tel Aviv, December.

Evans, J. (1982) *Negotiating Technological Change*, Brussels, ETUI.

Fricke, W. (1986) 'New Technologies and German co-determination', *Economic and Industrial Democracy* 7 (4).

Furstenburg, F. (1983) 'Technological change and industrial relations in Germany, *Bulletin of Comparative Labour Relations*, Vol. 12.

Jenkins, C. and Sherman, B. (1979) *The Collapse of Work*, London, Eyre Methuen.

Jones, B. and Rose, M. (1985) 'Management strategy and trade union response in work organisation schemes at factory level', in D. Knights, D. Collinson and H. Wilmott (eds), *Job Redesign*, Aldershot, Gower.

Levie, H. (1985) *The Control of Frontiers; Workers and New Technology, the Disclosure and use of Company Information*, Oxford, Ruskin College.

—— and Moore, R. (1985) *Workers and New Technology; Disclosure and Use of Company Information*, Summary Report and Case Studies, Oxford, Ruskin College.

Lorentzen, B. (1988) 'Experience of participation and involvement in technological change in Danish firms', Paper presented to European Foundation Round Table Conference Copenhagen, November.

MacInnes, J. (1988) 'New technology in Scotbank: gender, class and work', in R. Hyman and W. Streeck (eds), *New Technology and Industrial Relations*, Oxford, Blackwell.

Marsden, D. (1978) *Industrial Democracy and Industrial Control in W. Germany, France and Great Britain*, Department of Employment Research Paper No. 4.

Noble, D. (1979) 'Social choice in machine design; the case of automatically controlled machine tools', in A. Zimbalist (ed.), *Case Studies in the Labour Process*, New York, Monthly Review Press.

Pollert, A. (1988) 'Dismantling flexibility', *Capital and Class*, No. 34.

Price, R. (1988) 'Information, consultation and the control of new technology', in R. Hyman and W. Streeck (eds), *New Technology and Industrial Relations*, Oxford, Blackwell.

Romano, A. (1984) *The Role of the Parties Involved in the Introduction of New Technology*, Italian National Report, Dublin, European Foundation for the Improvement of Living and Working Conditions.

Safarti, H. and Cove, M. (1986) 'New technologies, skill mis-match and the challenge to industrial relations', Paper to IRRA conference Hamburg; also reprinted in G. Bamber and R. Lansbury (eds), *New Technology: International Perspectives on Human Resources and Industrial Relations*, London, Unwin Hyman.

Sandberg, A. and Ehn, P. (1982) *Local Union Influence on Technology and Work Organisation*, Results of the Demos Project Arbeitslivcentrum, Stockholm (mimeo).

Seivers, B., Rieckmann, H., Lawrence, W. and Foster, M. (1984) *The Role of the Parties Concerned in the Design and Setting up of New Forms of Work Organisation*, Dublin, European Foundation for the Improvement of Living and Working Conditions.

Sorge, A. and Streeck, W. (1988) 'Industrial relations and technical change:

the case for an extended perspective', in R. Hyman and W. Streeck (eds), *New Technology and Industrial Relations*, Oxford, Blackwell.

Streeck, W. (1987) 'The uncertainties of management in the management of uncertainty: employers , labour relations and industrial adjustment in the 1980s', *Work, Employment and Society* 1 (3).

Wilkinson, B. (1983) *The Shopfloor Politics of New Technology*, London, Heinemann.

Williams, R. (1985) 'Technology agreement in Great Britain: a survey 1977–1983', *Industrial Relations Journal* 16 (3).

—— (1986) 'United Kingdom' section in G. Berta (ed.), *Industrial Relations in Information Society: A European Survey*, Rome, Adriano Olivetti Foundation.

—— and Moseley, R. (1982) 'Technology agreements', Paper presented to EEC/FAST Conference, University of Aston.

—— and Steward, F. (1985) National UK Report in *The Role of the Parties Involved in the Introduction of New Technology*, Dublin, European Foundation for the Improvement of Living and Working Conditions.

Willman, P. (1986) *New Technology and Industrial Relations: A Review of the Literature*, Research Paper No. 56, Dept of Employment.

Index